D1035217

The Whole Truth About Man

John Paul II
to University Faculties
and Students

Edited with an Introduction
by James V. Schall, S.J.

Indexed by the
Daughters of St. Paul

ST. PAUL EDITIONS

Reprinted with permission from *L'Osservatore Romano*, English Edition.

ISBN 0-8198-8201-1 cloth
       0-8198-8202-X paper

COVER PHOTO:
Curt Clark

Printed in the U.S.A. by the Daughters of St. Paul
50 St. Paul's Ave., Boston, MA 02130

The Daughters of St. Paul are an international congregation of religious women serving the Church with the communications media.

Contents

IV. Familiar Homilies to University Students
About Faith and Knowledge

V. Addresses About Science and Faith

VI. Addresses to
Roman Ecclesiastical Universities

VII. A Papal Doctrinal Homily, On Seeking the Lord

VIII. Pastoral Addresses to University Faculty and Students About Christianity and Intelligence

From the first centuries, the Church has felt the importance of an apostolate of the intellect....

John Paul II, February 24, 1980, Rome.

It is not knowledge as such that justifies in the first place your belonging to the Institut Catholique, *but the light it contributes to offer you about your reasons for living. In this field, every man needs certainty.*

John Paul II, June 1, 1980, Paris.

The best friends, followers and apostles of Christ have always been those who heard within them one day the definitive, inescapable question, before which all others become secondary and derivative: "For you, whom am I?" The life, the destiny, the present and future history of a young person depends on the clear and sincere answer, without rhetoric or subterfuges, that he gives to this question.

John Paul II, July 1, 1980, Belo Horizonte.

INTRODUCTION

The present Roman Pontiff, John Paul II, was himself, among other things, a university student and a professor of philosophy. He seems to have acted a bit in his university days, written poetry, and worked in a factory. He has given many talks on sports and seems to enjoy a good game. One of the characteristics of this Pope is his love for and insight into the nature of university life, particularly his awareness of what students search for through, or sometimes, in spite of their formal curricula. He knows too what professors, aging and otherwise, are obliged to, to the truth, that is, in their university lives. He seems to be acutely aware of the different university situations and problems throughout the world.

On each of his many now famous journeys throughout the world, John Paul II has sought the occasion to address himself familiarly to university students and, more academically, to faculties and administrations. In Rome also, he has often given addresses and homilies to university groups from the city, from Europe, or from almost anywhere else, who come to see him. These addresses and talks are a rich source of teaching of particular interest to anyone personally concerned about what a university is and ought to be, of how Christianity relates directly and indirectly to academic life and the persons engaged in it.

John Paul II, thus, never forgets that human persons are the main subjects of university life, especially those persons who are ready to pursue intelligence directly and openly. He considers university students on the whole to be a privileged group in their society and, therefore, he treats them accordingly, constantly recalling to them their subsequent duties to God and neighbor that arise from their education itself. He never allows the narrow purpose of the university as a specific institution to blind a student or a professor to the ultimate questions about the purpose and destiny of human life itself. He is quite aware that many universities, in fact, do not allow such deeper questions to be properly and adequately posed. This is why it is worthwhile to gather many of his addresses in this area into one collection so that a student or professor will have some criterion, some test against which to measure what is actually being taught or not taught in his college or university.

The most common theme we find in John Paul's talks to university students, however, is a more personal one, wherein he reminds them to ask themselves who they are, to know the whole truth about themselves and man, a truth that must include the truth about God. A university that knows nothing of the truth of God is not really complete even on its own terms. The Pope asks this in the name of truth itself. He is not asking for something that does not by right belong. He argues also from philosophy as well as from religion and man's need of it. Often he warns university departments and faculties of the dangers of "reductionism," wherein the deeper sides of man are deliberately or ignorantly cut off from serious consideration, even in the name of "science." This pursuit of all truth for which the Pope stands includes a free openness to the religious truth which is man's goal and destiny. This is more than "academic"—the Pope does not hesitate to tell even professors, even himself, the Pope, that they must also pray—but there is a definite intellectual content to faith. No student's or professor's level of religious knowledge should be inferior to the level of his academic knowledge. He told a group of young students from colleges in Rome that this disproportion can cause students or faculty serious problems if they do not take means to know the intelligence of faith along with their secular or technical knowledges (cf. no. IV, I).

John Paul II understands in a unique way that modern philosophies and ideologies offer a university student or faculty member a kind of explanation about the meaning of life and society. Often he reminds students of how narrow and one-sided many of these explanations are in honest comparison with the full reality to which young students often feel themselves to be called. The Pope knows there are partial truths in most systems. This is why he stresses, by contrast, the whole truth about man, a central theme in his first Encyclical, *Redemptor hominis,* which university teachers and students should carefully read and reflect upon, as the Pope considers this admittedly rather complicated document to be a basic statement of what he is about, of what Christianity means in the modern world.

John Paul II is a man who will tell university audiences what practically no one else will tell them. And this is as often true, almost, in universities of Christian foundations as those with civil or philanthropical origins. John Paul II is himself one of the great intellects of this century. Perhaps, as Daniel Patrick Moynihan said of him, he is the only figure in public life today to have himself lived through and given a reasoned, philosophic response to the principal problem of the 20th Century, that of totalitarianism (Cf. *The Washington Post,* October 7, 1979, Supplement). Consequently, it is important for any student—students often tend to skepticism anyhow—to have some sense of the Holy Father's own intellectual depth and how he arrived at it; often through the same confusing conditions students everywhere encounter in universities with regard to the whole truth about man.

The student and the professor likewise need to know how the Church looks on university life, how the enterprise of science and knowledge relates to Christian truth, how all truth is ultimately one. John Paul II is at his best in this area. Moreover, the Pope is a pastor and a father, not just a professor or an ecclesiastic. His affection for students shines through all his addresses and homilies. But he is not condescending. He has no intention of telling anyone the burden of intelligence and truth is easy. Indeed, he is blunt and frank. He challenges the student at every point, intellectual, moral, religious, social. And to the objection given by the youth in Paris that belief and morality are difficult, he simply agrees (Cf. p. 326). Only he goes on to point out that this is the nature of anything worthwhile, worth living for. He will not "change" a truth to make us comfortable. On almost every occasion, the Pope stresses the need for self-discipline and even mortification, for prayer and sacrifice, along with the joy and generosity of serving God and others, of knowing the truth for oneself. He knows also that Christianity has its own sources of life and truth, a spiritual life in which students and professors must also participate.

John Paul II, furthermore, does not "apologize" for the truth of Christianity. He is not embarrassed to be a Christian in a university, any university. He knows that any serious pursuit of truth must include the challenge of the truth of Christ, that men have thought long and hard about the relation between God and the world, reason and revelation, so that to be deprived of such reflections is also to be uneducated. The Pope is quite concerned that religious truth be part of the pursuit of the truth found in any discipline or faculty. He challenges directly any university's claim to authenticity that, in principle, reduces the scope of truth to something less than all truth. He knows that there are many, many saints without B.A.'s or Ph.D.'s, and many a sinner with them. Yet, he does not minimize the central place of this very important institution.

The Holy Father thinks there should also be Catholic universities, that any honest notions of religious freedom—which he holds to be the first human and civil right—would include this possibility. His addresses to Catholic universities often suggest that they themselves should be much more than they are. And he does not cease to challenge students and faculty in state or secular universities to be likewise open to theological and metaphysical and moral truth, to be critical of faculties, states, and administrations that only allow a part of reality. He urges students constantly to be attentive to what it is they ultimately search for in all they study, in all their personal lives. He knows of service to the neighbor and constantly refers to it, but he also realizes this itself is not all and is ultimately nothing apart from the love and worship of God.

Many of John Paul II's conversations with students are almost meditations with them, addressing themselves to what is deepest in young men and women. John Paul II knows he is the Roman Pontiff. He does not apologize for this but explains how he looks at himself in this office to which he has somehow been called, how he too is obliged to the truth God has revealed in the Church. He tells students with candor that his first duty is to this truth. He knows that they first expect him to talk to them of the truth of God. And he knows instinctively that today practically no one else will so speak to them; few know how as he does. It will be noted too that this Pope, while addressing himself to the anguishing problems he knows are in the minds of students and faculty, speaking often bluntly as in Galway, never talks down to them as if they also did not somehow need to know the truth of God (cf. pp. 38ff.). Many others can talk of popular or faddish topics to university students. What John Paul II is, the Pope, means that he is expected to be qualified to speak of God and how God means something to each human person. And he pays each person—the Pope's philosophy and personality are profoundly directed to each human person in his or her particularity and uniqueness—the compliment of directing his teaching to each one, not to some abstract man or species. The Pope senses that students and faculty do want to hear the truth about God, the whole truth about themselves as revealed in Christ. Ironically, the modern media and John Paul's own unique personality have conspired to make his teaching a reality on a vast scale even where cultural, political, or religious reasons work against considering what he teaches.

Collected here, then, are many of the most significant addresses and homilies John Paul II has given to university audiences. It should be emphasized, however, that this Holy Father, as many of his modern Predecessors, is a very energetic and productive man, who will continue to travel and talk to university audiences. He is worth following. John Paul II has a vast range of concern, often much broader than that of a university, while many of the things he says are of particular interest to various faculties. Thus, his addresses to the United Nations, to UNESCO, FAO, to the Latin American and African bishops, to various presidents and diplomatic corps, on the Mall in Washington or at Notre Dame in Paris, are of great moment. These can easily be found and are not included here (cf. Bibliography).

The emphasis in the addresses and homilies presented here is rather on the university world itself and on the moral, spiritual, and intellectual life of those found in it. John Paul II teaches here in various ways. None of the materials presented here are cut or edited since it seems important to the university reader to have a feeling and an exposure to the whole of his approach. Italics are often added for special emphasis in the text. They should be read carefully and with full realization that the religious part of what he says is also a part of his understanding, the part the average student or professor is not likely to hear elsewhere. Often there will be in these talks references to Scripture, to the Church Fathers, to ancient or modern philosophers, to the documents of earlier Popes or to the works of Councils of the Church, particularly Vatican II. The student may not be familiar with this matter, though they ought to be in some sense a part of any good education. But these are parts of the Pope's context and ought not to be neglected as if they served no purpose. One of the things John Paul teaches indirectly is an awareness of history, especially the history of Christianity itself, a history which is also too often neglected in modern universities.

Included here is a wide variety of approaches and topics from the simple homily to the profound formal address on the Philosophy of Thomas Aquinas (cf. pp. 262-280). Sometimes the most profound things are found in unlikely places. Also included are several major addresses to Roman ecclesiastical universities. These are included both because they are of great value in themselves, but also because it is important for university students and professors to know the ideals of specifically ecclesiastical education. John Paul II, moreover, does not doubt that many young men and women are called to religious life. He wants them to think about it. He tells young men to consider the priesthood. And he expects as a matter of course that a healthy relation of fondness and mutual comprehension will exist between laity and clerics, that university faculties will have an appreciation of uniquely Christian intelligence. But mainly the reason for this collection is to give university students and faculties a chance to know what is expected in the way of Christian intelligence. This will not substitute for the hard work of learning or the need of a spiritual life, but it should give some goal, some sense of the validity of religion in the university context, some sense that university life is not itself complete if it neglects the whole truth about God and man, that truth to which John Paul II constantly refers when speaking to university students and faculty.   *James V. Schall, S.J.*

I. Three Brief Homilies to University Students on Who They Are

1) *To Students at Catholic University before the National Shrine. October 7, 1979.*

2) *To Group of Italian Students from "Communion and Liberation" Group before Lourdes Shrine in Vatican Gardens. July 13, 1979.*

3) *To Pilgrimage of French University Students in Rome. April 5, 1980.*

ENJOY THE PRIVILEGES
OF YOUR YOUTH

On Sunday, October 7, 1979, His Holiness, Pope John Paul II arrived at the National Shrine of the Immaculate Conception. He was welcomed by students from the Catholic University of America with loud applause, cheering and the repeated chant: "We love you!" The Holy Father greeted them as follows:

Dear students,

...My first greeting, on arriving at this campus, is for you! To all of you, I offer the peace and joy of our Lord Jesus Christ.

I am told that you have held an all night prayer vigil...to ask God's blessing on my visit. Thank you most cordially for such a wonderful expression of communion with me and for such a beautiful gift.

I would like to talk to you at length. *I would like to listen to you and know what you think about yourselves and the world,* but the time I have been given is so short...short time.

One thing you have taught me already. By choosing to welcome me with the offering of your prayers, you have demonstrated that *you understand what is most important in your lives: your contact with God, your searching for the meaning of life, by listening to Christ as He speaks to you in the Scriptures.* I am pleased to know that reflection on spiritual and religious values is part of your desire to live fully this time of your lives. *Materialistic concerns and one-sided values are never sufficient to fill the heart and the mind of a human person.* A life reduced to the sole dimension of possessions, of consumer goods, of temporal concerns, will never let you discover and enjoy the full richness of your humanity. *It is only God, in Jesus, God made man, that you will fully understand what you are.* He will unveil to you the true greatness of yourselves, that you are redeemed by Him and taken up in His love, that you are made truly free in Him, in Him who said about Himself: "If the Son frees you, you will be free, indeed."

I know that you, like students all over the world, are troubled by the problems that weigh on society around you and on the whole world. Look at those problems, explore them, study them and accept them as a challenge. But do it in the light of Christ. He is the Way, and the Truth, and the Life. He put all human life in the true dimension of truth and of authentic love. *True knowledge and true freedom are in Jesus. Make Jesus always part of your hunger for truth and justice, and part of your dedication to the well-being of your fellow human beings.*

Enjoy the privileges of your youth: the right to be dynamic, creative and spontaneous, the right to be full of hope and joy, the opportunity to explore the marvelous world of science and knowledge, and above all, the chance to give of yourself to others in generous and joyful service.

I leave you now with this prayer, that the Lord Jesus will reveal Himself to each one of you, that

He will give you the strength to go out and profess that you are Christians, that He will show you that He alone can fill your hearts. Accept His freedom and embrace His truth and be messengers of the certainty that you have been truly liberated through the death and resurrection of the Lord Jesus. This will be the new experience, the powerful experience that will generate through you a more just society and a better world. God bless you!

God bless you and may the joy of Jesus be always with you!

Thank you very much! Thank you very much!

And now, with your permission, I enter. I enter our Lady's shrine and I introduce you, at least spiritually, in this shrine, in this marvelous shrine.

(Transcribed from a live recording.)

WHO ARE WE?
WHAT ARE WE TO DO?
HOW CAN WE DO IT?

On July 13, 1979, the Holy Father celebrated Mass for a group of young people of Communion and Liberation *in the grotto of Our Lady of Lourdes in the Vatican.*
John Paul II delivered the following homily.

1. We listened with deep veneration to the words which the liturgy of the Church dedicates to this Sunday. Now, it is necessary to stop for a little and accept these words, that is, adapt them to the hearts of listeners. Adapt them to our lives. Here are some thoughts along these lines.

2. In the first place: who are we all, members of this assembly, listeners to the Word of God and, shortly, participants in the body and blood of the Lord?

The question "Who am I?" conditions all other questions and all the answers concerning the subject "What must I do?"

Today, in the letter to the Ephesians, St. Paul replies to this first and fundamental question. He replies: we are chosen by God in Christ Jesus.

"Blessed be the God and Father of our Lord Jesus Christ, who has blessed us in Christ with every spiritual blessing in the heavenly places, even as he chose us in him before the foundation

16

of the world, that we should be holy and blameless before him. He destined us in love to be his sons through Jesus Christ, according to the purpose of his will, to the praise of his glorious grace which he freely bestowed on us in the Beloved" (Eph. 1:3-6).

This is the answer that St. Paul gives us today to the question "Who am I?", and he develops it in the other words of the same text of the letter to the Ephesians.

Here is a further stage of this answer:

We are redeemed; we are brimming over with the forgiveness of sins and grace; we are called to union with Christ and, consequently, to unify everyone in Christ.

And this is not yet the end of this answer in St. Paul.

We are called to exist for the glory of the Divine Majesty; we participate in the Word of truth, in the Gospel of salvation; we are marked with the seal of the Holy Spirit; we are participants in the inheritance, while waiting for complete redemption, which will make us the property of God.

3. This is St. Paul's answer to our question. It gives us a lot to think about.

Forgive me if I confine myself to making a few references.

The words of the letter to the Ephesians cannot stop ringing out after one reading, after listening to them only once. They must remain with us. They must continue with us. These are words in keeping with the whole of life. In keeping with eternity.

It would be a good thing if they could continue together with each of you during these weeks and months of summer rest. In whatever direction you turn: whether to some temporary commitment,...or to apostolic work,...or perhaps, as you have already done more than once, to the pilgrimage from Warsaw to Jasna Gora.... Let these words go with you. The answer to the question "Who am I?" "Who are we?"

May they mold and form your personality, inserted, as we are, in the same root, in the dimension of the mystery, which Christ has imprinted on the life of each of us.

The sacrifice in which we participate, holy Mass, also gives us every time the answer to the fundamental question "Who are we?"

4. What must we do?

The answer to this second question does not emerge, perhaps, from today's liturgy of the divine Word, with the same forcefulness as the answer to the question "Who are we?" But it, too, is strong and firm. God says to Amos: "Go, prophesy to my people!" (Amos 7:15)

Christ calls the Twelve and begins to send them out two by two (Mk. 6:7). And He bids them enter individual houses and thus bear witness. The Second Vatican Council recalled that all Christians, not only ecclesiastics, but also laity, have their part in Christ's prophetic mission. There is no doubt about "What we must do."

5. The question "How are we to do it?" still remains, however, a topical one at present.

I am glad that you are looking for an answer to this question, both individually and together with the whole of your community. He who looks for this answer, finds it in due time.

The responsorial psalm of today reassures us that "mercy and truth will meet...."

"Truth will spring from the earth."

Yes, truth must spring from each of us; from each heart.

Be faithful to truth.

Faithful to your vocation.

Faithful to your commitment.

Faithful to your choice.

Be faithful to Christ, who liberates and unites (communion and liberation).

6. Finally, a fervent wish for each of you and for all.

Like a ray of sunshine from today's liturgy, may the God of our Lord Jesus Christ penetrate our hearts with His light to make us understand what the hope of our vocation is (cf. Eph. 1:17-18).

May this wish come true through the intercession of our Lady, before whom we have meditated on the divine Word of today's liturgy, in order to be able to continue to carry out the Eucharistic Sacrifice.

EACH MUST ANSWER

On Saturday, April 5, 1980, the Holy Father received in audience the pilgrimage of French Catholic university students and delivered the following address.

Dear friends,

I am very happy to meet you, French university students, linked with the Sacred Heart of Montmartre. You have come to end the paschal Triduum in Rome. I know how earnestly you are attached to the Church, and how you desire to deepen your faith incessantly, not only in study, but also in personal prayer of worship, in the liturgy, celebrated well, in sharing and in witness.

I offer all of you my best Easter wishes. *Christ asks you as He asked the Apostles gathered round Peter: "Who do you say that I am?" Each one of you must answer in his soul and conscience.* Actually, left to your own resources, to your reason alone, influenced perhaps by the climate of uncertainty and doubt that reigns around you, you would be unable to do so. But the Church herself, in the steps of the Apostle Peter, has proclaimed for you the only fitting faith: "You are the Christ, the Son of the living God." This faith was instilled into you by Baptism in the form of a seed, capacity, virtue. You have made it your own gradually in the course of your childhood and your adolescence, with ups and downs, perhaps. From within, the Holy Spirit has enlightened and strengthened this faith, spreading love of God in your hearts. I am glad to tell you again with the first of the Apostles, the first of the Bishops of Rome: "Without having seen him (Jesus Christ) you love him; though you do not now see him you believe in him and rejoice with unutterable and exalted joy. As the outcome of your faith you obtain the salvation of your souls" (1 Pt. 1:8-9).

May your attachment to Christ and His Church never fail. Accept Him with trust, serenity and joy, for we know in whom we have put our faith. Tonight, we are going to celebrate His resurrection. The risen Christ is there to "seize" you, as St. Paul said—and He has already done so—to deliver you from your sins, from what would prevent you from living in religious faith, in peace with others, in truth, purity, forgiveness and charity; to infuse into you His divine life and His power of renewal. No barrier can prevent Him from exercising His salvation, as soon as anyone opens to it freely. Be confident, even if you have the impression that you are still far from it.

This love of God that takes possession of you is a gratuitous gift. Receive it with thanksgiving. And set out along the ways of the world, to your families, your cities, your schools, in the midst of other young people, to be witnesses of this God, to be in a way the sacrament of His love for each of your brothers, inviting them to welcome the Savior in their own life. *This is the secret of happiness! For our world, grown old in its doubts, its irresponsiveness and its hate, it is its chance of renewal. It is its salvation.*

A Happy Easter! With the apostolic blessing which I willingly give you in the Lord's name.

BE YOUNG PEOPLE
OF TRUE, DEEP
CHRISTIAN FAITH

On Sunday, October 5, 1980, the Holy Father delivered the following talk to the youth of Apulia at Otranto. The young people gathered in the Piazzale degli Eroi represented ecclesiastical associations active in the area.

Beloved young people!

1. At the conclusion of this intense and splendid day of pilgrimage, which has brought me to your Otranto to venerate the Eight Hundred Martyrs on the fifth centenary of their testimony of faith and of blood, I meet you, who are and represent the future of your city, of your country, of the Church. You bear in your hearts, as a very precious heritage, the admirable example of those people of Otranto, who on August 14, 1480—at the dawn of what is historically considered the "modern age"—preferred to sacrifice their very lives rather than renounce the Christian faith.

This is a shining and glorious page for the secular and religious history of Italy, but especially for the history of the pilgrim Church in this world, which must pay, through the centuries, her price of suffering and persecution to keep intact and immaculate her faithfulness to the

Bridegroom, Christ, the Man-God, man's Redeemer and Liberator.

You, beloved young people, are legitimately proud of belonging to a generous, courageous and strong stock, which is happy to see itself reflected in those eight hundred inhabitants of Otranto who, after defending with all means the survival, the dignity, and the freedom of their beloved city and their homes, were also able to defend in a sublime way the treasure of faith, communicated to them in Baptism.

TO DIE FOR CHRIST

2. We cannot read today without intense emotion the accounts of the eyewitnesses of the dramatic episode: The citizens of Otranto, over fifteen years of age, were faced with the tremendous alternative: either to deny faith in Jesus Christ, or to die an atrocious death. *Antonio Pezzulla, a cloth cutter, answered for everyone: "We believe in Jesus Christ, the Son of God; and for Jesus Christ we are ready to die!"* And immediately afterwards, all the others, exhorting one another, confirmed: "We die for Jesus Christ, all of us; we die willingly, in order not to deny His holy faith!"

Were they, perhaps, deluded? Were they men outside their time? No, beloved young people! Those were men, real, strong, decided, consistent men, deeply rooted in their history; they were men who intensely loved their city; they were strongly bound to their families; among them there were young people, like you, and they longed, like you, for joy, happiness, and love; they dreamed of an honest and secure job, a holy home, a serene and tranquil life in the civil and religious community!

And they made their choice for Christ, with clarity and with firmness!

In five hundred years the history of the world has undergone many changes; *but man, in his deepest interiority, has kept the same desires, the same ideals, the same demands; he has remained exposed to the same temptations, which—in the name of fashionable systems and ideologies, try to empty the meaning and the value of the religious deed and of Christian faith itself.*

Before the suggestions of certain contemporary ideologies, which exalt and proclaim theoretical or practical atheism, I ask you, young people of Otranto and of Apulia: are you ready to repeat, with full conviction and awareness, the words of the Blessed Martyrs: "We choose to die for Christ with any kind of death, rather than deny Him"?

AUTHENTIC FAITH

3. The Blessed Martyrs have left us—and in particular they have left you—two fundamental orders: *love of one's earthly country; authenticity of Christian faith.*

The Christian loves his earthly country. Love of one's country is a Christian virtue; following the example of Christ, His first disciples always manifested sincere *pietas,* deep respect and a clear loyalty towards their earthly country, even when they were outraged and persecuted to the point of death by the civil authorities.

During the course of two millennia, Christians have made, and continue to make today, their contribution of work, dedication, sacrifice, preparation, and blood for the civil, social, and economic progress of their country!

The second order left to us by the Blessed Martyrs is authenticity of faith. The Christian must always be *consistent with his faith.* "Martyrdom"—Clemente Alessandrino wrote—"consists in bearing witness to God. But every soul that seeks knowledge of God with purity, and obeys God's commandments, is a martyr, both in life and in words. For, if it does not shed its blood, it pours out its faith, since for faith it separates from the body even before dying" *(Stromata,* 4, 4, 15: ed. Staehlin II, p. 255).

Be young people of faith! of true, deep Christian faith! My great Predecessor, Paul VI, on October 30, 1968, after speaking on the authenticity of faith, recited a prayer of his "to obtain faith."

Keeping in mind that incisive and profound text, I express the wish that, following the example of the Blessed Martyrs of Otranto, your faith, O young people, may be certain, that is, founded on the Word of God, on deep knowledge of the Gospel message, and especially of the life, person, and work of Christ; and also on the interior witness of the Holy Spirit.

May your faith be strong; may it not hesitate, not waver, before the doubts, the uncertainties which philosophical systems or fashionable movements would like to suggest to you; may it not descend to compromises with certain concepts, which would like to present Christianity as a mere ideology of historical character, and therefore to be placed at the same level as so many others, now outdated.

May your faith be joyful, because it is based on awareness of possessing a divine gift. When you pray and dialogue with God and when you converse with men, manifest the joy of this enviable possession.

Let your faith be active; let it manifest itself and take on concrete shape in laborious and generous charity towards brothers, who live crushed in sorrow and in need; let it be manifested in your serene adherence to the teaching of the truth; let it be expressed in your availability for all apostolic initiatives, in which you are called upon to participate for the expansion and the building up of the kingdom of Christ!

RENEWED COMMITMENT

I entrust these thoughts of mine to the Blessed Martyrs, whose intercession I invoke today, particularly for you young people, in order that, like them, you may be able to live with renewed commitment the requirements of Christ's message.

With my apostolic benediction.

Amen!

II. Addresses to University Students and Faculties About the Nature of University Life

1) *To University Students in Krakow. June 8, 1979.*

2) *To Irish Students at Galway. September 30, 1979.*

3) *To Italian Students in Norcia, Home of St. Benedict. March 23, 1980.*

4) *To African University Students at Yamoussoukro, Ivory Coast. May 10, 1980.*

GET TO KNOW CHRIST AND MAKE YOURSELVES KNOWN TO HIM

Late on Friday evening, June 8, 1979, John Paul II met the university students of Krakow at the Church of St. Michael the Archangel, erected at Skalka in the mid-eighteenth century on the spot where St. Stanislaus was martyred on April 11, 1079. The Holy Father conversed with them at length and delivered the following address.

Dear young friends,

1. Allow me to begin with my recollections, since it is still only a short time ago that I used to meet you regularly in the many pastoral centers for the university students of Krakow. We saw each other on various occasions and I think that we understood each other well. I shall never forget our exchange of Christmas good wishes with the shared Eucharist, the Advent and Lenten spiritual exercises and our other meetings.

This year I had to spend Lent in Rome and for the first time I spoke not to the Polish university students of Krakow but to the Roman university students. I shall quote you some passages of what I said to them in the Basilica of St. Peter:

"Christ is...the One who made a radical change in the way of understanding life. He showed that life is a passing over, not only to the

limit of death, but to a new life. Thus the cross became for us the supreme Chair of the truth of God and of man. We must all be pupils—no matter what our age is—of this Chair. Then we will understand that the cross is also the cradle of the new man.

"Those who are its pupils look at life in this way, perceive it in this way. And they teach it in this way to others. They imprint this meaning of life on the whole of temporal reality: on morality, creativity, culture, politics, economics. It has very often been affirmed—as, for example, the followers of Epicurus sustained in ancient times, and as some followers of Marx do in our times for other reasons—that this concept of life distracts man from temporal reality and that it cancels it in a certain sense. The truth is quite different. *Only this conception of life gives full importance to all the problems of temporal reality.* It opens the possibility of placing them fully in man's existence. And one thing is certain: this conception of life does not permit shutting man up in temporary things, it does not permit subordinating him completely to them. It decides his freedom.

"Giving human life this 'paschal' meaning, that is, that it is a passing over to freedom, Jesus Christ taught with His word and even more with His own example that it is a test...the test of thought, of the 'heart' and of the will, the test of truth and love. In this sense, it is at the same time the test of the Covenant with God....

"The concept of 'test' is closely connected with the concept of responsibility. Both are addressed to our will, to our acts. Accept, dear friends, both these concepts—or rather both realities—as elements of the construction of one's own humanity. *This humanity of yours is already mature and, at the same time, is still young. It is in the phase of the definitive formation of one's life project.* This formation takes place particularly in the 'academic' years, in the time of higher studies....

"It is necessary to undertake this test with all responsibility. It is at the same time a personal responsibility—for my life, for its future pattern, for its value—and also a social responsibility, for justice and peace, for the moral order of one's own native environment and of the whole of society. It is a responsibility for the real common good. A man who has such an awareness of the meaning of life does not destroy, but constructs the future. Christ teaches us this."

After the evening I spent with the youth of Rome, during which nearly all received their Easter Communion, *I thought to myself: How alike students are everywhere! Everywhere they listen to the Word of God and participate in the liturgy with the same attention.* I then thought of you, of the spiritual retreats of the Polish university students of Krakow, of the similar moment of recollection. reflection and living the silence in the Church of St. Ann, or in that of the Mother of God at Nowa Wies, or in that of the Dominicans or of the Jesuits, during like encounters.

2. I thought of you also in Mexico, when I met the local university students in the shrine of Our Lady of Guadalupe. Allow me to quote also some

phrases from the letter that after my return from
Mexico I wrote specially to the university students of Latin America:

"During my meeting with you I saw that you
feel very deeply the evil that weighs upon the
social life of the nations whose sons and daughters you are. You are troubled by the need of
change, the need to build a better world, one that
is more just and also more worthy of man. In this
manner your desires coincide with the outlook
that has become more and more marked through
the teaching and apostolate of the present-day
Church. The Second Vatican Council often responds to this aspiration to make life on earth
more human, more worthy of man. This basically
has reference to each human being and so to all
human beings. It cannot lead to restrictions,
exploitation, falsification or discrimination of
any kind. It must bring with it the full truth
concerning man and lead to full actualization of human rights. The correct actualization
of this noble inspiration beating in the heart and
will of the young requires that man be seen in the
whole of his human dimension. *Man must not be
reduced to the sphere of his merely material needs.*
Progress cannot be measured by economic categories alone. The spiritual dimension of the
human being must be given its right place.

"Man is himself through the maturity of his
spirit, his conscience and his relationship with
God and neighbor.

"*There will be no better world, no better ar-
rangement of social life, unless preference is first
given to the values of the human spirit.* Remem-

ber this well, you who are justly longing for changes bringing a better and more just society, you who rightly oppose every kind of evil, of discrimination, of violence and of torture inflicted on human beings. Remember that the order that you desire is a moral order and you will not attain it in any way, if you do not give first place to all that constitutes the strength of the human spirit—justice, love and friendship" (*AAS* 71 [1979] 253-254).

3. I rejoice today in meeting you again in the context of the jubilee of St. Stanislaus in which I have the good fortune to participate. When we listen to the Gospel that the liturgy of the solemnity of St. Stanislaus each year recalls to us, we see in our mind's eye Christ, the Good Shepherd who "lays down his life for the sheep" (Jn. 10:11), who knows His own sheep and His own know Him (cf. Jn. 10:14), who goes after the lost sheep and, when He has found it, "he lays it on his shoulders, rejoicing" (Lk. 15:5), and brings it back with joy to the fold.

All that I can say to you is summed up in the words: Get to know Christ and make yourselves known to Him. He knows each one of you in a particular way. It is not a knowledge that arouses opposition and rebellion, a knowledge that forces one to flee in order to safeguard his own inward mystery. It is not a knowledge made up of hypotheses and reducing man to his dimensions of social utility. *The knowledge of Christ is a knowledge full of the simple truth about man and, above all, full of love.* Submit yourselves to this simple and loving knowledge of the Good

Shepherd. *Be certain that He knows each one of you more than each one of you knows himself.* He knows because He has laid down His life (cf. Jn. 15:13).

Allow Him to find you. A human being, a young person, at times gets lost in himself, in the world about him, and in all the network of human affairs that wrap him round. Allow Christ to find you. Let Him know all about you and guide you. It is true that following someone requires also making demands on ourselves. That is the law of friendship. If we wish to travel together, we must pay attention to the road we are to take. If we go walking in the mountains, we must follow the signs. If we go mountain climbing, we cannot let go of the rope. We must also preserve our unity with the divine Friend whose name is Jesus Christ. We must cooperate with Him.

Many times I have spoken of this and have done so more amply and in greater detail than today. Remember what I said before and am saying now. I said it and I am saying it from personal experience. *I have always been amazed at the wonderful power that Christ holds over the human heart: He holds it not for just any reason or motive, not for any kind of career or profit, but only because He loves us and lays down His life for His brethren* (cf. Jn. 15:13).

4. You are the future of the world, of the nation, of the Church. "Tomorrow depends on you." Accept with a sense of responsibility the

simple truth contained in this song of youth and ask Christ, through His Mother, that you may be able to face it.

You must carry into the future the whole of the experience of history that is called "Poland." It is a difficult experience, perhaps one of the most difficult in the world, in Europe, and in the Church. *Do not be afraid of the toil; be afraid only of thoughtlessness and pusillanimity.* From the difficult experience that we call "Poland" a better future can be drawn, but only on condition that you are honorable, temperate, believing, free in spirit and strong in your convictions.

Be consistent in your faith.

Be faithful to the Mother of fair love. Have trust in her, as you shape your love and form your young families.

May Christ always be for you "the Way, and the Truth, and the Life."

ONLY IN CHRIST
WILL YOU DISCOVER
THE TRUE GREATNESS
OF YOUR LIVES

On September 30, 1979, at Galway, an Irish city on the west coast, the Pope met a large concourse of young persons coming from all parts of Ireland, to assist at the concelebrated Mass at Ballybrit Racecourse.

After an enthusiastic welcome by the youth of Ireland both in English and Gaelic, accompanied with song and music, the Holy Father delivered the following homily during the Mass.

Dear young people, brothers and sisters of our Lord Jesus Christ,

1. This is a very special occasion, a very important one. This morning, the Pope belongs to the youth of Ireland! I have looked forward to this moment; I have prayed that I may touch your hearts with the words of Jesus. Here I wish to recall what I said so often before as Archbishop of Krakow and what I have repeated as Successor of St. Peter: I believe in youth. I believe in youth with all my heart and with all the strength of my conviction. And today I say: I believe in the youth of Ireland! I believe in you who stand here before me, in every one of you.

When I look at you, I see the Ireland of the future. Tomorrow, you will be the living force of your country; you will decide what Ireland will be. Tomorrow, as technicians or teachers, nurses or secretaries, farmers or tradesmen, doctors or engineers, priests or religious—tomorrow you will have the power to make dreams come true. Tomorrow, Ireland will depend on you.

When I look at you assembled around this altar and listen to your praying voices, I see the future of the Church. God has His plan for the Church in Ireland, but He needs you to carry it out. What the Church will be in the future depends on your free cooperation with God's grace.

When I look at the thousands of young people here before me, I also see the challenges that you face. You have come from the parishes of Ireland as the representatives of those that could not be here. You carry in your hearts the rich heritage that you have received from your parents, your teachers and your priests. You carry in your hearts the treasures which Irish history and culture have given you, but you also share in the problems that Ireland faces.

2. Today, for the first time since St. Patrick preached the faith to the Irish, the Successor of St. Peter comes from Rome and sets foot on Irish soil. You rightly ask yourselves what message he brings and what words he will speak to Ireland's youth. *My message can be none other than the message of Christ Himself;* my words can be none other than the Word of God.

I did not come here to give you an answer to all your individual questions. You have your bishops, who know your local circumstances and local problems; you have your priests, especially those who devote themselves to the demanding but rewarding pastoral care of youth. They know you personally and will help you to find the right answers. *But I, too, feel that I know you, for I know and understand young people.* And I know that you, like other young people of your age in other countries, are affected by what is happening in society around you. Although you still live in an atmosphere where true religious and moral principles are held in honor, you have to realize that your fidelity to these principles will be tested in many ways. The religious and moral traditions of Ireland, the very soul of Ireland, will be challenged by the temptations that spare no society in our age. Like so many other young people in various parts of the world, you will be told that changes must be made, that you must have more freedom, that you should be different from your parents, and that the decisions about your lives depend on you, and you alone.

The prospect of growing economic progress, and the chance of obtaining a greater share of the goods that modern society has to offer, will appear to you as an opportunity to achieve greater freedom. The more you possess—you may be tempted to think—the more you will feel liberated from every type of confinement. In order to make more money and to possess more, in order to eliminate effort and worry, you may be tempted to take moral shortcuts where honesty, truth and work are concerned. The progress of science and technology seems inevitable and you may be enticed to look towards the technological society for the answers to all your problems.

3. The lure of pleasure, to be had whenever and wherever it can be found, will be strong and it may be presented to you as part of progress towards greater autonomy and freedom from rules. The desire to be free from external restraints may manifest itself very strongly in the sexual domain, since this is an area that is so closely tied to a human personality. The moral standards that the Church and society have held up to you for so long a time, will be presented as obsolete and a hindrance to the full development of your own personality. Mass media, entertainment, and literature will present a model for living where all too often it is every man for himself, and where the unrestrained affirmation of self leaves no room for concern for others.

You will hear people tell you that your religious practices are hopelessly out of date, that they hamper your style and your future, that with everything that social and scientific progress has to offer, you will be able to organize your own lives, and that God has played out His role. Even many religious persons will adopt such attitudes, breathing them in from the surrounding atmosphere without attending to the practical atheism that is at their origin.

A society that, in this way, has lost its higher religious and moral principles will become an easy prey for manipulation and for domination by the forces, which, under the pretext of greater freedom, will enslave it ever more.

Yes, dear young people, *do not close your eyes to the moral sickness that stalks your society today, and from which your youth alone will not protect you.* How many young people have already warped their consciences and have substituted the true joy of life with drugs, sex, alcohol, vandalism and the empty pursuit of mere material possessions.

4. Something else is needed: something that you will find only in Christ, for He alone is the measure and the scale that you must use to evaluate your own life. *In Christ you will discover the true greatness of your own humanity;* He will make you understand your own dignity as human beings "created to the image and likeness of God" (Gn. 1:26). Christ has the answers to your questions and the key to history; He has the power to uplift hearts. He keeps calling you, He keeps inviting you, He who is "the way, and the truth, and the life" (Jn. 14:6). *Yes, Christ calls you, but He calls you in truth. His call is demanding, because He invites you to let yourselves be "captured" by Him completely, so that your whole lives will be seen in a different light. He is the Son of God, who reveals to you the loving face of the Father. He is the Teacher, the only One whose teaching does not pass away, the only One who teaches with authority.* He is the friend who said to His disciples, "No longer do I call you servants...but I have called you friends" (Jn. 15:15). And He proved His friendship by laying down His life for you.

His call is demanding for He taught us what it means to be truly human. Without heeding the call of Jesus, it will not be possible to realize the fullness of your own humanity. You must build on the foundation which is Christ (cf. 1 Cor. 3:11); only with Him will your life be meaningful and worthwhile.

You come from Catholic families; you go regularly and meet Christ in Holy Communion on Sundays or even during the week. Many of you pray with your families every day; and I hope you all will continue to do so throughout later life. And yet it can happen that you will be tempted to walk away from Christ. This can happen especially if you see the contradiction in the life of some of your fellowmen between the faith they profess and their way of living. *But I wish to insist and to plead that you always heed the call of Christ, for He alone can teach you the true meaning of life and of all temporal realities.*

5. Permit me, in this context, to recall still another phrase of the Gospel, a phrase that we must remember even when its consequences are particularly difficult for us to accept. It is the phrase that Christ pronounced in the Sermon on the Mount: "Love your enemies, do good to those who hate you" (Lk. 6:27). You have guessed already that even by my reference to these words of the Savior, I have before my mind the painful events that for over ten years have been taking place in Northern Ireland. I am sure that all young people are living these events very deeply and very painfully, for they are tracing deep furrows in your young hearts. These events, painful as they are, must also be an incitement to reflection. *They demand that you*

*form an interior judgment of conscience to deter-
mine where you, as young Catholics, stand on the
matter.*

You heard the words of Jesus: "Love your
enemies." The command of Jesus does not mean
that we are not bound by love for our native
land; they do not mean that we can remain indifferent before injustice in its various temporal
and historical aspects. These words of Jesus
take away only hate. *I beg you to reflect deeply:
what would human life be if Jesus had never
spoken such words?* What would the world be if
in our mutual relations we were to give primacy
to hatred among people, between classes, between nations? What would the future of humanity be if we were to base on this hatred the future
of individuals and of nations?

Sometimes, one could have the feeling that,
before the experiences of history and before concrete situations, love has lost its power and that
it is impossible to practice it. And yet, in the long
run, love always brings victory, love is never
defeated. If it were not so, humanity would only
be condemned to destruction.

6. Dear young friends, this is the message I
entrust to you today, asking you to take it with
you and share it with your family at home and
with your friends in school and at work. On
returning home, tell your parents, and everyone who wants to listen, that the Pope believes
in you and that he counts on you. Say that the
young are the strength of the Pope, who wishes
to share with them his hope for the future and
his encouragement.

I have given you the words of my heart. Now let me also ask you for something in return. *You know that from Ireland I am going to the United Nations. The truth which I have proclaimed before you is the same that I shall present, in a different way, before that supreme forum of the nations.* I hope that your prayers—the prayers of the youth of Ireland—will accompany me and support me in this important mission. *I count on you, because the future of human life on this earth is at stake, in every country and in the whole world.* The future of all peoples and nations, the future of humanity itself depends on this: whether the words of Jesus in the Sermon on the Mount, whether the message of the Gospel will be listened to once again.

May the Lord Jesus be always with you! With His truth that makes you free (cf. Jn. 8:32); with His word that unlocks the mystery of man and reveals to man his own humanity; with His death and resurrection that makes you new and strong.

Let us place this intention at the feet of Mary, Mother of God and Queen of Ireland, example of generous love and dedication to the service of others.

Young people of Ireland, I love you! Young people of Ireland, I bless you! I bless you in the name of our Lord Jesus Christ.

THE NEED TO MEET
THE ABSOLUTE

About 5.00 p.m. in the afternoon of Sunday, March 23, 1980, the Holy Father met a very large number of young people in St. Benedict's Square in Norcia. With the young people of Norcia, and those of the other towns of Valnerina stricken by the earthquake, there were various groups from different regions of Italy, who were among the first to bring aid to the people immediately after the earthquake. John Paul II delivered the following address.

Beloved young people,

Now at the conclusion of this day, so intense and rich in deep emotions and interior joy, I am happy to meet you, young people of Valnerina and the whole of Umbria, together with those of you who have gathered here to strengthen your spirit in that generous dedication that you jointly displayed immediately after the disastrous earthquake which struck these hard-working people last year. You bore at that time a luminous witness all the more to be appreciated because it was a spontaneous expression springing from your dynamic and serene spirit of sacrifice, and emulating in the work of assistance and solidarity the example of precocious maturity offered by the young Benedict, whose mind—as St. Gregory the Pope says—matured from childhood, anticipating age with virtues (cf. *Dialogues,* II, Prol.).

Inspired by such a resolution to cooperate in the good of the community and especially of those living in painful conditions of hardship, you set yourselves in the true light of the "Christian humanism" proposed and lived by the Saint of Norcia, and which can be summed up in true respect for man in every expression of his value, in efficacious love for him, especially when he reveals the countenance and the voice of suffering.

Accept, therefore, dear young people of Caritas, Agesci, the Community of St. Giles, Communion and Liberation, the Focolare, Catholic Action and the various ecclesial groups, my affectionate greeting in this birthplace of St. Benedict and, above all, my congratulations on what you have carried out with youthful enthusiasm.

Your commitment of charity and altruism has found its place in the age-old course of the Benedictine message. *The latter is valid and relevant today also because it is firmly attached to perennial values, which, if they require ever new expression and verification, are such as to vivify and elevate the human experience of all times. This message must attract and win over also the young people of the present generation, who are often disappointed and confused in the maze of a hedonistic and permissive society.*

In fact, also the sad times in which Saint Benedict's spiritual experience found its place, were full of deep contradictions, ambiguous and utopian aspirations, vain resolutions of grandeur; those times, too, were marked by desolate moral wretchedness, and very low living standards, under the impact of peoples in expansion, but still dominated by promptings of violence. The Saint of Norcia, however, nourished by the certainties of the Faith, reasserted the power of a Christianity that taught moral dignity and spiritual freedom and was at the same time the architect of civilization.

As you have clearly experienced, the conquest of interior spaces, that offer God His rightful place in the human spirit, all that commitment, in a word, which we could distinguish with the primacy of "ORA," "pray," is absolutely not in conflict, but on the contrary brings relief and grants creative intuition to true openness to the social sphere, to daily duty deeply felt, to the living forces of work and culture, thus animating with fervent inspiration and spirit of service the great and agitated world of "WORK."

What can I say to you in particular in this picturesque setting of crags and valleys which tempered the strong and courageous spirit of the predestined youth, and at a moment so charged with brotherhood and communion pervaded by the spiritual presence of the Father of our European civilization?

Continue, dear young people, with the witness you generously bear, because, while it is in harmony with the values of Benedictine tradition, it is at the same time faithful to modern men, interpreting their deepest aspirations.

IMPORTANCE OF SILENCE
AND MEDITATION

1. *You have felt the urgent need of meeting the Absolute and, therefore, you have discovered the importance of interiority, silence, and meditation, to be able to grasp the definitive and reconciling meaning of your own existence.* You have tasted the sweetness of prayer and of that ever renewed and persevering reconciliation of friendship with the Lord established in hearts by an existential attitude of humble and active obedience to the heavenly Father. With Saint Benedict, then, I will address to you the fatherly invitation: *"Ausculta, fili, verba magistri";* listen, sons, to the teachings of true teachers, and make your hearts attentive in prayerful silence, in order to return, through the effort of docile obedience, to wholesome precepts, to Him from whom a position of indolence or rebellion takes us away (cf. *Rule,* Prol.). Place yourselves often before the interior Master, and those who represent Him, in the attitude of the true disciple, who knows how to be silent and listen.

PREMISES FOR COMPLETE
HUMAN REVIVAL

2. You, dear young people, have discovered charity and love, which are manifested in solicitude for your neighbor and in an open dialogue with brothers, respecting their dignity and being available for a diffusion of reciprocal contribution. They are values that St. Benedict estab-

lished in a socio-economic context in which exploitation and arbitrary action predominated, by opposing the spirit of brotherhood to violence, and industrious commitment to sloth, in order to lay down the premises for a complete human revival.

The Benedictine monastery will be almost a forerunner of the new *societas;* within its walls discriminations between nobles and plebeians, between rich and poor, between free men and slaves, are canceled. In it persecuted settlers and barbarian oppressors will find refuge setting aside, before God, old rivalries and recent rancor, in order to dedicate themselves to prayer, work and mutual support. The Saint, full of delicacy in treating the monks, in welcoming the pilgrims, in looking after the sick, lists among the means to act rightly: *"Pauperes recreare,...infirmum visitare,...in tribulatione subvenire, dolentem consolari; nihil amori Christi praeponere;* help the poor,...visit the sick,...assist those who are victims of misfortune, console the afflicted,...put nothing before love of Christ" (*Rule,* Chap. IV).

VIOLENCE BORN OF HATE

3. You love beauty which is the splendor of order and, therefore, mainly innocence of life and harmony of the spirit. The Rule, on the writing of which the Saint was engaged for a long time, and which indicates with wisdom and moderation the ways and the times of prayer and work, shows the importance he attached to

this beauty emerging from an orderly rhythm of life. He harmonizes, indeed, in himself the sense of authority, order and discipline, borrowed from the classical world, with a delicacy of spirit that matured during his long progress towards perfection.

It is the order, primarily of a spiritual nature, that reigns there which enables the monasteries to be great centers of life and creative activity, in the mature awareness that Christianity is at the same time asceticism in regard to God and also earthly commitment, so that prayer leads to work not only as a means of ensuring monks the necessary maintenance, but also as a most valuable opportunity for personal discipline and social advancement.

The powerful call of the Benedictine message to seek God and His will, to establish a social context permeated by brotherhood and order, takes on an extraordinarily topical note on this day of prayer and reflection, in regard to the very serious problem of terrorism in Italy.

The violence that is upsetting the social fabric of the Italian nation is not fortuitous: it is based on a precise program, it is born of the spirit of hate. The origin of violence is here, only here. People must not let themselves be deceived by other motivations. *That is why it is so necessary for Christians to be able to discern this spirit, understand its intrinsic perversion (cf. Jn. 3:15), and not let themselves be contaminated, so that they can withdraw themselves from the spiral of hate and not let themselves be taken in by its promptings.* On the contrary, be clear-sighted and generous apostles of love.

Dear young people, you have picked out the ideal and main values of St. Benedict's witness and, with the grace of God, you have undertaken to put them into practice in your lives. Continue to interpret them and embody them with courage, generosity and enthusiasm, convinced that the Lord Himself is the only Guarantor, as the Psalmist says, of a building with solid foundations, and therefore of a just and human future, a peaceful and productive society, and harmonious and brotherly order. With my affectionate blessing.

CHRIST CALLS YOU TO CONSTRUCT A NEW SOCIETY

In the afternoon of May 11, 1980, John Paul II traveled by helicopter from Abidjan to Yamoussoukro. On his arrival there he concelebrated Mass with thirteen young priests for the student youth of the country. The celebration was held in the largest square of Yamoussoukro, which by presidential decree of May 10 is now known as John Paul II Square. It was estimated that more than 200,000 were present. During the Mass the Holy Father preached the following homily.

Dear students, boys and girls,

1. How can I thank you for having come in such large numbers, so joyful and trusting around the Father and Head of the Catholic Church? I hope and I ask God that this meeting may be a moment of deep communion of our hearts and minds, an unforgettable moment for me and a decisive one for you.

Your problems and aspirations as Ivory Coast students have come to my knowledge. They make me both happy and moved. It is, therefore, young people, in a concrete setting and as bearers of great human and Christian hopes, that I address you with perfect confidence. The Liturgy of the Word which has just ended has certainly contributed to putting your souls in a state of receptiveness. These three readings constitute an ideal framework for the demanding meditation we shall make shortly.

The Church, of which you are members through the sacraments of Baptism and Confirmation—I shall have, moreover, the joy of conferring the latter on some of you—is a Church that has been open, since her foundation, to all men and all cultures: a Church assured of a glorious conclusion through the humiliations and persecutions inflicted upon her in the course of history; a Church mysteriously animated by the Spirit of Pentecost and eager to reveal to men their inalienable dignity and their vocation as "members of God's family," creatures inhabited by God, Father, Son and Spirit. How bracing it is to breathe this atmosphere of a Church always young and resolute!

Your bishops have recently addressed to you, but also to your parents and those in charge of you, a letter intended to diagnose the dangers that threaten youth and bring about, in its ranks as well as among adults, a generous spiritual outburst. Many of you are very conscious of the difficulties and miseries affecting the environments of the young. Without generalizing, they are not afraid to call a spade a spade and to question their elders, referring to the famous words of the prophet Ezekiel: "The fathers have eaten sour grapes, and the children's teeth are set on edge" (Ez. 18:2).

A CALL TO
PERSONAL CONVERSION

2. Today, on my part, I would like to convince you of a truth of common sense, but of fundamental importance, which applies to every man and every society that is suffering physically or morally: namely, that a sick person cannot get better unless he himself takes the necessary remedies. That is what the apostle St. James wished to make the first Christians understand (cf. Jas. 1:23-26). What is the use of diagnosing the disease in the mirror of individual and collective conscience, if we forget it immediately or refuse to treat it? Everyone in society bears responsibilities with regard to this situation and each one is called, therefore, to a personal conversion which is truly a form of participation in the evangelization of the world (cf. *Evangelii nuntiandi,* nos. 21, 41). But I ask you: is it not true that if all the young agree to change their own lives, the whole of society will change? Why wait longer for ready-made solutions to the problems from which you are suffering? Your dynamism, your imagination, your faith, are capable of moving mountains!

Let us look together, calmly and realistically, at the ways that will lead you towards the society of which you are dreaming. A society built on truth, justice, brotherhood, peace; a society worthy of man and in conformity with God's plan. These ways are inescapably those of your ardent preparation for your responsibilities tomorrow and those of a true spiritual awakening.

Young people of the Ivory Coast, find again together the courage to live! The men who cause history to advance, at the humblest or at the highest level, are those who remain convinced of man's vocation: the vocation of a searcher, of one who strives vigorously, and of a builder. What is your conception of man? It is a fundamental question, since the answer will determine your future and the future of your country, because it is your duty to make a success of your lives.

YOU ARE A PRIVILEGED YOUTH

3. You have, indeed, obligations towards the national community. The past generations carry you invisibly. It is they who enabled you to have access to studies and a culture destined to make you the executives of a young nation. The people count on you. Forgive it for considering you privileged persons. You really are privileged, at least on the plane of the distribution of cultural goods. How many young people of your age—in your country and in the world—are at work and are contributing already, as workers or farmers, to the production and economic success of their country! Others, alas, are unemployed, without a trade, and sometimes without hope. Others again have not and will not have the chance to have access to schooling of quality. You have a duty of solidarity towards all. And they have the right to be demanding with regard to you. Dear

young people, do you want to be the thinkers, the technicians, the leaders that your country and Africa need? Avoid like the plague carelessness and the easy way out. Be indulgent to others and severe with regard to yourselves! Be men!

PRESERVE ROOTS AND SAFEGUARD VALUES

4. Allow me, further, to stress a very important aspect of your human, intellectual and technical preparation for your future tasks. It is also part of your duties. Preserve carefully your African roots. Safeguard the values of your culture. You know them and are proud of them: respect for life, family solidarity and support for relatives, respect for the old, the sense of hospitality, judicious preservation of traditions, the taste for feasts and symbols, attachment to dialogue and palaver to settle differences. All that is a real treasure from which you can and must draw something new for the building up of your country, on an original and typically African model, made up of harmony between the values of its cultural past and the most acceptable elements of modern civilization. On this precise plane, remain very vigilant, with regard to models of society which are based on the selfish pursuit of individual happiness and on the god of money, or on the class struggle and violent means. All materialism is a source of degradation for man and of enslavement of social life.

LOOK WITH NEW EYES
TOWARDS JESUS

5. Let us go even further in clear vision of the road to take or to continue. Who is your God? Without ignoring any of the difficulties that the social and cultural changes of our time cause all believers, but also thinking of all those who struggle to keep the faith, I venture to say concisely and insistently: Look up! Look with new eyes towards Jesus Christ! I take the liberty of asking you in a friendly way: have you read the letter I wrote last year to all Christians about Christ the Redeemer? In the wake of the Popes who preceded me, Paul VI especially, I endeavored to ward off the temptation and error of modern man and modern societies to exclude God and to put an end to the expression of the religious sentiment.

The death of God in men's hearts and lives is the death of man. I wrote in that letter: "The man who wishes to understand himself thoroughly—and not just in accordance with immediate, partial, often superficial, and even illusory standards and measures of his being—must with his unrest, uncertainty and even his weakness and sinfulness, with his life and death, draw near to Christ. He must, so to speak, enter into Him with all his own self; he must 'appropriate' and assimilate the whole of the reality of the Incarnation and Redemption in order to find himself. If this profound process takes place within him, he then bears fruit not only of adoration of God but also of deep wonder at himself. How precious must man be in the eyes of the Creator, if he 'gained so great a Redeemer' and if God 'gave his only Son' in order that man 'should not perish but have eternal life!' " (*Redemptor hominis,* no. 10) Yes, beloved young people, Jesus Christ is not a kidnapper of men, but a Savior. And He wants to free you, to make you, one and all, saviors in the student world of today as in the professions and important responsibilities that you will assume tomorrow.

FAITH IS TRULY A GIFT FROM GOD

6. *So stop thinking to yourself or saying out loud that the Christian faith is good only for children and simple people. If it still appears to be so, it is because adolescents and adults have seriously neglected to make their faith grow at the same rate as their human development.* Faith is not a pretty garment for childhood days. Faith is a gift from God, a stream of light and power that comes from Him, and must enlighten and give dynamic impulse to all sectors of life, in proportion as it takes root in responsibilities. Make up your minds, and persuade your friends and fellow students, to adopt the means of a personal religious formation, worthy of the name. Take advantage of the chaplains and animators placed at your disposal. With them, train yourselves to make a synthesis between your human knowledge and your faith, between your African culture and modernity, between your role as citizens and your Christian vocation. Celebrate your faith and learn to pray together.

You will find again in this way the sense of the Church which is communion in the same Lord among believers, who then go out into the midst of their brothers and sisters to love them and serve them in the way of Christ. You have a vital need of integration in Christian, brotherly and dynamic communities. Frequent them assiduously. Inspire them with the breath of your youth. Build them, if they do not exist. In this way your temptation to go and seek elsewhere—in esoteric groups—what Christianity brings you fully, will disappear.

APOSTOLIC COMMITMENT

7. Logically, the personal and community deepening of faith of which we have just spoken, must lead you to concrete apostolic commitments. Many of you are already on this way, and I congratulate them. Young people of the Ivory Coast, today Christ calls you through His representative on earth. He calls you exactly as He called Peter and Andrew, James and John, and the other Apostles. He calls you to construct His Church, to build a new society. Come in crowds! Take your place in your Christian communities. Offer royally your time and your talents, your heart and your faith to animate liturgical celebrations, to take part in the immense amount of catechetical work among children, adolescents and even adults, and to be integrated in the numerous services for the benefit of the poorest, illiterates, the handicapped, the isolated, refugees and migrants, to animate your student

movements, to work with the authorities for the defense and promotion of the human person. Truly, the workyard is immense and stirring for young people who feel overflowing with life.

It seems to me the very moment to address those young people who are going to receive the sacrament of Confirmation, precisely in order to enter a new stage of their baptismal life: the stage of active service in the immense workyard of the evangelization of the world. The laying on of hands and the anointing with the holy chrism will really and effectively signify the plenary coming of the Holy Spirit into the very depth of your person, at the crossroads, in a way, of your human faculties of intelligence in search of truth and freedom, in pursuit of an ideal. Your confirmation today is your Pentecost for life! Realize the seriousness and grandeur of this sacrament.

What will be your lifestyle from now on? That of the Apostles when they came out of the Upper Room! That of Christians of every era, energetically faithful to prayer, to deepening of, and bearing witness to, faith, to the breaking of the Eucharistic Bread, to service of one's neighbor and especially of the poorest (cf. Acts 2:42-47). Young confirmed persons of today or yesterday, advance, all of you, along the ways of life as fervent witnesses of Pentecost, an inexhaustible source of youth and dynamism for the Church and for the world.

Expect to meet sometimes with opposition, contempt, mockery. True disciples are not above the Master. Their crosses are like the passion and cross of Christ: a mysterious source of fruitfulness. This paradox of suffering offered and fruitful has been confirmed for twenty centuries by the history of the Church.

Allow me finally to assure you that such apostolic commitments prepare you not only to bear your heavy responsibilities in the future, but also to found solid homes, without which a nation cannot hold out long; and what is more, Christian homes, which are so many basic cells of the ecclesial community. There are commitments which will lead some of you towards complete donation to Christ, in the priesthood or religious life. The dioceses of the Ivory Coast, like all the dioceses of Africa, have the right to rely on your generous response to the call that the Lord certainly makes many of you hear: "Come, and follow me."

A flash in the pan, this celebration? A flash in the pan, this meditation? The liturgical texts of this Sixth Sunday of Easter affirm the contrary. The Gospel of John assures us that the Holy Spirit dwells in the loving and faithful hearts of the disciples of Christ. His role is to refresh their memory as believers, to enlighten them in depth, to help them to solve the problems of their time, in the peace and hope of the new world conjured up in the reading from Revelation.

May this same Holy Spirit unite us all and dedicate us all to the service of God our Father and of men our brothers, through Christ, in Christ, and with Christ! Amen.

III. Addresses to University Convocations and Meetings About the Nature of a Christian University

1) *To Students of Mexican Catholic Universities. January 31, 1979.*

2) *To Members of the Council of International Federation of Catholic Universities. February 24, 1980.*

3) *To the* Institut Catholique *of Paris. June 1, 1980.*

4) *To the Faculty and Students of the Catholic University of America. October 7, 1979.*

5) *To Faculty and Students of the Italian Catholic University of the Sacred Heart in Milan. December 8, 1978.*

THE MISSION OF CATHOLIC UNIVERSITIES

On January 31, 1979, John Paul II met tens of thousands of students of the Catholic universities of .Mexico on the esplanade in front of the Guadalupe Sanctuary, and delivered the following address.

Beloved brothers and daughters of the Catholic university world,

1. With immense joy and hope I come to this appointment with you, students, professors and lecturers of the Catholic universities of Mexico, in whom I also see the university world of the whole of Latin America.

Receive my most cordial greeting. It is the greeting of one who feels so much at home among the young, in whom he lays so many hopes; especially when it is a question of such qualified sectors and those that pass through university halls, preparing for a future that will be determinant in society.

Allow me to recall in the first place the members of the Catholic University La Salle, within which this meeting was to have taken place. I recall no less cordially, however, the other Mexican Catholic universities: the Iberian American University, the Anahuác University, Monterrey University, the Superior Institute of Educational Sciences in Mexico City, the Faculty of Public Accountancy at Vera Cruz, the Western Institute of Technology and Higher Studies at Guadalajara, Montolinia University, Puebla University for Women, the canonical Faculty of Philosophy in this city, and the Faculty—still in embryo—of Theology, also in this metropolis.

These are young universities. You have, however, a venerable ancestor in the "Royal and Pontifical University of Mexico," founded on September 21, 1551, with the explicit purpose that in it "the natives and sons of Spaniards should be instructed in matters of the holy Catholic Faith and in the other faculties."

There are also among you—and they are certainly extremely numerous in the whole Mexican territory—Catholic professors and students who teach or study in universities of different denominations. I address my affectionate greeting to them, too, and express my deep joy at knowing that they are all engaged in the same way in establishing the kingdom of Christ.

Let us now extend our view to the vast Latin-American horizon. Thus my greeting and thought will dwell with satisfaction on so many other Catholic university centers, which are a motive of legitimate pride in every nation, where so many enthusiastic looks converge, from whence Christian culture and civilization irradiate. *There, persons are formed in the atmosphere of an integral concept of the human being, with scientific precision, and with a Christian view of man, life, society, moral and religious values.*

2. And now what more can I say to you in these moments that will necessarily be short?

What can the Mexican and Latin-American Catholic university world expect from the words of the Pope?

I think I can sum it up, quite synthetically, in three observations, following the line of my venerated Predecessor, Paul VI.

a) The first one is that the Catholic university must offer a specific contribution to the Church and society, setting itself at a high level of scientific research, deep study of problems and an adequate historical sense. But that is not sufficient for a Catholic university. *It must find its ultimate and deep meaning in Christ, in His message of salvation which embraces man in his totality, and in the teaching of the Church.*

All this presupposes the promotion of an integral culture, that is, one that aims at the complete development of the human person; one in which emphasis is laid on the values of intelligence, will, conscience, and brotherhood, all of which are based on God the Creator and have been marvelously exalted in Christ (cf. *Gaudium et spes*, no. 61): a culture that aims in a disinterested and genuine way at the good of the community and of the whole of society.

b) The second observation is that the Catholic university must form men who are really outstanding for their knowledge, ready to exercise important functions in society and to bear witness to their faith before the world (*Gravissimum educationes*, no. 10). This aim is unquestionably decisive today. *Moral and Christian formation must not be considered as something added from outside, but rather as an aspect with which the academic institution is, so to speak, specified and lived.* It is a question of promoting and realizing in professors and students a more and more harmonious synthesis between faith and reason, between faith and culture, between faith and life. This synthesis must be obtained not only at the level of research and teaching, but also at the educative-pedagogical level.

c) The third observation is that the Catholic university must be an environment in which Christianity is alive and operating. *It is an essential vocation of the Catholic university to bear witness that it is a community seriously and sincerely engaged in scientific research, but also visibly characterized by a real Christian life.* That presupposes, among other things, a revision of the figure of the professor, who cannot be considered a mere transmitter of knowledge, but also and above all a witness and educator to true Christian life. In this privileged environment of formation, you, dear students, are called to conscientious and responsible collaboration, free and generous, to realize your formation itself.

3. The establishment of a university apostolate, both as *an apostolate of intelligences* and as a source of liturgical life, and which must serve the whole university sector of the nation, will not fail to yield precious fruits of human and Christian elevation.

Dear sons, who dedicate yourselves completely or partially to the Catholic university sector in your respective countries, and all you who, in any university environment, are engaged in establishing the kingdom of God:

—create a real university family, engaged in the pursuit, which is not always easy, of truth and good, the supreme aspirations of the rational being and the foundations of a solid and responsible moral structure;

—pursue a serious research activity, directing the new generations towards truth, towards human and religious maturity;

—work indefatigably for real and complete progress in your countries. Without prejudices of any kind, take the hand of those who propose, like you, to construct the real common good;

—unite your forces as bishops, priests, religious men and women, laity, in the planning and implementation of your academic centers and of their activities;

—walk joyfully and tirelessly under the guidance of holy mother Church. Her Magisterium, the prolongation of Christ's, is the only guarantee not to stray from the right path, and is a reliable guide to the imperishable inheritance that Christ reserves for those who are faithful to Him.

I recommend you all to eternal Wisdom: "Wisdom is radiant and unfading, and she is easily discerned by those who love her, and is found by those who seek her" (Wis. 6:12).

May the Seat of Wisdom, which Mexico and the whole of Latin America venerate in Guadalupe sanctuary, protect you all under her motherly mantle! Amen. And many thanks for your presence.

CATHOLIC UNIVERSITIES FOR AN APOSTOLATE OF CULTURE...

On February 24, 1980, the Holy Father received in audience members of the Council of the International Federation of Catholic Universities and Rectors of the Catholic Universities of Europe, meeting then in Rome. At the beginning of the audience, Father Herve Carrier, president of the International Federation of Catholic Universities, delivered an address of homage to the Holy Father in the course of which he recalled the last meeting of the Council, which took place at Lublin and in which the then Cardinal Wojtyla took part.

John Paul II delivered the following address.

Dear brothers and sons,

Is it necessary to say how happy I am to be again with you, members of the Council of the International Federation of Catholic Universities or Rectors of the Catholic Universities of Europe? The Pontifical Yearbook of 1978 still named me among the members of the Congregation for Catholic Education, where I became familiar with your problems. I have also kept an excellent memory of my participation in the meeting at Lublin, which you have just recalled so kindly. As for the work of university professor, I quite naturally gauge its interest and importance, after the years I myself spent teaching in the Theological Faculty of Krakow, the most ancient in Poland, at Lublin University.

THE POPE'S INTEREST

1. You are certainly quite convinced, but *I am anxious to stress again that the Catholic universities have a select place in the Pope's heart, as they must have in the whole Church and in the concerns of her pastors in the midst of the many activities of their ministry.* Dedicated to a work of research and teaching, they have also thereby a role of witness and an apostolate without which the Church could not fully and durably evangelize the vast world of culture, or simply the rising generations, more and more highly educated, who will also be increasingly demanding to face up to, in faith, the many questions raised by sciences and the various systems of thought. *From the first centuries the Church has felt the importance of an apostolate of the intellect*—let it be enough to recall St. Justin, Saint Augustine—and her initiatives are numberless in this field. I do not need to quote the texts of the recent Council which you know by heart. For some time now, the attention of leaders of the Church has rightly been drawn by the spiritual needs of social environments that are quite dechristianized or little christianized: workers, peasants, migrants, poor people of every kind. It is certainly necessary, and the Gospel makes it a duty for us. *But the university world also needs a*

Church presence more than ever. And, in the specific framework which is yours, you help to provide it.

SPECIFIC AIMS

2. Addressing teachers and students in Mexico recently, I indicated three aims for Catholic university institutes: to make a specific contribution to the Church and society—thanks to a really complete study of the different problems—with the concern to show the full significance of man regenerated in Christ and thus permit his complete development; to form pedagogically men who, having made a personal synthesis between faith and culture, will be capable both of keeping their place in society and of bearing witness in it to their faith; to set up, among teachers and students, a real community which already bears witness visibly to a living Christianity.

AN ORIGINAL ROLE

3. I stress here some fundamental points. Research at the university level presupposes all the loyalty, the seriousness and, for that very reason, the freedom of scientific investigation. It is at this price that you bear witness to the truth, that you serve the Church and society, that you deserve the esteem of the university world; and this in all branches of knowledge.

But when it is a question of man, of the field of human sciences, it is necessary to add the fol-

lowing: if it is right to take advantage of the contribution of the different methodologies, it is
not sufficient to choose one, or even make a synthesis of several, to determine what man is in
depth. The Christian cannot let himself be
hemmed in by them, all the more so in that he is
not taken in by their premises. He knows that he
must go beyond the purely natural perspective;
his faith makes him approach anthropology in
the perspective of man's full vocation and salvation; it is the light beneath which he works, the
line that guides his research. *In other words, a
Catholic university is not only a field of religious
research open in all directions. It presupposes in
its teachers an anthropology enlightened by faith,
consistent with faith, in particular with the creation and with the redemption of Christ.* In the
midst of the swarm of present-day approaches,
which too often lead, moreover, to a minimizing
of man, Christians have an original role to play,
within research and teaching, precisely because
they reject any partial vision of man.

As for theological research properly speaking, by definition it cannot exist without seeking
its source and its regulation in Scripture and
Tradition, in the experience and decisions of the
Church handed down by the Magisterium
throughout the course of the centuries. These
brief reminders mark the specific exigencies of
the responsibility of the teaching staff in
Catholic faculties. It is in this sense that *Catholic
universities must safeguard their own character.*
It is in this framework that they bear witness not
only before their students, but also before other

universities, to the seriousness with which the Church approaches the world of thought, and, at the same time, to a real understanding of faith.

COLLABORATION NEEDED

4. Before this great and difficult mission, collaboration between Catholic universities of the whole world is highly desirable, for themselves and for the development, in an opportune way, of their relations with the world of culture. This shows all the importance of your Federation. I warmly encourage its initiatives, and in particular the study of the subject of the next Assembly on the ethical problems of the modern technological society. A fundamental subject, to which I am very sensitive myself, and to which I hope to have the opportunity to return. May the Holy Spirit guide you with His light and give you the necessary strength! May the intercession of Mary keep you available for His action, for the will of God! You know that I remain very close to your concerns and to your work. I willingly give you my apostolic blessing.

THE TRUTH ABOUT MAN
AND GOD IS INSEPARABLE

On Sunday, June 1, 1980, John Paul II met the professors and students of the Catholic Institute, where he himself, as a young priest, had been a student in the Canon Law Faculty. After an address of homage by the Rector, Most Reverend Paul Poupard, Auxiliary Bishop of Paris, the Holy Father spoke as follows.

Most Reverend Rector,

1. I thank you heartily for your words of welcome, as I thank also with all my heart all those who surround me this morning for this reception which touches me deeply. In my turn, I address to you my most cordial greeting, as well as to the high personalities who have kindly wished to accept your invitation and who honor this meeting with their presence. I greet all the members of the university community whom I am particularly happy to meet in this place, the heir to the most impressive university tradition. In this setting, so evocative and so pregnant with history, you will allow me, I am sure, Monsignor, ladies and gentlemen, to reflect as a former professor and address especially those for whom the Catholic Institute exists: its students.

2. Dear friends, the situation that is yours, here in Paris, calls for reflection on the profound reasons for your presence in this Institute. Is not

the university world of Paris, illustrious for so many reasons, rich in competence of all orders, literary and scientific? In how many centers could you not find, with learning and love of truth, the foundation of that intellectual freedom without which there cannot be, anywhere, either the university spirit or a university worthy of the name?

However, the magnificent scientific development of the modern age has also its weaknesses, of which almost exclusive attachment to the natural sciences and their technical applications is not the least. Is not humanism itself often reduced to loving cultivation of the great testimonies of the past without finding again their roots? Finally, the human sciences, the fundamental discoveries of our age, also bear within them, in spite of the horizons they open up to us, the limits inherent in their methodological models and their premises.

At the same time, how many persons are in search of a truth capable of unifying their lives? A moving search, even when the appeal of the fundamental values inscribed in the deepest recesses of being is suffocated, as it were, by the influence of the environment. The search is often an anxious one: many are "groping," like the Athenians addressed by St. Paul, for the God that we proclaim to them. All the more so since the upheavals of our age manifest before our eyes, in many respects, the more and more obvious failure of all the forms of what can be called "atheistic humanism."

3. I do not think I am mistaken, then, when I say that the students ask of the Catholic Institute of Paris, at the same time as the various branches of knowledge that are offered to them and through them, personal access to another order of truth, the complete truth about man, inseparable from the truth about God such as He revealed it to us, for it can come only from the Father of lights, from the gift of the Holy Spirit, He who, the Lord assured us, would lead us to the entire truth.

That is why, although your Institute has also distinguished itself in the university world through the work of eminent men in the different branches of learning, *it is not knowledge as such that justifies in the first place your belonging to the* Catholic *Institute, but the light it contributes to offer you about your reasons for living. In this field, every man needs certainty.* We Christians find it in the mystery of Christ who is, in His own words, our way, our truth, our life. It is He who is at the starting-point of our spiritual quest, He is its soul, He will be its goal. Thus, religious knowledge and spiritual progress go hand-in-hand. St. Augustine has left us an incomparable formula of this interior proceeding typical of one who is in search of God: *Fecisti nos ad Te, et inquietum est cor nostrum donec requiescat in Te. (God, You made us for Yourself, and our heart is restless until it rests in You.)*

4. I do not doubt, dear friends, dear students, men and women, that I meet your deep convictions here, evoking in this way the reasons for your presence, but I am happy to point out the ir-

replaceable specific role of your Institute and, addressing you, I am thinking also of the Catholic universities of France, represented by their rectors, and of similar institutes. Their specific task is to initiate into intellectual research while at the same time meeting your thirst for certainty and truth. They enable you to unify existentially, in your intellectual work, two orders of realities that people too often tend to oppose to each other as if they were antithetical, *the search for truth and the certainty of already knowing the source of truth.*

This sketch, though too rapid, will be enough to stress the importance I attach to Catholic education in general at its different levels, and in particular to Catholic university thought today. The Catholic atmosphere you desire goes far beyond a mere environment. It includes the desire to be formed to a Christian view of the world, a way of apprehending reality and also of conceiving your studies, however different they may be. I am speaking here, as you well understand, of a perspective which goes beyond the limits and methods of particular sciences to reach the understanding you must have of yourselves, of your role in society, of the meaning of your life.

5. In your university community as a whole, specialized philosophical and theological studies have the first place. It is natural that they should be the heart of the Institute. It is natural and also necessary that these sections should be distinguished by the seriousness of their work, their

researches and their publications. How glad I am to see that theological teaching is addressed also to lay students in ever larger numbers, offering them the possibility of a Christian formation equal to their culture and professional responsibilities! For what do you seek here, dear friends, but the truth of faith? It is this truth that inspires love of the Church, to which the Lord entrusted it: it is this truth also which requires, by virtue of its internal existence, convinced and faithful adherence to the Magisterium, which alone has been entrusted with the task of interpreting the Word of God written and transmitted (cf. *Dei Verbum,* no. 10), and of defining the Faith in conformity with this revelation (cf. *Lumen gentium,* no. 25). All theological work is in the service of the Faith. I know that it is a particularly demanding and meritorious service when it is carried out in this way. It has an essential place in the Church, and on its quality depends the Christian authenticity of the researchers themselves, the students and finally the generations to come.

"Let faith think," according to St. Augustine's admirable saying! In Paris, you have long lived in this seething of thought, which can be so creative, as St. Thomas so brilliantly showed in your ancient university, where he was a model student before becoming a model professor. Today as in his time, it is in the same faithfulness that it is necessary to construct anew, but always taking as a basis the Gospel, inexhaustible in its eternal newness, and the doctrine that the Church has clearly formulated.

6. Such is the pastoral commitment of the Catholic Institute. I am thinking in the first place of the laity who benefit from its teaching. I am happy to see them so numerous, so varied. I find again among you a little of Africa, which is even dearer to me now; Latin America, so well represented here, to which I will go soon. I cannot enumerate all your countries, but I greet you all affectionately. Dear friends, I hope that your studies at the Catholic Institute will enable you to form a deeply Christian and ecclesial conscience.

I am happy to see that the life of prayer flourishes here. Is it not, as it were, the spontaneous blooming of the knowledge of the Lord? May it, by His grace, be strengthened more and more. You cannot progress in it, however, without the question being raised one day, in its widest sense: "How shall I live for Christ?" A question inseparable from the personal consciousness of the requirements of a true Christian life. Such a question matures slowly and develops its vital force only gradually. It is this question that contributes powerfully to direct your family and professional life, according to your Christian convictions strengthened by the time you spent here. I, too, pray for all you men and women who are listening to me, at the essential moment when you give your life its interior orientation, that you may be able to accept this question if it becomes more urgent, more immediate: "What must I do for the Lord?" May He inspire the answer in you Himself!

Saying this to you, I have already approached the consideration of your responsibilities. As the first beneficiaries of the formation you receive, you cannot ignore what it commits you to. Monsignor d'Hulst, the founder of the Catholic Institute over a century ago now, said that it had been established "to cast a Christian ferment in the thinking world." That creates obligations for you, for today and for tomorrow, in your various countries and also beyond.

7. I have just referred to the Lord's call. I now turn to the priests, seminarians, men and women religious who are continuing their formation here. Rest assured that you have a great place in my heart and in my prayer. Prepare ardently for the task of evangelization that awaits you. In France, the Church has long been a missionary Church, anticipating in this way the orientations of the Second Vatican Council. Without going back further, this missionary activity would amply suffice for the glory of the last century, a magnificent century in which the dynamism of faith, far from letting itself be disheartened by the immensity of the task, blossomed in a host of Christian families, priestly and religious vocations, institutions of every kind that have gone far beyond the frontiers of France. During the days I spent in the Churches of Africa, so much alive, I was the admiring witness of the harvests that are ripening, the fruit of the obscure and persevering work to which so many missionaries sacrificed their lives. The Catholic Institute was founded in this period. According to its specific vocation, it took its part in this work. Today

more than ever, the harvest is plentiful! You are preparing here to enter the field of the Master of the harvest. Tomorrow, in France as in your respective countries: you know how much the Church counts on you.

8. I said that I was addressing the students particularly. But now, I wish to turn also to all those who are dedicated to their service here, because they have realized the importance of this ecclesial task and have in many cases dedicated most of their lives to it: in the first place the teaching staff as a whole which is particularly numerous and competent, to deal with the many specializations; the administrators of the Catholic Institute and all those who enable it to live. I am happy to express deep gratitude to them.

9. Ladies and gentlemen, dear friends, men and women students, concluding this too short visit I say to you: Be faithful to the heritage received. Continue to be sensitive to the appeals that reach you. Do not let yourselves be suffocated by the weight of secularization; reject the ferment of doubt, the suspicion of the human sciences, the encroaching practical materialism.... In this historic place, I wish to call you to share my hope and to tell you of my trust. Here, the disciples of St. Teresa and St. John of the Cross have left you the memory and the example of a life entirely consecrated to contemplation of the one Truth. Here, priests who came from very different horizons, among whom were some of your predecessors in the university of that time, have given the testimony of com-

plete faithfulness. Here, a new stage opened, just over a century ago, with the foundation of the Catholic Institute.

May the Holy Spirit, the Spirit of Pentecost, help you to clarify what is ambiguous, to give warmth to what is indifferent, to enlighten what is obscure, to be before the world true and generous witnesses of Christ's love, for "no one can live without love."

I express the most fervent wishes for your teaching, for your studies, and for your future. I pray to the Lord, with all my heart, to give you His light and to bless you.

A DEEP COMMITMENT
TO AUTHENTIC
CHRISTIAN LIVING

At the Catholic University of America where he met the professors and theologians, on October 7, 1979, Pope John Paul II addressed them as follows.

Dear brothers and sisters in Christ,

1. Our meeting today gives me great pleasure, and I thank you sincerely for your cordial welcome. My own association with the university world, and more particularly with the Pontifical Theological Faculty of Krakow, makes our encounter all the more gratifying for me. I cannot but feel at home with you. The sincere expressions with which the Chancellor and the President of the Catholic University of America have confirmed, in the name of all of you, the faithful adherence to Christ and the generous commitment to the service of truth and charity of your Catholic associations and institutions of higher learning are appreciated.

Ninety-one years ago Cardinal Gibbons and the American bishops requested the foundation of the Catholic University of America, as a university "destined to provide the Church with worthy ministers for the salvation of souls and the propagation of religion and to give the republic most worthy citizens." It seems appropriate to me on this occasion to address myself not only to this great institution, so irrevocably linked to the bishops of the United States, who have founded it and who generously support it, but also to all the Catholic universities, colleges, and academies of post-secondary learning in your land, those with formal and sometimes juridical links with the Holy See, as well as all those which are "Catholic."

2. Before doing so, though, allow me first to mention the Ecclesiastical Faculties, three of which are established here at the Catholic University of America. I greet these Faculties and all who dedicate their best talents in them. I offer my prayers for the prosperous development and the unfailing fidelity and success of these Faculties. In the Apostolic Constitution *Sapientia Christiana,* I have dealt directly with these institutions in order to provide guidance and to ensure that they fulfill their role in meeting the needs of the Christian community in today's rapidly changing circumstances.

I also wish to address a word of praise and admiration for the men and women, especially priests and religious, who dedicate themselves to all forms of campus ministry. Their sacrifices and efforts to bring the true message of Christ to the university world, whether secular or Catholic, cannot go unnoticed.

The Church also greatly appreciates the work and witness of those of her sons and daughters whose vocation places them in non-Catholic universities in your country. I am sure that their Christian hope and Catholic patrimony bring an enriching and irreplaceable dimension to the world of higher studies.

A special word of gratitude and appreciation also goes to the parents and students who, sometimes at the price of great personal and financial sacrifice, look toward the Catholic universities and colleges for the training that unites faith and science, culture and the Gospel values.

To all engaged in administration, teaching or study in Catholic colleges and universities I would apply the words of Daniel: "They who are learned shall shine like the brightness of the firmament; and those that instruct many in justice, as stars for all eternity" (Dan. 12:3). Sacrifice and generosity have accomplished heroic results in the foundation and development of these institutions. Despite immense financial strain, enrollment problems, and other obstacles, divine Providence and the commitment of the whole People of God have allowed us to see these Catholic institutions flourish and advance.

3. I would repeat here before you what I told the professors and students of the Catholic universities in Mexico when I indicated three aims that are to be pursued. *A Catholic university or college must make a specific contribution to the Church and to society through high quality scientific research, in-depth study of problems, and a just sense of history, together with the concern to show the full meaning of the human person regenerated in Christ, thus favoring the*

complete development of the person. Furthermore, the Catholic university or college must train young men and women of outstanding knowledge who, having made a personal synthesis between faith and culture, will be both capable and willing to assume tasks in the service of the community and of society in general, and to bear witness to their faith before the world. And finally, to be what it ought to be, a Catholic college or university must set up, among its faculty and students, a real community which bears witness to a living and operative Christianity, a community where sincere commitment to scientific research and study goes together with a deep commitment to authentic Christian living.

This is your identity. This is your vocation. *Every university or college is qualified by a specific mode of being. Yours is the qualification of being Catholic, of affirming God, His revelation and the Catholic Church as the guardian and interpreter of that revelation.* The term "Catholic" will never be a mere label, either added or dropped according to the pressures of varying factors.

4. *As one who for long years has been a university professor, I will never tire of insisting on the eminent role of the university, which is to instruct but also to be a place of scientific research.* In both these fields, its activity is closely related to the deepest and noblest aspiration of the human person: the desire to come to the knowledge of truth. No university can deserve the rightful esteem of the world of learn-

ing unless it applies the highest standards of scientific research, constantly updating its methods and working instruments, and unless it excells in seriousness and, therefore, in freedom of investigation. *Truth and science are not gratuitous conquests, but the result of a surrender to objectivity and of the exploration of all aspects of nature and man.* Whenever man himself becomes the object of investigation, no single method, or combination of methods, can fail to take into account, beyond any purely natural approach, the full nature of man. Because he is bound by the total truth about man, the Christian will, in his research and in his teaching, reject any partial vision of human reality, but he will let himself be enlightened by his faith in the creation of God and the redemption of Christ.

The relationship to truth explains, therefore, the historical bond between the university and the Church. Because she herself finds her origin and her growth in the words of Christ, which are the liberating truth (cf. Jn. 8:32), the Church has always tried to stand by the institutions that serve, and cannot but serve, the knowledge of truth. The Church can rightfully boast of being in a sense the mother of universities. The names of Bologna, Padua, Prague and Paris shine in the earliest history of intellectual endeavor and human progress. The continuity of the historic tradition in this field has come down to our day.

5. An undiminished dedication to intellectual honesty and academic excellence are seen, in a Catholic university, in the perspective of the Church's mission of evangelization and service.

This is why the Church asks these institutions, your institutions, to set out, without equivocation, your Catholic nature. This is what I have desired to emphasize in my Apostolic Constitution *Sapientia Christiana,* where I stated: "Indeed, the Church's mission of spreading the Gospel not only demands that the Good News be preached ever more widely and to ever greater numbers of men and women, but that the very power of the Gospel should permeate thought patterns, standards of judgment, and the norms of behavior; in a word, it is necessary that the whole of human culture be steeped in the Gospel. The cultural atmosphere in which a human being lives has a great influence upon his or her way of thinking and, thus, of acting. Therefore, a division between faith and culture is more than a small impediment to evangelization, while a culture penetrated with the Christian spirit is an instrument that favors the spreading of the Good News" *(Sapientia Christiana,* no. 1). The goals of Catholic higher education go beyond education for production, professional competence, technological and scientific competence; they aim at the ultimate destiny of the human person, at the full justice and holiness born of truth (cf. Eph. 4:24).

6. If then your universities and colleges are institutionally committed to the Christian message, and if they are part of the Catholic community of evangelization, it follows that they have an essential relationship to the hierarchy of the Church. And here I want to say a special word of gratitude, encouragement and guidance

for the theologians. The Church needs her theologians, particularly in this time and age so profoundly marked by deep changes in all areas of life and society. The bishops of the Church, to whom the Lord has entrusted the keeping of the unity of the faith and the preaching of the message—individual bishops for their dioceses; and bishops collegially, with the Successor of Peter for the universal Church—we all need your work, your dedication and the fruits of your reflection. We desire to listen to you, and we are eager to receive the valued assistance of your responsible scholarship.

But true theological scholarship, and by the same token, theological teaching, cannot exist and be fruitful without seeking its inspiration and its source in the Word of God as contained in Sacred Scripture and in the Sacred Tradition of the Church, as interpreted by the authentic Magisterium throughout history (cf. *Dei Verbum*, no. 10). True academic freedom must be seen in relation to the finality of the academic enterprise, which looks to the total truth of the human person. *The theologian's contribution will be enriching for the Church only if it takes into account the proper function of the bishops and the rights of the faithful.* It devolves upon the bishops of the Church to safeguard the Christian authenticity and unity of faith and moral teaching, in accordance with the injunction of the Apostle Paul: "Proclaim the message and, welcome or unwelcome, insist on it. Refute falsehood, correct error, call to obedience..." (2 Tm. 4:2). *It is the right of the faithful not to be troubled by theories and hypotheses that they are not expert in judging, or that they are easily simplified or manipulated by public opinion for ends that are alien to the truth.* On the day of his death, John Paul I stated: "Among the rights of the faithful, one of the greatest is the right to receive God's word in all its entirety and purity..." (September 28, 1979). It behooves the theologian to be free, but with the freedom that is openness to the truth, and the light of that comes from faith and from fidelity to the Church.

In concluding, I express to you once more my joy in being with you today. I remain very close to your work and your concerns. May the Holy Spirit guide you. May the intercession of Mary, Seat of Wisdom, sustain you always in your irreplaceable service of humanity and the Church. God bless you.

INTELLIGENCE
AND RESEARCH
IN THE SERVICE OF GOD
AND MAN

On December 8, 1978, John Paul II received in audience over seven thousand of the governing body, professors, pupils and "friends" of the Catholic University of the Sacred Heart, which was celebrating the first centenary of the birth of its founder, Father Agostino Gemelli. The Holy Father delivered the following address.

Mr. Rector,

1. The noble expressions with which you have wished to confirm, in this first meeting with the new Successor of Peter, the faithful adherence to Christ in the person of His Vicar and the generous commitment of service for truth in charity, which animate the members of the large family of the Catholic University of the Sacred Heart, have aroused sentiments of deep emotion and sincere appreciation in my heart. To you, therefore, to the eminent representatives of the academic body, to the dear students, to the members of the administrative and auxiliary personnel and to all those gathered here, there goes the attestation of my fatherly gratitude and my special benevolence.

I am happy to extend to you my cordial welcome, beloved sons, and to greet in you the qualified exponents of an institution which, for many years now, has carried out in Italy a role of primary importance for the Christian animation of the world of culture. With this meeting, which you requested and I granted joyfully, you wished to conclude in a significant way the celebrations for the centenary of the birth of Father Agostino Gemelli, the illustrious Franciscan who, with far-sighted wisdom, apostolic charity and indomitable courage, created that splendid complex of persons and works, life and thought, study and action, which your University is.

In the course of this year you have paused to reflect, with renewed intensity of affection, on the figure, thought and work of the outstanding religious, to whom the community of Italian Catholics and the world of culture and of scientific research itself, owes so much. You have taken his writings in your hands again and you have meditated again on their teachings. It seemed clear to you, in fact, that you could not offer him a better tribute of gratitude than by making room for his voice, whose echo many of you still keep in their hearts, in order that "the Father" might speak again—to those who are at present continuing his work—of ideal aims and concrete plans of action, of inviting prospects and insidious dangers, of fears that still loom up and hopes that never fail.

2. At this moment, too, our thoughts go to him, to gather some significant aspects of his message and draw from it comfort and a stimulus in the great difficulties of the present time. Well, there is a "constant"—at least it

seems so to me—which directs and sustains Father Gemelli's action throughout his whole existence: it is *interest in man:* individual man, endowed with certain physical and psychical capacities, conditioned by certain environmental factors, weakened by certain illnesses, straining towards the conquest of certain ideals.

Was it not this interest that drove the young student to the Faculty of Medicine, towards that science which makes service of human life its own program and banner? And was it not again the same interest that prompted him—now a friar—to specialize in experimental psychology, directing him towards the science on which his attention and his effort as a brilliant and indefatigable researcher were focused for the rest of his life?

Interest in man induced him to turn with particular passion to the most painful and difficult situations: those of the worker, to study "the human factor in work" and to arrive, after experiments carried out directly in the sulfur mines of Sicily or in the workshops of the North, at the conclusion, which was then a pioneering one, that it is not man who must be adapted to machines, but the latter that must be constructed to fit man; the situations of soldiers exposed to the shattering experiences of the violence of war, or those of aviators, contending with rudimentary and extremely dangerous aircraft, in order to prepare specific remedies for the increasingly numerous psychological traumas among soldiers in the front lines; finally, the situations of prisoners sentenced to penal servitude, to a group of whom he offered hospitality in the premises of the psychology laboratory of the Catholic University, to study their reactions from close at hand and deduce from them the norms for an effective intervention to rehabilitate them.

3. The biographical references just made show what kind of interest Father Gemelli took in man: not the interest of the scientist uprooted from reality, who considers man as a mere subject of analysis, but the heartfelt passion of one who feels deeply involved in the problems of which his fellowmen are victims. Interest in man meant for Father Gemelli the desire to serve man. How? Experience taught the courageous friar that the most necessary and urgent service to offer one's neighbor was to help him "à bien penser" (to think well), to use the words of Pascal (*Pensées*, no. 347), because "la pensée fait la grandeur de l'homme" (thought makes man's greatness) (*ibid.*, no. 346). In right thought lies the premise for right action; and in right action lies the hope of a lasting solution for the serious evils that torment mankind.

"Ideas are what the world needs above all": this was his conviction (cf. A. Gemelli, "L'Universita per la pace sociale," in *Vita e Pensiero,* January 1950). And as ideas are worked out and communicated in teaching, he conceived the bold project of an institute that would gather together good students, sustained by the ideal of serious and disinterested scientific research, and willing young people, animated by the desire to proceed with their teachers in search of truth, in order to adhere to it passionately and then generously to transmit to others its riches, which had now become the substance of their own lives (cf. A. Gemelli, "Il progresso degli study scientifici fra i cattolici italiani," in *Studium,* June 1907).

But is human reason able to reach, by itself, the satisfying shores of truth? The painful turmoil of his youth, solved only with the tranquillizing experience of conversion, had caused Father Gemelli to feel tangibly the necessity of faith for a fully satisfying answer to the fundamental problems of human existence. He will not be afraid, therefore, to declare: "The solution of these problems must not be sought from sciences, pure or applied; it must not be sought from philosophy, but from religion." And he will establish with programmatic clarity: "We must go back to God, not to just any God, presented to us by a natural religion, but to a living God, to Jesus Christ, the supreme reason for our life, the supreme beauty to contemplate, the supreme goodness to imitate, the supreme reward to reach" (A. Gemelli, "La funzione religiosa della cultura," in *Vita e Pensiero,* April 1919).

4. The Catholic University came into being to meet these requirements. This was the intention of its founder, who wished to constitute in it a "real and effective center of Catholic culture," as he declared when the great project was about to be realized (cf. A. Gemelli, "Perchè i cattolici italiani debbono avere una loro Università," in *Vita e Pensiero,* July 1919), and as he confirmed immediately after its official launching,

when he stressed that: "The Catholic University was conceived with the bold dream of making Catholicism known, loved and followed in Italy" (*Bollettino degli Amici,* no. 1, January 1922).

It was not a matter, obviously, of questioning in any way the method and freedom to which the individual scientific disciplines are entitled: Father Gemelli described their nature and advocated their safeguarding on various occasions. It was a question rather of carrying out, at the university level, that "union of faith and science," to which the then Apostolic Nuncio, Msgr. Achille Ratti, referred in a letter from Poland (cf. Letter to Father Gemelli of March 28, 1921) and which the official Magisterium, in particular that of the Second Vatican Council, has recognized so many times as possible, desirable and fruitful (cf. Declaration *Gravissimum educationis,* nos. 8 and 10 and the preceding magisterial documents quoted in it).

In faith that is understood and lived, in fact, cultural progress finds, not an obstacle, but an incomparable aid to solve and overcome the antinomies to which it is dramatically exposed today: just think, for example, of the necessity of promoting the dynamism and expansion of culture without jeopardizing the ancestral wisdom of peoples; think also of the urgency of safeguarding the necessary synthesis, in spite of the division of the single disciplines; think, finally, of the problem of recognizing, on the one hand, the legitimate autonomy of culture, while avoiding, on the other hand, the risk of a humanism that is closed, limited to a purely earthly horizon and exposed, consequently, to decidedly inhuman developments (cf. H. De Lubac, *Le drame de l'humanisme athée,* Paris, 1945).

Father Gemelli sees in the Catholic University the privileged place in which it would be possible to throw a bridge between the past and the future, between the ancient classical culture and the new scientific culture, between the values of modern culture and the eternal message of the Gospel. From this fruitful synthesis there would be derived—he rightly trusted—a most effective impulse towards the implementation of a full humanism, dynamically open to the boundless horizons of divinization, to which historical man is called. This would lead to reaching in the best way that purpose to which—as I said just before—Father Gemelli's life was completely directed, the purpose of serving man. "I am of the opinion"—he stated in the inaugural lecture for the academic year 1957-58, that is, at the end of his hard-working existence—"I am of the opinion that the contemporary university, while it has the duty of collaborating for the progress of sciences and of following the methodology required by each of them, must never, however, give second place to what demands recognition of its primacy, that is, man, the human person, the world of spirituality" (A. Gemelli, "Le conquiste della scienza e i diritti dello spirito," in *Vita e Pensiero,* January 1958).

5. These were the convictions that guided and sustained Father Gemelli's action in starting and carrying out, in the midst of difficulties of every kind, the titanic project of a private

Catholic university in Italy. These are the convictions that must continue to direct, also today, the effort of those who have freely chosen to enter, as leaders, teachers or pupils, the Catholic University of the Sacred Heart.

I am certain that I am expressing the deep feeling of Father Gemelli when I say to you today: Be proud of the title "Catholic" which describes your university. It does not mortify your commitment for the advancement of every true human value. If it is true that *"l'homme passe infinement l'homme"* (man transcends man infinitely), as Pascal divined (cf. *Pensées*, no. 434), then it must be said that the human person does not find full self-fulfillment except in reference to Him who is the fundamental reason of all our judgments on being, good, truth and beauty. And since the infinite transcendence of this God, who has been indicated as the "completely Other," has approached us in Christ Jesus, who became flesh in order to take part completely in our history, then it must be concluded that Christian faith qualifies us believers to interpret, better than anyone else, the deepest aspirations of the human being and to indicate, with serene and tranquil certainty, the ways and the means to satisfy them fully.

This is, therefore, the testimony which the Christian community and even the world of culture expect from you, teachers and pupils of the University, set up by Father Gemelli's intrepid faith: *to prove with facts that intelligence is not only not impaired, but on the contrary stimulated and strengthened by that incomparable source of understanding human reality, which is the Word of God;* to show with facts that it is possible to build around this Word a community of men and women (the *universitas personarum* of the origins) who carry on their research in the different areas without losing contact with the essential frame of reference of a Christian view of life; a community of men and women who seek particular answers to particular problems, but who are sustained by the joyful awareness of possessing together the ultimate answer to ultimate problems; a community of men and women, above all, who endeavor to incarnate, in their existence and in the social environment to which they belong, the proclamation of salvation which they received from Him who is "the true light that enlightens every man" (Jn. 1:9); a community of men and women who feel committed— while respecting the legitimate autonomy of earthly realities, created by God, depending on Him and subordinated to Him—"to see that the divine life is inscribed in the life of the earthly city" *(Gaudium et spes,* no. 43).

The title "Catholic" also prides itself on containing the commitment of a distinct faithfulness of the University to the Church, to the Pope and the bishops, to whom it has always been and is extremely dear and to the whole Italian ecclesial community, by which it is sustained with sacrifices and considered with affection, but also with demanding hope. This faithfulness—so insistently instilled and so consistently lived by Father Gemelli—is the guarantee of that unity and brotherly charity, which are the distinguishing marks of your institution, as of any other one destined for service of the People of God.

This is your task, beloved sons, this is the order the Pope entrusts to you; and this is also his wish. A wish which I address in a very special way to the young, in whose hands are laid not only the future destiny of the glorious Catholic University, but above all the hopes of Christian animation of the future society. Let there ring out again for them, on the Pope's lips, a warning that the rector addressed to them at a difficult hour of Italian and world history: "It is not the hour for empty chatter and arrogant attitudes," he said. "It is the hour for great tasks. It falls upon you, the young, especially to construct the future, to construct the new era of history. Wherever you may be, show that you are aware of this mission of yours. Be flames that burn, illuminate, guide and comfort. Nobility of sentiment, purity of life, hatred for vulgarity and for everything that degrades, are a duty now more than ever" (*Foglio agli studenti,* October 1940).

And now, in taking leave of you, beloved sons, my thought rises in imploration to her whom we are venerating today in the privilege of her Immaculate Conception. Father Gemelli loved the Blessed Virgin with filial devotion and defended her against disparagers with passionate ardor, to an extent that won him among his friends the name of "Knight of the Virgin." May Mary keep a glance of motherly predilection for the Catholic University of the Sacred Heart, for which this generous son of hers worked, suffered and prayed so much. May she, whom the Church invokes as *Sedes Sapientiae*, enlighten and strengthen lavishly those who are now continuing a work to which the Holy See and the whole Italian Church look with unchanged affection, constant trust and ever living hope.

With these wishes I am happy to grant to you, to your families and to all friends of the Catholic University, my fatherly apostolic blessing.

I know that also members of the Association of Parents of the Catholic Schools are present at this meeting. In these days it is holding in Rome the first congress of its regional delegates.

I extend my greeting and my blessing to them, too, hoping that the Lord will assist them in their generous effort in favor of an adequate cultural, moral and religious formation of youth.

IV. Familiar Homilies to University Students About Faith and Knowledge

1) *To Collegiate Students of Two Roman Catholic Colleges. February 9, 1980.*

2) *To University Students in Rome for Congress of International University Cooperation. April 10, 1979.*

3) *Easter Mass for Roman University Students. April 5, 1979.*

4) *Prepared Address of John Paul II for University Students in Paris. June 1, 1980.*

5) *Address to Students in Turin. April 13, 1980.*

6) *To University Students in Warsaw. June 3, 1979.*

IN YOUR WITNESS
LIES THE VITALITY
OF THE CATHOLIC SCHOOL

On Saturday, February 9, 1980, the Holy Father received in audience about eight thousand teachers, pupils and former pupils of the Roman schools "Massimo" and "Santa Maria," which celebrated respectively the hundredth, and the ninetieth anniversary of their foundation. John Paul II delivered the following address.

Beloved brothers and sisters!

"Grace to you and peace from God the Father and the Lord Jesus Christ!" (2 Thes. 1:2)

1. I am really glad to be able to meet today the superiors, teachers, and pupils with the members of their families, of two of the most renowned Catholic schools of Rome: the "Massimo" Institute of the Jesuit Fathers, which has celebrated the first centenary of its foundation, and the "Santa Maria" Institute of the Marianist Religious, which remembers its ninetieth anniversary.

These two dates sum up two histories, lived with commitment, enthusiasm, dedication and sacrifice.

The "Massimo" College, founded on November 9, 1879, under the direction of a committee formed of the archeologist Msgr. Pietro Crostarosa, the parish priest of St. Mary Major, Don Cesare Boccanera, and the Jesuit Father Massimiliano Massimo, intended to revitalize the cultural traditions of the famous "collegio Romano"; but it can be said that the "Massimo" was also in perfect continuation and harmony with the great ideal of St. Ignatius of Loyola, who, in a period in which it seemed that there was an absolute incompatibility between humanistic culture and the Christian message, dreamed of a great school, in Rome, the center of Christianity, which could serve as a model for so many others scattered all over the world; and in 1551, at the foot of the capitol, he had placed on the door of a modest house the notice: "Schola de Grammatica, de humanità e Dottrina christiana."

In these hundred years of life, the "Massimo" school has followed this humanistic and Christian program of St. Ignatius and has developed and spread intensely: from the twenty-five pupils of 1879, it reached a thousand in the old premises at Terme, and it has arrived at over one thousand six hundred in the new buildings at EUR.

No less glorious is the history of the ninety years of the "Santa Maria" Institute, run by the sons of the Servant of God Giuseppe Chaminade, who wished to bring to Rome the experience they had acquired in education at the "College Stanislas" in Paris and in other educational establishments in Europe and North America: from forty pupils and nine religious in 1889, it has reached 1,260 pupils, thirty-six religious and forty-four external teachers in this period. Nor can we forget the *Centro Universitario Marianum,* in which as many as one hundred and six university students reside at present.

2. These figures, beloved brothers and sisters, are eloquent and bear witness effectively and concretely to the dynamism and vitality of your institutes and of what is called the "Catholic" school itself. For, behind these figures, there is the whole indefatigable cultural, educational and formative work, carried out by you in this long lapse of time, day by day, hour by hour, in continual contact with the boys and youths with whom you have traveled together not only along the paths of human sciences, history, philosophy, and literature, but, owing to the specific qualification of your institutions and your ideals, also and above all along the ways of Christian faith.

Who could evaluate today the good, open or concealed, which so many pupils of yours—some of whom have already disappeared from the scene of this world, others now mature men—received and were then able, in turn, to transmit to their friends, their families, their children and to civil society? How many exemplary heads of households, how many competent and appreciated professionals are still deeply indebted, and no less deeply grateful, to you, to your apostolic action, and to your institutes, in which their personality was molded with serene thoroughness, in order to be able to face the complex responsibilities of life? How many priests and religious discovered, deepened and matured their priestly or religious vocation, helped and supported by the exemplary priestly and religious life of their teachers?

Sometimes, unfortunately, when people speak of "Catholic" schools they consider them only as in competition or even in opposition to other schools, particularly state schools. But this is not so! Catholic schools have always intended, and still do, to form Christians who are only exemplary citizens, capable of making their whole contribution of intelligence, seriousness, and competence, for the sound and orderly construction of the civil community.

3. Your institutes are and make a point of proclaiming themselves "Catholic" schools. But what is a Catholic school? What are its main tasks, its specific purposes? The subject is one of such deep and continual topicality that the Second Vatican Council dedicated to these problems a whole document, the Declaration on Christian Education. And this Declaration presents, in pregnant synthesis, the threefold characteristic peculiar to Catholic schools, which, like others, pursue cultural purposes and the human formation of the young. "It is, however, the special function of the Catholic school"—the conciliar document affirms—"to develop in the school community an atmosphere animated by a spirit of liberty and charity based on the Gospel. It enables young people, while developing their own personality, to grow at the same time in that new life which has been given them in baptism. Finally, it so orients the whole of human culture to the message of salvation that

the knowledge which the pupils acquire of the world, of life and of men is illumined by faith" (*Gravissimum educationis*, no. 8). This is a text very rich in precious indications, dynamic ferments, and concrete applications. But it is clearly affirmed in it that *in the Catholic school it is Christian faith that illuminates knowledge of the whole of reality (world, life, man)*.

It is true that the school is, as such, the place or the community of learning and culture; but the Catholic school is also, or rather first and foremost, a place and a special community for the education and maturation of faith. I laid special stress on this subject in my recent apostolic exhortation on catechesis in our time. A Catholic school—I said—would no longer deserve this title "if, no matter how much it shone for its high level of teaching in non-religious matters, there were justification for reproaching it for negligence or deviation in strictly religious education. Let it not be said that such education will always be given implicitly and indirectly. The special character of the Catholic school, the underlying reason for it, the reason why Catholic parents should prefer it, is precisely the quality of the religious instruction integrated into the education of the pupils" (*Catechesi tradendae*, no. 69). *It is the right of pupils of Catholic schools to receive in them a catechesis that is permanent, thorough, articulated, qualified and adapted to the requirements of their age and their cultural preparation.* And this religious teaching must be entire in its content, because every disciple of Christ has the right to receive the word of faith in a form that is not mutilated, not distorted, not reduced, but complete and whole, in all its rigor and vigor (cf. *ibid.*, no. 3).

4. *At the center of academic teaching, at the culminating point of all interest, must be the person, the work and the message of Christ*: He is our true Teacher (cf. Mt. 23:8-10). He is our Way, Truth and Life (cf. Jn. 14:6). He is our Redeemer and Savior (cf. Eph. 1:7; Col. 1:14). The priority and irreplaceable commitment, both of teachers and of pupils, is to get to know Jesus, by studying, examining and meditating on Holy Scripture, not as a mere history book, but as the perennial witness of One who is alive, because Jesus rose again and "sits at the right hand side of the Father." Furthermore, when it is a question of Jesus, it is not enough to stop at the plane of theoretical knowledge: His person, His message, continue to challenge us, to involve us, to impel us to live by Him and in Him. *Then one is truly a Christian when, day by day, one carries out the requirements, not always easy, of the Gospel of Jesus.* Let not the words of Saint Augustine be applicable in any way to you, brothers and sisters: "Those who style themselves with a name and do not correspond to it, what good is the name to them if there is not the reality?... In this way, many people call themselves Christians, but are not found to be such in reality, because they are not what they say they are, that is, in life, in morals, in hope, in charity" (Jn. Epist. Joann. tract. IV, 4: PL 35, 2007).

My wish for you, priests and religious, is that in the midst of your dear pupils you may always be joyful witnesses to complete dedication and consecration to God, and that you consider it a real honor, as well as a serious duty, to transmit and communicate the Christian faith to them in the teaching of religion. But let your evangelical life be a living and luminous catechesis for the boys and youths entrusted to your educational apostolate.

My wish for you, lay teachers, is that you may live intensely the sense of responsibility of teaching in a Catholic school. In this way your pupils will appreciate you and love you not only for your specific professional and cultural competence, but above all for your Christian consistency.

My wish for you, fathers and mothers, rightly concerned about the cultural preparation, but even more about the human, civil and religious formation of your sons, is that you may always be aware that you are the first true and irreplaceable educators of your children! Always follow them with that extraordinary love, which God the Father has sown in your heart! Learn to understand them, listen to them, guide them!

And today at this meeting, charged with promises and enthusiasm, what will the Pope say to you, beloved students, who are the real protagonists of the school? You are the point of convergence of the affection, cares and interest of your parents, your teachers, your superiors. Respond to this sum of love with a constant commitment for your human, cultural and Christian maturation. Prepare, in serious and assiduous study, for the tasks that divine Providence has in store for you tomorrow within civil society and the ecclesial community. The future of the nation, nay more of the world, depends on you! The society of the future will be the one constructed by you; and you are already constructing it, in these years, in your classrooms, at your meetings, in your associations.

May the Pope be able to repeat to you too, with joy, the words that St. John addressed to the young: "I write to you, young men, because you are strong, and the word of God abides in you, and you have overcome the evil one" (1 Jn. 2:14).

Yes, beloved young people! Be strong in faith; let Christ, the Incarnate Word of God, direct your lives; in this way you will overcome evil, which is manifested in selfishness, divisions, hatred and violence!

My apostolic blessing to everyone!

CONVERSION OF THE HEART
IS REAL WISDOM

On the afternoon of April 10, 1979, the Holy Father received some 6,000 students from all over the world who had come to Rome for the International Congress organized by the Institute for University Cooperation (I.C.U.). The Pope addressed them as follows.

Beloved brothers and sisters,

Through the words of the President of your University Congress, you have sketched an effective summary of the purposes of these days you are spending in Rome, and you have spoken to me of the aspirations and ideals by which you are inflamed.

I thank you sincerely for your expressions of affection for me and for my universal ministry as Peter's Successor.

I know that you represent here as many as two hundred and seventeen Universities all over the world, and this is already a positive sign of the universality of Christian faith, even if it does not always have an easy life. I know very well, indeed, the anxieties of the University world, but I also know your youthful commitment in assuming personally the responsibility that Christ entrusts to you: to be His witnesses in circles in which, through study, science and culture are elaborated.

In these days, you are reflecting on the efforts that are being made in the world for the purpose of developing unity and solidarity among peoples. You rightly ask yourselves on what values these efforts must be based, in order not to fall into the danger of the rhetoric of empty words. And you are asking yourselves, at the same time, in the name of what ideals it is possible to bring together cultures and peoples so different as, for example, those I see represented here by you.

For this reason, it already comforts me to see in your eyes the desire to seek in Christ the revelation of what God says to man and how man must answer God.

Here, beloved, is the central point: we must look to Christ, with all our attention. We know that God's plan is "to unite all things in him" (Eph. 1:10), by means of the exceptional nature of His person and His salvific destiny of death and life. Just in these days, in which we are living again His blessed passion, all this becomes more evident: Christ shows Himself to us, in fact, with features that are even more similar to those of our weak nature as men. The Church points out to us Jesus raised on the cross, "a man of sorrows and acquainted with grief" (Is. 53:3); but also risen from the dead, "he always lives to make intercession for (us)" (Heb. 7:25).

Here, then, is the one at whom the Pope calls on you to look: Christ crucified for our sins and risen for our salvation (cf. Rom. 4:25), who becomes a universal and irresistible point of convergence: "and I, when I am lifted up from the earth, will draw all men to myself" (Jn. 12:32).

"ROYAL BANNER"

I know you place your hope in that cross, which has become for us all a "royal banner" (Liturgical hymn of Passiontide). Continue to be imbued, every day and in every circumstance, with the wisdom and strength which come to us only from Christ's paschal cross. Try to draw from this experience an ever new purifying energy. The cross is the pressure point to act as a lever for a service of man, so as to transmit to so many others the immense joy of being Christians.

In these days, while I contemplate Christ raised and nailed to the cross, there often comes into my mind the expression with which Saint Augustine comments on the passage in John's Gospel just mentioned: "The wood of the cross to which the limbs of the dying One had been nailed, became the chair of the Master who teaches" (In Io. 119:2). Just think: what voice, what master of thought can found unity among men and nations, if not He who, giving His own life, obtained for all of us adoption as children of the same Father? Precisely this divine filiation, obtained for us by Christ on the cross and realized by sending His Spirit into our hearts, is the only solid and indestructible foundation of the unity of a redeemed humanity.

My sons and daughters, you have pointed out at your Congress the sufferings and the contradictions by which a society is seen to be overwhelmed when it moves away from God. The wisdom of Christ makes you capable of pushing on to discover the deepest source of evil existing in the world. And it also stimulates you to proclaim to all men, your companions in study today, and in work tomorrow, the truth you have learned from the Master's lips, that is, that evil comes "out of the heart of man" (Mk. 7:21). *So sociological analyses are not enough to bring justice and peace. The root of evil is within man. The remedy, therefore, also starts from the heart.* And—I am happy to repeat—the door of our heart can be opened only by that great and definitive word of the love of Christ for us, which is His death on the cross.

It is here that the Lord wishes to lead us: within ourselves. All this time that precedes Easter is a constant call to conversion of the heart. This is real wisdom: *Initium sapientiae timor Domini* (Sir. 1:16).

Beloved sons, have therefore the courage to repent; and have also the courage to draw God's grace from sacramental confession. This will make you free! It will give you the strength that you need for the undertakings that are awaiting you, in society and in the Church, in the service of men. *The true service of the Christian, in fact, is qualified on the basis of the active presence of God's grace in him and through him.* Peace in the Christian's heart, moreover, is inseparably united with joy, which in Greek *(chara)* is etymologically akin to grace *(charis)*. The whole teaching of Jesus, including His cross, has precisely this aim: "that my joy may be in you, and that your joy may be full" (Jn. 15:11). When it pours from a Christian heart into other men, it brings forth hope, optimism, and impulses of generosity in everyday toil, infecting the whole of society.

JOY AND PEACE

My sons, only if you have in you this divine grace, which is joy and peace, will you be able to construct something worthwhile for men. Consider your university vocation, therefore, in this magnificent Christian perspective. Study today, professional work tomorrow, become for you a way in which to find God and serve men your brothers; that is, they become a way of holiness, as beloved Cardinal Albino Luciani said pithily just before he was called to this See of Peter, with the name of John Paul I: *"There, right in the very street, in the office, in the factory, one becomes holy, provided one carries out one's duty competently, for love of God, and joyfully;* in such a way that daily work will not become a 'daily tragedy,' but almost 'a daily smile' "* (from *Il Gazzettino*, July 25, 1978).

Finally, I recommend to the Blessed Virgin, *Sedes sapientiae*, whom we find in these days *iuxta crucem Jesu* (Jn. 19:25), to help you always to listen to this wisdom which will give you and the world the immense joy of living with Christ.

And in whatever environment you find yourselves living and bearing witness to the Gospel, may my fatherly apostolic blessing always accompany you.

THE CROSS:
SUPREME TEACHER
OF TRUTH ABOUT GOD
AND MAN

On April 5, 1979, John Paul II celebrated Easter Mass for the university students of Rome. Over ten thousand students, lecturers and researchers took part.

The Holy Father delivered the following homily.

1. "I have earnestly desired to eat this passover with you!" (Lk. 22:15)

These words of Christ come into my mind today, as we meet together round the altar of St. Peter's Basilica to take part in the celebration of the Eucharist. Right from the beginning, since I have been granted the privilege of standing at this altar, *I have greatly desired to meet you, young people studying at the university and colleges of this city.* I missed you, university students of the Pope's diocese. I had the desire, let me tell you, to feel you near. I have been accustomed to such meetings for years. In the period of Lent—and also of Advent—I often had the privilege of finding myself in the midst of university students in Krakow, on the occasion of the closing of the spiritual exercises which gathered thousands of participants. On this day

I meet you. I greet cordially all of you here present. And in you and through you I greet all your fellow students, your professors, researchers, your faculties, organizations, and those in charge of your circles. I greet the whole of "academic" Rome.

In this period in which, every year, Christ speaks to us again in the life of the Church with His "Passover," the need of being with Him is revealed in human hearts, particularly in young hearts. The time of Lent, Holy Week, the sacred Triduum, are not just a memory of events that occurred nearly two thousand years ago, but constitute a special invitation to participation.

MEANING OF PASSOVER

2. Passover means "passing over."

In the Old Testament it meant the exodus from the "house of slavery" of Egypt and the passing over the Red Sea, under the special protection of the Lord God, towards the "Promised Land." The wandering lasted for forty years. In the New Testament this historic Passover was accomplished in Christ during three days: from Thursday evening to Sunday morning. And it means the passing through death to the resurrection, and at the same time the exodus from the slavery of sin towards participation in God's life by means of grace. Christ says in today's Gospel: "If anyone keeps my word, he will never see death" (Jn. 8:51). *These words indicate at the same time what the Gospel is. It is the book of eter-*

nal life toward which go the innumerable ways of man's earthly pilgrimage. Each of us walks on one of those roads. The Gospel teaches about each one of them. And the mystery of this sacred book consists just of this. The fact that it is read a great deal springs from this, and its relevance today comes from this. In the light of the Gospel our life acquires a new dimension. It acquires its definitive meaning. Therefore, life itself is shown to be a passing over.

HUMAN LIFE PASSES

3. Human life, a passing over.

This life is not one whole, enclosed definitively between the date of birth and the date of death. It is open to the last fulfillment in God. Each of us feels painfully the close of life, the limit set by death. Each of us is in some way conscious of the fact that man is not contained completely in these limits, and that he cannot die definitively. Too many questions not spoken and too many problems unsolved—if not in the dimension of personal, individual life, at least in that of the life of human communities: families, nations, humanity—stop at the moment of the death of every man. In fact, none of us lives alone. Various circles pass through each man. Also St. Thomas said: *Anima humana est quodammodo omnia* (Comm. in Arist. *De Anima*, III, 8, lect. 13). We bear in us the need of "universalization." At a given moment, death interrupts all this....

Who is Christ? He is the Son of God, who assumed human life in its temporal orientation towards death. He accepted the necessity of death. Before death overtook Him, He was repeatedly threatened by it. The Gospel of today reminds us of one of these threats: "...they took up stones to throw at him" (Jn. 8:59).

Christ is He who accepted the whole reality of human dying. And for that very reason He is the One who made a radical change in the way of understanding life. He showed that life is a passing over, not only to the limit of death, but to a new life. Thus the cross became for us the supreme chair of the truth of God and of man. We must all be pupils—no matter what our age is—of this chair. Then we will understand that *the cross is also the cradle of the new man.*

Those who are its pupils look at life in this way, perceive it in this way. And they teach it in this way to others. They imprint this meaning of life on the whole of temporal reality: on morality, creativity, culture, politics, economics. It has very often been affirmed—as, for example, the followers of Epicurus sustained in ancient times, and as some followers of Marx do in our times for other reasons—that this concept of life distracts man from temporal reality and that it cancels it in a certain sense. The truth is quite different. Only this conception of life gives full importance to all the problems of temporal reality. It opens the possibility of placing them fully in man's existence. And one thing is certain: this conception of life does not permit shutting man up in temporal things, it does not permit subordinating him completely to them. It decides his freedom.

LIFE IS A TEST

4. Life is a test.

Giving human life this "paschal" meaning, that is, that it is a passing over, that it is a passing over to freedom, Jesus Christ taught with His word and even more with His own example that it is a test. The test corresponds to the importance of the forces accumulated in man. Man is created "for" the test, and called to it right from the beginning. It is necessary to think deeply of this call, meditating on the first chapters of the Bible, especially the first three. Man is described there not only as a being created "in the image of God" (Gn. 1:26-27), but at the same time he is described as a being who undergoes a test. And this is—if we analyze the text properly—the test of thought, of the "heart" and of the will, the test of truth and love. In this sense, it is at the same time the test of the covenant with God. When this first covenant was broken, God made another one. Today's readings recall the covenant with Abraham, which was a way of preparation for the coming of Christ.

Christ confirms this meaning of life: it is man's great test. And for this very reason it has a meaning for man. It has not a meaning, on the contrary, if we believe that in life man must only take advantage, use, "take," and even struggle implacably for the right to take advantage, use, "take"....

Life has its meaning when it is considered and lived as a test of an ethical character. Christ confirms this meaning, and at the same time defines the adequate dimension of this test that human life is. Let us re-read carefully, for example, the Sermon on the Mount, and also chapter twenty-five of Matthew's Gospel—the image of the judgment. This alone is enough to renew in us the fundamental Christ conscious-ness of the meaning of life.

The concept of "test" is closely connected with the concept of responsibility. Both are addressed to our will, to our acts. Accept, dear friends, both of these concepts—or rather both realities—as ele-ments of the construction of one's own humanity. This humanity of yours is already mature and, at the same time, is still young. It is in the phase of the definitive formation of one's life project. This formation takes place particularly in the "aca-demic" years, in the time of higher studies. *Per-haps that personal life project is suspended at present over many unknown factors. Perhaps you still lack a precise vision of your place in society, of the work for which you are preparing through your studies.* This is certainly a great difficulty; but difficulties of the kind must not paralyze your initiatives. They must not give rise only to aggression. Aggression itself will not solve anything. It will not change life for the better. Ag-gression can only make "bad in another way."

I hear you denounce, in your language which is so frank, the senility of ideologies and the ideal of inadequacy of the "social machine." *Well, to promote man's true dignity—also intellectual dignity—and not let yourselves, in your turn, be trapped in various forms of sectarianism, do not forget that it is indispensable to acquire a deep formation based on the teaching that Christ left us in His words and in the example of His own life.* Try to accept the difficulties you must face precisely as a part of that test which is the life of every man. It is necessary to undertake this test with all responsibility. It is at the same time a personal responsibility—for my life, for its future pattern, for its value—and also a social responsibility, for justice and peace, for the moral order of one's own native environment and of the whole of society. It is a responsibility for the real common good. A man who has such an awareness of the meaning of life does not destroy, but constructs the future. Christ teaches us this.

TRUTH AND LOVE

5. And He also teaches us that *human life has the meaning of a testimony to truth and to love.* Not long ago, I had the opportunity to express myself on this subject, speaking to University students of Mexico and of the many nations of Latin America. I take the liberty of quoting some thoughts of that address, which is perhaps of interest to European and Roman students too. Today there exists a worldwide involvement of commitments, fears and at the same time, hopes, ways of thinking and evaluating, which trouble your young world. On that occasion I pointed out, among other things, that it is necessary to promote an "integral

culture, which will aim at the complete development of the human person, in which there will stand out the values of intelligence, will, conscience, and brotherhood, which are all based on God the Creator and which have been marvelously exalted in Christ (cf. *Gaudium et spes,* no. 61)." To scientific formation, that is, it is necessary to add a deep moral and Christian formation, that will be deeply lived and will bring about a more and more harmonious synthesis between faith and reason, between faith and culture, between faith and life. To unite dedication to precise scientific research and the testimony of a true Christian life, that is the stirring commitment of every university student (cf. *AAS* LXXI, 1979, pp. 236-237). And I repeat to you too what I wrote in February to the students of Latin American schools: "Studies must comprise not only a given quantity of knowledge acquired in the course of specialization, but also a special spiritual maturity which presents itself as a responsibility for truth: for truth in thought and in action" *(ibid.,* p. 253).

TODAY'S TENSIONS

Let these few quotations suffice.

A great tension exists in the modern world. All things considered, this is a tension over the sense of human life, the meaning we can and must give to this *life* if it is to be *worthy of man,* if it is to be *such that it is worth living.* There also exist clear symptoms of moving away from these dimensions; in fact, materialism in different forms, inherited from the last centuries, is capable of coercing this meaning of life. *But materialism does not at all form the deepest roots of European or world culture. It is not at all a correlative or a full expression of epistemological or ethical realism.*

Christ—allow me to put it in this way—*is the greatest Realist in the history of man.* Reflect a little on this formulation. Meditate on what it can signify.

It is precisely by virtue of this realism that Christ bears witness to the Father, and bears witness to man. He Himself, in fact, knows "what is in man" (Jn. 2:25). He knows! I repeat it without wishing to offend any of those who have tried at any time or are trying today to understand what man is, and wish to teach it.

And precisely on the basis of this realism, Christ teaches that human life has a meaning insofar as it is a testimony of truth and love.

Think this over, you who as students *must be particularly sensitive to truth* and to the testimony of truth. You are, so to speak, the professionals of intelligence, since you are engaged in the study of humanistic and scientific disciplines, in view of preparation for the office that is waiting for you in society.

Think it over, you who having *young hearts feel how much need of love is born in them.* You who are looking for a form of expression for this love in your lives. There are some who find this expression in exclusive dedication of themselves to God. The vast majority are those who find the expression of this love in marriage, in family life.

Prepare for that thoroughly. *Remember that love as a noble sentiment is a gift of the heart; but at the same time it is a great task that must be assumed in favor of the other one, in favor of her, in favor of him. Christ is waiting for such a love of yours.* He wishes to be with you when it is formed in your hearts, and when it matures in the sacramental oath. And afterwards, and always.

LOVE ONE ANOTHER

6. Christ says, "I have earnestly desired to eat this passover with you!" (Lk. 22:15) When He ate it for the first time with the disciples, He spoke *words that are particularly cordial and particularly binding:* "No longer do I call you servants...but I have called you friends..." (Jn. 15:15); "This is my commandment, that you love one another" (Jn. 15:12). Remember these words of Christ's farewell speech, from the Gospel of John, now, in the period of the Lord's passion. Think about them again.

Purify your hearts in the sacrament of Reconciliation. Those who accuse the call of the Church to repentance as coming from a "repressive" mentality are lying. Sacramental confession is not a repression but a liberation; it does not restore feelings of guilt, but cancels the guilt, dissolves the evil done, and bestows the grace of forgiveness. *The causes of evil are not to be sought outside man, but first and foremost inside his heart; and the remedy starts also from the heart.* Then Christians, through the sincerity of their commitment of conversion, must rebel against the leveling down of man and proclaim with their own lives the joy of true liberation from sin by means of Christ's forgiveness. *The Church does not have a project of her own ready for the university, for society, but she has a project of man, of the new man, born again from grace.* Find the interior truth of your consciences again. May the Holy Spirit grant you the grace of a sincere repentance, of a firm purpose of amendment, and of a sincere confession of sins.

May He grant you deep spiritual joy.

"The day which the Lord has made" (Ps. 117/118:24) is approaching.

Be prepared for this day!

RAISE YOUR EYES
TOWARDS JESUS CHRIST!

The address prepared by the Holy Father for the meeting with young Parisians at Parc des Princes, June 1, 1980, which was replaced by the one that the Pope actually delivered in reply to the questions submitted to him, was left to the young in the form of a message. The text is as follows.

Thank you, thank you, dear young people of France, for having come this evening for this vigil with the Pope! Thank you for your trust! I thank, too, all those who have written to me! The meeting with the young is always a very special moment of my pastoral visits. Thank you for what you have prepared this evening for the eyes and for the heart! You now give me your testimony, you profess your faith. And I will then speak of your lives as young people, bearing in mind your questions, and with you I will profess the whole faith of the Church.

Dear young people of France,

1. My hearty thanks for having come in such large numbers, so joyful, so confident, so united with one another! My thanks to the young people of Paris and of the Paris region! My thanks to the young people who have come enthusiastically from all over France! I would have liked so much to shake hands with each of you, look into your eyes, and say a personal and friendly word. This

practical impossibility is not an obstacle .to the deep communion of spirits and hearts. Your exchanges of testimonies are the proof.

Your assembly is a delight to my eyes and overwhelms my heart. Your assembly of young people has wished to be worthy of the crowds of young people I have already met in the course of my apostolic journeys, in Mexico first of all, then in Poland, in Ireland, in the United States, and recently in Africa. I can confide to you: God has bestowed on me—as on so many bishops and priests—the grace of loving the young passionately. Though they are certainly different from one country to another, they are so similar in their enthusiasm and their disappointments, their aspirations and their generosity!

Those of you who have had the possibility of establishing contacts and making friends with young people of another province, another country, another continent than their own, will understand better, perhaps, and certainly share my faith in youth, because it is everywhere, today as yesterday, the bearer of great hopes for the world and for the Church. Young people of France, convinced Christians or sympathizers with Christianity, I would like us, on this unforgettable evening, to make a climb, all roped together, in the direction of the difficult and at the same time bracing, peaks of the vocation of man, of Christian man. *I wish, in fact, to share with you, as a friend with his friends, my own convictions as a man and as a servant of the faith and unity of the People of God.*

AN EXISTENCE REALLY HUMAN

2. Your problems and your sufferings as young people are known to me, at least in general: a certain instability inherent in your age and increased by the acceleration of the changes of history; a certain mistrust with regard to certainties, aggravated by the knowledge learned at school and the frequent atmosphere of systematic criticism; concern about the future and the difficulties of professional integration; the stimulation and superabundance of desires in a society which makes pleasure the purpose of life; the painful feeling of powerlessness to master the ambiguous or fatal consequences of progress; the temptations of revolt, escape or resignation. You know all that, to the extent of being saturated with it. I prefer, with you, to reach the heights. *I am convinced that you want to get out of this debilitating atmosphere and deepen or rediscover the meaning of existence that is really human because it is open to God: in a word, your vocation as a man in Christ.*

3. The human being is a corporeal being. This very simple statement is pregnant with consequences. However material it may be, the body is not an object among other objects. It is in the first place some one, in the sense that it is a manifestation of the person, a way of being present to others, of communication, of extremely varied expression. The body is a word, a language. What a marvel, and what a risk at the same time! Young men and women, have very

great respect for your body and for the bodies of others! Let your body be in the service of your inner self! Let your gestures, your looks, always be the reflection of your soul! Worship of the body? No, never! Contempt for the body? Again, no! Control of the body? Yes! Transfiguration of the body! Even more! It often happens to you to admire the marvelous transparency of the soul in many men and women in the daily accomplishment of their human tasks. Think of the students or sportsmen who put all their physical energies in the service of their respective ideal. Think of the father and the mother whose faces, bending over their child, reveal so deeply the joys of fatherhood and motherhood. Think of the musician or the actor identified with the authors whom they bring to life again. See the Trappist or the Carthusian, the Carmelite or the Poor Clare, radically abandoned to contemplation and letting God shine through them.

MASTERY OF SELF

I really hope that you will take up the challenge of this time and be, one and all, champions of Christian mastery of the body. Sports rightly understood, which is springing up again today beyond the circle of professionals, is a very great help. This mastery is decisive for the integration of sexuality in your lives as young people and adults. It is difficult to speak of sexuality at the present time, marked by a lack of inhibitions which is not without an explanation but which is, alas, stimulated by a real exploitation of the sexual instinct. Young people of France, the union of bodies has always been the most forceful language in which two beings can communicate with each other. That is why this language, which touches the sacred mystery of man and woman, demands that the gestures of love should never be performed without the conditions of a complete and definitive assumption of responsibility for the partner, and that the commitment should be undertaken publicly in marriage. Young people of France, preserve or find again a healthy view of corporal values! Contemplate more Christ the Redeemer of man! He is the Word made flesh whom so many artists have painted with realism in order to signify to us clearly that He assumed everything of human nature, including sexuality, sublimating it in chastity.

A MIND TO THINK

4. The mind is the original element that fundamentally distinguishes man from the animal world and that gives him the power to master the universe. I cannot resist quoting to you your incomparable French writer, Pascal: "Man is only a reed, the weakest one in nature; but he is a thinking reed. It is not necessary for the whole universe to take up arms to crush him...; but even if the universe were to crush him, man would still be nobler than what kills him, because he knows that he is dying; and the universe knows nothing of the advantage it has over him. Our whole

dignity, therefore, consists in thought...; so let us work at thinking well" *(Pensees,* no. 347).

Speaking of the mind in this way, I mean the mind capable of understanding, willing, loving. It is precisely through these that man is a man. Safeguard the sacred sphere of the mind at all costs in you and around you! You know that in the modern world there still exist, alas, totalitarian systems which paralyze the mind, and seriously impair the integrity, the identity of man, by reducing him to the state of an object, a machine, by depriving him of his interior resilience, of his impulses of freedom and love. You know also that there are economic systems which, while priding themselves on their formidable industrial expansion, accentuate, at the same time, the degradation, the decomposition of man. Even the mass media, which should contribute to the complete development of men and to their mutual enrichment in growing brotherhood, are sometimes guilty of hammering at the intelligence and the imagination and even bewitching them, in a way that is harmful to the health of the mind, of judgment and of the heart, and distorts man's capacity of discerning what is healthy from what is unhealthy.

Yes, what is the use of social and political reforms, even very generous ones, if the mind, which is also conscience, loses its lucidity and its vigor? *In practice, in the world such as it is and which you must not flee, learn more and more to reflect, to think! The studies that you are carrying out must be a very special moment of apprenticeship to the life of the mind.* Unmask slogans, false values, mirages, dead-ends! I wish you the spirit of meditation, of interiority. Each one of you, at his or her level, must promote the primacy of the spirit and even contribute to bringing back into honor what has value for eternity even more than for the future. Living in this way, believers or non-believers, you are all close to God. God is Spirit!

A HEART TO LOVE

5. You are also worth what your heart is worth. The whole history of mankind is the history of the need of loving and being loved. This end of the century—especially in regions of accelerated social change—makes the development of healthy emotions more difficult. That is probably why many young and not so young people seek the atmosphere of little groups, in order to escape from anonymity and sometimes from distress, in order to find again their deep vocation for interpersonal relations. If we are to believe a certain type of advertising, our age is even enamored of what could be called a doping of the heart.

It is important in this sphere, as in the preceding ones, to see things clearly. Whatever use humans make of it, the heart—the symbol of friendship and love—has also its norms, its ethics. To make room for the heart in the harmonious construction of your personality has nothing to do with mawkishness or even sentimentality. The heart is the opening of the whole being to the existence of others, the capacity of divining them, of understanding them. Such a sensitiveness, true and deep, makes one vulnerable. That is why some people are tempted to get rid of it by hardening their hearts.

To love is, therefore, essentially to give oneself to others. Far from being an instinctive inclination, love is a conscious decision of the will to go towards others. *To be able to love truly, it is necessary to detach oneself from many things and above all from oneself, to give gratuitously, to love to the end.* This dispossession of oneself—a long and demanding task—is exhausting and exalting. It is the source of balance. It is the secret of happiness.

Young people of France, raise your eyes more often towards Jesus Christ! He is the Man who loved most, and most consciously, most voluntarily and most gratuitously! Meditate on Christ's testament: "There is no greater proof of love than to give one's life for those one loves." Contemplate the Man-God, the man with the pierced heart! Do not be afraid! Jesus did not come to condemn love but to free love from its ambiguities and its counterfeits. It was He who changed the heart of Zacchaeus, of the Samaritan woman, and who still operates similar conversions today, all over the world. It seems to me that tonight, Christ is whispering to each one of you: "Give me your heart!... I will purify it, I will strengthen it, I will turn it towards all those who need it: towards your own family, your school or university community, your social environment, towards the unloved, towards foreigners living on the soil of France, towards the inhabitants of the Third World who do not have enough to live on and to develop, towards the most humble of men. Love demands sharing!"

Young people of France, it is more than ever the time to work hand-in-hand at the civilization of love, according to the expression dear to my great Predecessor, Paul VI. What a gigantic workyard! What a stirring task!

On the plane of the heart, of love, I have something else to confide to you. I believe with my whole strength that many of you are capable of risking the complete gift, to Christ and to your brothers, of all your powers of loving. You understand perfectly that I mean the vocation to the priesthood and to religious life. Your towns and villages in France are waiting for ministers with hearts burning to proclaim the Gospel, celebrate the Eucharist, reconcile sinners with God and with their brothers. They are also waiting for women radically consecrated to the service of Christian communities and their human and spiritual needs. Your answer to this call lies along the direct line of Christ's last question to Peter: "Do you love me?"

MYSTERY OF CHRIST'S LOVE FOR US

6. I have spoken of the values of the heart, the mind and the heart. But at the same time I have given glimpses of an essential dimension without which man becomes again a prisoner of himself or of others: it is openness to God. *Yes, without God, man loses the key to himself, he*

loses the key to his history. For, since creation, he has borne within him the likeness of God. This remains in him in the state of an implicit wish and unconscious need, in spite of sin. And man is destined to live with God. There, too, Christ will reveal Himself as our way. But this mystery requires, perhaps, greater attention.

Jesus Christ, the Son of God made man, lived everything that constitutes the value of our human nature, body, mind and heart, in a fully free relationship with others, marked by the seal of truth and filled with love. His whole life, as much as His words, manifested this freedom, this truth, this love, and especially the voluntary gift of His life for men. In this way He was able to proclaim the charter of a blessed world—yes, blessed—on the way of poverty, sweetness, justice, hope, mercy, purity, peace, faithfulness even in persecution; and two thousand years afterwards, this charter is inscribed in the heart of our gathering. But Christ did not only give an example and teach. He actually freed men and women from what held their bodies, their minds and their hearts captive. And since His death and resurrection for us, He continues to do so, for men and women from all walks of life and from all countries, from the moment when they give Him their faith. He is the Savior of man. He is the Redeemer of man. *"Ecce homo,"* Pilate said, without being clearly conscious of the significance of his words: "there is the man."

How do we dare to say that, dear friends? Christ's earthly life was a short one, His public life even shorter. But His life is unique, His personality is unique in the world. He is not only a brother for us, a friend, a man of God. We recognize in Him the only Son of God, who is one with God the Father and whom the Father gave to the world. With the apostle Peter, whose humble Successor I am, I profess: "You are the Christ, the Son of the living God." *It is precisely because Christ shares at once the divine nature and our human nature that the offering of His life, in His death and His resurrection, reaches us, the men of today, saves us, purifies us, frees us, elevates us:* "The Son of God in a certain way united Himself with each man." And I'd like to repeat here the wish of my first encyclical: "That each person may be able to find Christ, in order that Christ may walk with each person the path of life, with the power of the truth about man and the world that is contained in the mystery of the Incarnation and the Redemption and with the power of the love that is radiated by that truth" *(Redemptor hominis,* no. 13).

If Christ liberates and raises our humanity, it is because He introduces it into the covenant with God, with the Father, with the Son, and with the Holy Spirit. This morning we celebrated the feast of the Holy Trinity. That is the real opening to God to which every human must aspire even without knowing it and which Christ offers the believer. It is a question of a personal God and not just the God of philosophers and scholars; it is the God revealed in the Bible, the God of Abraham, the God of Jesus Christ, He who is at the heart of our history. He is the God who can seize all the resources of your body, your mind and your heart, to make them bear fruit; in a word, who can seize your whole being to renew it in Christ, now and beyond death.

That is my faith, that has been the faith of the Church since the origins, the only one that is founded on the witness of the Apostles, the only one that resists fluctuations, the only one that saves man. I am sure that many of you have already experienced it. May you find in my coming an encouragement to deepen it by all the means that the Church puts at your disposal.

Others are undoubtedly more hesitant to adhere fully to this faith. Some consider themselves to be unbelievers and perhaps incapable of believing, or indifferent to faith. Others still reject a God whose face has been badly presented to them. Others, finally, shaken by the fall-out of philosophies of suspicion which present religion as an illusion or alienation, are perhaps tempted to construct a humanism without God. I hope, however, that all those will at least, out of honesty, leave their window open to God. Otherwise, they run the risk of missing the way to man which Christ is, of shutting themselves up in attitudes of revolt and violence, of contenting themselves with sighs of helplessness or resignation. *A world without God is constructed, sooner or later, against man.* Certainly, many social or cultural influences, many personal events, may have obstructed your way to faith, or turned you away from it. But actually, if you wish—in the midst of these difficulties which I understand—you have still, finally, a good chance, in your country of religious freedom, to clear this way and have access, with the grace of God, to faith! You have the means to do so! Are you really taking them? In the name of all the love that I bear you, I do not hesitate to call upon you: "Throw open your doors to Christ!" What do you fear? Trust Him. Take the risk of following Him. That requires, of course, that you should come out of yourselves, your reasonings, your "wisdom," your indifference, your self-complacency, the non-Christian habits that you may have acquired. Yes, that calls for sacrifice, a conversion, which you must first dare to desire, ask in prayer and begin to practice. Let Christ be for you the way, the truth and the life. Let Him be your salvation and your happiness. Let Him seize your whole life in order that it may reach all its dimensions with Him, that all your relationships, activities, feelings and thoughts may be integrated in Him, one could say "Christified." I hope that with Christ you will recognize God as the Source and End of your existence.

These are the men and women that the world needs, that France needs. You will personally have the happiness promised in the beatitudes and you will be, in all humility and respect for others, and in their midst, the leaven of which the Gospel speaks. You will build a new world; you will prepare a Christian future. It is a way of the cross, yes, it is also a way of joy, for it is a way of hope.

With all my trust and all my affection I call upon the young people of France to raise their heads and walk together along this way, their hands in the Lord's hand. "Arise, young women. Arise, young men."

CHRISTIANITY CROWNS YOUR PERSONALITY

After meeting with the religious sisters in the church of Maria Ausiliatrice in the afternoon, John Paul II went out into the large square in front of the basilica, and from a specially erected platform in front of the statue of St. John Bosco he gave the following address to the thousands of young people of Turin who had come to greet him on April 13, 1980.

Beloved young people of the city and of the Church of Turin, could there fail to be a special appointment with you on the occasion of this visit of mine? Yes or no?

(Crowd: no!)

So here we have a fixed point. We must thank the organizers who made provision for this appointment and this program.

Finding myself in your land, I felt, more than the opportuneness, the necessity of addressing to you my word of exhortation and incentive, also to strengthen the hope of all those who, in the difficult years that we are living, turn to you with renewed confidence.

1. Turin is a city which has remarkable and literally exemplary traditions in the religious-educational field. It presents to us chosen figures of men and youths who, though they lived in different periods from ours, are surprisingly relevant today and can offer the modern world very

precious lessons. Among the many names that I could mention, I will select only two.

The first is that of St. John Bosco, who was a great educator of the young, to the extent that his work on their behalf has had a far-reaching influence not only here and in the surrounding region, but also in Italy and in the world. What can I say of my Krakow, of my Poland? There are so many Salesians! I was in a Salesian parish for several years. So I cannot fail to speak about St. John Bosco.

I would like to ask, then: what does it mean to be a great educator? It means, first of all, being a man who is able "to understand" the young. And, in fact, we know that Don Bosco had special insight into young souls. He was always ready to listen attentively and understand the youths who flocked in large numbers to him in the youth club of Valdocco and in the church of Our Lady Help of Christians. But it must be added at once that the reason for this peculiar depth in "understanding" the young was that he "loved" them just as deeply.

To understand and to love: here we have the unequalled pedagogical formula of Don Bosco, who—I think—if he were in your midst today, with his mature experience as an educator and with the common sense of the genuine Piedmontese, would be able to pick out and distinguish clearly in you the echo, never extinguished, of the words that Christ addresses to those who wish to be His disciples: "come, follow me" (Mt. 19:21; Lk. 18:22). *Follow me* with faithfulness and constancy; *follow me* right from this moment;

follow me along the various, possible ways of your life! The whole action of St. John Bosco—it seems to me—can be summed up and defined in this successful and masterly "start" of the young on their way to Christ.

The second name is that of Pier Giorgio Frassati, a figure nearer to our own age (he died, in fact, in 1925). He shows us in real life what it really means, for a young layman, to give a concrete answer to the "Come, follow me." Even a rapid glance at his life, consummated in the span of barely twenty-four years, is enough to understand what the answer was that Pier Giorgio gave to Jesus Christ. It was that of a "modern" young man, open to the problems of culture, sport (he was a good mountaineer), to social questions, to the real values of life. At the same time it was that of a deep believer, nourished on the Gospel message; of a staunch, consistent character, passionately eager to serve brothers and consumed by burning charity which led him to approach, in an order of absolute precedence, the poor and the sick.

TWO OUTSTANDING MODELS FOR YOUTH

2. Why, speaking to you now, did I wish to take an example from these two figures? Because they serve to show, in a certain sense, from two different aspects, what is essential for the Christian view of man. Both of them—Don Bosco as a true Christian educator and Pier Giorgio as a genuine young Christian—indicate

to us that *what counts most in this view is the person and his vocation, as was established by God. You know very well that this reference to the person is now a frequent one on my part, because it is really a question of a fundamental element, which can never be disregarded.* When I say person, I do not intend to speak of an autonomous humanism, limited to the realities of this earth. *Man—it is worth recalling—is of immense value in himself, but he does not have it from himself because he has received it from God, by whom he was created "in his image and likeness"* (Gn. 1:26, 27). There is no adequate definition of man but this one! This value is like a "talent" and, according to the teaching of the well-known parable (Mt. 25:14-30), it must be used well, that is, used in such a way that it will bear fruit abundantly. Here, young people, is the Christian view of man, which, starting from God the Creator and Father, reveals the person in what he is and in what he should be.

FRUIT FOR ETERNITY

3. I spoke of bearing fruit, and here, too, the Gospel helps me, when it proposes—it is a reading that we have met with recently in the sacred liturgy—the metaphor of the barren fig tree, which runs the risk of being uprooted (Lk. 13:6-9). *Man must bear fruit in time, that is, during his earthly life, and not only for himself, but also for others, for the society of which he is an integral part.* However, this activity of his in time, precisely because he is "contained" in time, must

not make him forget or neglect his other essential dimension, that of a being directed towards eternity. Man, therefore, must bear fruit, at the same time, also *for eternity.*

If we deprive man of this perspective, he will remain a barren fig tree.

On the one hand, he must "fill time with himself" in a creative way, because the ultra-terrestrial dimension certainly does not dispense him from having to act in a responsible and genuine way, taking part effectively and in collaboration with all other men in the building up of society according to the concrete requirements of the historical moment, in which his life is cast. This is the Christian sense of man's "historicity."

On the other hand, this commitment of faith plunges the young into a contemporary dimension which brings with it, in a sense, a view that is contrary to Christianity. This anti-view presents the following characteristics, which I recall though in summary fashion. *The man of today often lacks the sense of the transcendental, of supernatural realities, of something that is beyond him.* Man cannot live without something that goes further, that is beyond him. Man lives his life if he is aware of this, if he must always go beyond himself, transcend himself. *This transcendence is deeply inscribed in the human constitution of the person.* Now, in the contemporary anti-view, as I said, the meaning of man's existence is, therefore, "determined" within a materialistic conception with regard to the various problems, such as, for example, justice, work, etc.: hence those multiform conflicts between social categories or nations, in which the various collective forms of egoism are manifested.

It is necessary, on the contrary, to go beyond this closed conception, fundamentally an alienating one, opposing to it that wider horizon of which sound reason itself, and still more so, the Christian faith, give us a glimpse. There, in fact, problems find a fuller solution; there, justice assumes completeness and implementation in all its aspects; there, human relations, with every form of selfishness excluded, correspond to the dignity of man, as a person on whom God's face shines.

CHOOSING WITH CHRIST

4. All this shows the importance of that choice which you young people must make! Make it *with Christ,* following Him courageously and adhering to His teaching, aware of the eternal love which found in Him its supreme expression and its definitive witness. In telling you this, I certainly cannot ignore the obstacles and the dangers, unfortunately neither slight nor infrequent, that you meet with in the various environments of today's social context. But you must not let yourselves be turned aside: you must never yield to the temptation, a subtle one and therefore all the more insidious, of thinking that this choice may contradict the formation of your personality.

I do not hesitate to affirm that this opinion is completely false: to consider that human life, in the process of its growth and maturation, may be "diminished" by the influence of faith in Christ, is an idea to be rejected. Exactly the opposite is true: just as civilization would be impoverished and mutilated without the presence of the religious element, of the Christian element, so the life of the individual man and, particularly, of the young person, would be incomplete without a strong experience of faith, drawn from direct contact with the crucified and risen Christ.

Christianity, the faith—believe me, young people—completes and crowns your personality. Centered as it is on the figure of Christ, true God and true Man and, as such, Redeemer of man, it opens you to consideration, understanding and enjoyment of everything great, beautiful and noble in the world and in man. Adherence to Christ does not repress, but expands and exalts the "drives" with which the wisdom of God the Creator has endowed you. Adherence to Christ does not mortify, but strengthens the sense of moral duty, giving you the desire and the satisfaction of committing yourselves for "something really worthwhile."

SOURCE OF REAL JOY

It gives you, I repeat, the desire and the satisfaction of committing yourselves in this way; and preserving the spirit against the tendencies that not infrequently make themselves felt in the spirit of the young, to "let themselves go" either in the direction of an irresponsible and lazy abdication, or along the way of blind and murderous violence. Above all—always remember this—adherence to Christ will be the source of real joy, deep joy. I repeat to you, adherence to Christ is the source of a joy that the world cannot give and that—as He Himself announced to His disciples—no one can ever take from you (cf. Jn. 16:22), even while you are in the world.

This joy, as the fruit of a paschal faith and—as I said this morning—the fruit "of contact" with Christ, as the ineffable gift of His Spirit, is intended as the point of arrival of my talk to you today. I want to arrive at this word "joy." I want to arrive at this word, because we are living the paschal week. *Christianity is joy,* and those who profess it and let it shine through their own lives, have the duty of bearing witness to it, communicating it and spreading it around them. That is why I mentioned these two figures. Don Bosco: I went again to visit his tomb, and he seemed to me always joyful, always smiling. And Pier Giorgio: he was a young man of joy, joy that swept everything along with it, a joy that also overcame so many difficulties in his life because the period of youth is always also a period of trial of strength.

LOVE AND FREEDOM

As young people, you are preparing to construct not only your future, but also that of the future generations. What is to be transmitted to them? You must ask yourselves this question. Only material goods, with the addition, perhaps, of a richer culture, a higher level of scientific knowledge, and a more advanced technology? Or, over and above this, or rather even prior to this, do you not want to transmit that higher perspective which I mentioned, those spiritual goods which are called love and freedom? True love, true freedom, I tell you, because these great words—love and freedom—can easily be exploited. They can easily be exploited.

In our age we are witnesses of a terrible exploitation of these words: love and freedom. The real meaning of these words—love and freedom—must be found again. I tell you: you must return to the Gospel. You must return to the school of Christ. Then you will transmit these spiritual goods: the sense of justice in all human relationships, the promotion and safeguarding of peace. And I tell you again, they are words that have been exploited, exploited many, many times. It is always necessary to return to the school of Christ, to find again the true, full and deep meaning of these words.

The necessary support for these values lies only in the possession of a certain and sincere faith, a faith that embraces God and man, man in God. Where there is God and where there is Jesus Christ, His Son, this foundation is a solid one; it is deep, it is very deep. There is not a more suitable, a deeper dimension to be given to this word "man," to this word "love," to this word "freedom," to these words "peace" and "justice": there is not any other, no other but Christ. Then, always returning to this school, here is the search for those precious gifts that you young people must transmit to future generations, to the world of tomorrow; with Him it will be easier and it cannot but succeed.

As I am about to take leave of you, I wish to raise you to this vision of transcendence and beauty, from which your Christian life will acquire solidity and go from strength to strength (Ps. 84:7) and bloom—because you are young, and you must bloom—bloom in works and also for earthly society. Let them be a premise and a promise of a more human and, therefore, more serene future. This is the major imperative of this age of ours, which is becoming sad, and will be even sadder, even more tragic, if it does not see that perspective which only you young people can give to it, to our century, to our generation, to our Italy, to our world!

And now, let us call forward the Cardinals, the bishops. Let us give the blessing to these young people. Let us say a prayer, the Our Father, and then, then we will give a blessing to all of you present here, the bishops together with the Bishop of Rome, who is a pilgrim in Turin today.

Blessed be Jesus Christ. Goodbye!

THE GIFTS OF
THE HOLY SPIRIT CAN LEAD
TO TRUE DEVELOPMENT OF
THE PERSON

Pope John Paul II addressed the following words to hundreds of thousands of university students in Warsaw who had spent a night in prayer-vigil in the Church of St. Anne and an adjacent square and assisted at Mass on Sunday morning, June 3, 1979, in the presence of His Holiness.

My very dear friends,

1. It is my ardent desire that today's meeting, which is marked by the presence of the university students, will be in keeping with the grandeur of the day and its liturgy.

The university students of Warsaw and those of the other seats of learning in this central metropolitan region are the heirs of specific traditions going back through the generations to the medieval "scholars" connected principally with the Jagellonian University, the oldest university in Poland. Today every large city in Poland has its university. Warsaw has several. They bring together hundreds of thousands of students who are being trained in various branches of knowledge and are preparing for intellectual professions and *particularly important tasks in the life of the nation.*

I wish to greet all of you who have gathered here. I wish also to greet in you and through you all the university and academic world of Poland: all the higher institutes, the professors, the researchers, the students. *I see in you, in a certain sense, my younger colleagues, because I too owe to the Polish university the basis of my intellectual formation.* I had a systematic connection with the lecture halls of the faculty of philosophy and theology at Krakow and Lublin. *Pastoral care of those in the universities* is something for which I have had a particular liking. I therefore wish on this occasion to greet also all those who dedicate themselves to this pastoral care, the groups of the spiritual assistants of university students, and the Polish Episcopate's Commission for University Pastoral Care.

2. We are meeting today on *the solemnity of Pentecost.* With the eyes of our faith we see appear before us the upper room in Jerusalem from which the Church came forth and in which the Church remains forever. There it was that the Church was born as the living community of the People of God, as a community aware of its own mission in the history of man.

Today the Church prays: "Come, Holy Spirit, fill the hearts of your faithful and enkindle in them the fire of your love" (liturgy of Pentecost). These words, so often repeated, today resound with particular ardor.

Fill the hearts.

Consider, young friends, *how great is the human heart,* if God alone can fill it with the Holy Spirit.

Through your university studies you see open up before you the wonderful world of human knowledge in its many branches. Step by step with this knowledge your self-awareness is certainly developing also. *Assuredly you have long been putting the question to yourselves: "Who am I?" This is, I would say, the most interesting question. The fundamental query. What is to be the measurement for measuring man? That of the physical forces at his command? That of the senses that enable him to have contact with the external world? Or that of the intelligence obtained by means of the various tests or examinations?*

Today's answer, the answer of the liturgy of Pentecost, points to two measurements: Man must be measured by the measurement of his "heart".... In Biblical language the heart means the inner spirituality of man; in particular it means conscience.... *Man must, therefore, be measured by the measurement of conscience, by the measurement of the spirit open to God.* Only the Holy Spirit can "fill" his heart, that is to say, lead it to self-realization through love · and wisdom.

3. Therefore, let this meeting with you today, in front of the upper room of our history, the history of the Church and of the nation, be above all a prayer to obtain the gifts of the Holy Spirit.

As once my father placed a little book in my hand and pointed out to me *the prayer to receive the gifts of the Holy Spirit,* so today I, who am also called "Father" by you, wish to pray with the university students of Warsaw and of Poland:

—for the gifts of wisdom, understanding, counsel, fortitude, knowledge, piety (that is to say, the sense of the sacred value of life, of human dignity, of the sanctity of the human body and soul) and, finally, for the gift of the fear of God, of which the Psalmist says that it is the beginning of wisdom (cf. Ps. 111:10).

Receive from me this prayer that my father taught me, and remain faithful to it. You will thus stay in the upper room of the Church, united with the deepest stream of its history.

4. Very much will depend on the measurement that each one of you will choose to use for your own life and your own humanity. You know well that there are different measurements. You know that there are many standards for appraising a human being, for judging him even during his studies and later in his professional work, his various personal contacts, etc.

Have the courage to accept the measurement that Christ gave us, in the upper room of Pentecost and the upper room of our history.

Have the courage to look at your lives from a viewpoint that is close up and yet detached, accepting as truth what St. Paul wrote in his letter to the Romans: "We know that the whole creation has been groaning in travail together until now" (Rom. 8:22). Do we not see this suffering before our eyes? "For the creation waits with eager longing for the revealing of the sons of God" (Rom. 8:19).

Creation is waiting not only for the universities and the various higher institutes to prepare engineers, doctors, jurists, philologists, historians, men of letters, mathematicians and technicians; it is waiting *for the revealing of the sons of God*. It is waiting for this revealing from you, you who in the future will be doctors, technicians, jurists, professors....

Try to understand that the human being whom God created in His image and after His likeness is also called in Christ, in order that in Him should be revealed what is from God, in order that in each one of us God Himself should to some extent be revealed.

5. Reflect on this.

As I make my way along the route of my pilgrimage through Poland towards the tomb of St. Wojciech (Adalbert) at Gniezno, to that of St. Stanislaus at Krakow, to Jasna Gora—everywhere I will ask the Holy Spirit with all my heart to grant you:

such an awareness,

such a consciousness of the value and the meaning of life,

such a future for you,

such a future for Poland.

And pray for me, that the Holy Spirit may come to the aid of my weakness.

V. Addresses About Science and Faith

THE PROBLEMS OF SCIENCE ARE THE PROBLEMS OF MAN

On March 30, 1979, the Holy Father received in audience members of the European Physical Society, who are taking part in Rome in the international seminar on the subject, "The great European projects."

John Paul II delivered the following address.

I would like first of all to express my gratitude to you, Professor, for this initiative to pay me a visit today. I cannot express how grateful I am for this initiative and for this presence of yours. For me it is a continuation of my previous experiences, when I was still in Poland, in Krakow, when it was a usual thing for me to meet scientists, and especially physicists, for different talks. So this day, and our meeting, are for me a first promise that this way of acting, these meetings, will have a future, that they do not belong just to my past but will have a future on another plane. I am also so grateful for what you said, and I think that all that you said was rather the essential talk of our meeting. What I can say now will be rather some allusion, some reference.

Actually, having the fortune to meet you today, I thought that I was not prepared. I would like to be better prepared, but I said to myself: well, let us go as things are, we must take a step, the first stage, as we are, and then, perhaps, we will prepare together with future meetings. But I must say that the things you expressed are really essential for the content of this meeting of ours because they are the fundamental problems: the problems of the very nature of science, and then the problems of the relationships of science and faith, religion. These are problems which are not just, let us say, internal problems of science, but problems of him who is the subject and who is the bearer, the author, of science, and who creates with science an environment of his own for himself: a cosmos of his own, a human cosmos for the problems of man. And so all the other things that you expressed are essential; but I am particularly happy that you should say that the effort that science is making will, perhaps, be a happier one than the effort made by others, such as, for example, politicians. They have not succeeded in reconstituting the unity of Europe, of our continent, while, on the contrary, scientists, you, are convinced that you will be able to obtain it. Then I am with the scientists; I am with you.

CONTACTS WITH
THE SCIENTIFIC WORLD

Allow me, Professor, to make a change of language now. I want now to speak in French because it will perhaps be easier for all the participants to translate my sentiments and then also some ideas.

Ladies and gentlemen, I am happy to greet in you a group of eminent scientists, members of the European Physical Society, presided over by Professor Antonino Zichichi. The meeting this morning gives me particular pleasure. In fact, if my personal formation has been rather, and still remains, humanistic (I must say that I know very little about your subject), geared, afterwards, to philosophical, theological, and moral questions, your concerns, however, are not alien to me. It was even a little strange, but I was always given a good reception by physicists, by the people, by the professors, who represent your profession, your specialization; and, though knowing so little of your problems, your science, I felt rather at home with them. It was possible to understand one another, and so we did so. In Krakow I always sought, and found very fruitful, contacts with the scientific world and particularly with specialists in physical sciences. This tells you the value this moment has for me, conjuring up so many other meetings, in particular, perhaps, the one with the "Rome Club"—the results of the work of this Club are well known in our country, in Poland—even if the circumstances do not make it possible to give it that aspect of personal exchange which I appreciated so much. But we will try to give, perhaps, more of this aspect of personal exchange to our meetings in the future.

IMPORTANT PROBLEMS

The problems you have set forth yourselves in the course of this international meeting are of great importance and are very topical, for they may constitute a point of reference for the development of modern physics. You have, in fact, dealt in your work with very topical scientific problems which range from very high energies for study of subnuclear phenomena to nuclear fusion, from astrophysical radio-interferometers to the light of synchrotrons. Excuse me if I utter these words and if I am unable to give a personal significance to all these expressions, to this terminology. But it is also, I think, our situation when we live in this highly specialized world; we lose the facility of speaking all possible languages, not just languages in the linguistic sense, but also languages in the scientific sense. Thanks to knowledge of the classical languages (Greek, Latin), we understand a little of what these words mean, but the real significance, the correspondence with the reality determined by this terminology, must certainly be brought by you. Your society, furthermore, which comprises several thousand physicists belonging to twenty-eight European nations, is also an appeal to the cultural unity of the whole community of European countries.

WORK OF RESEARCHERS

I do not intend to make a profound speech today but just some remarks on the problem, always new and relevant, of the mutual position of scientific knowledge and faith. You are in the first place researchers; I must say that this is a word particularly dear to me. Researchers! It is opportune to point out this characteristic of your activity and to encourage the rightful freedom of your research in its own object and method, according to "the legitimate autonomy of culture and especially of the sciences," recalled by the Second Vatican Council (Pastoral Constitution *Gaudium et spes,* no. 59). I must say that this paragraph of *Gaudium et spes* is really important for me. *Science in itself is good since it is knowledge of the world, which is good, created and regarded by the Creator with satisfaction,* as the book of Genesis says: "And God saw everything that he had made, and behold, it was very good" (Gn. 1:31). I am very attached to the first chapter of Genesis. Original sin has not completely spoilt this original goodness. Human knowledge of the world is a way of participating in the Creator's knowledge. It is, therefore, a first degree of man's resemblance to God, an act of respect towards Him, for everything that we discover pays tribute to basic truth.

HUMANIZING MAN

The scientist discovers the still unknown energies of the universe and puts them in man's service. Through his work, he must, therefore, cause man and nature to grow at the same time. He must humanize man more, while respecting and perfecting nature. The universe has a harmony in all its parts and every ecological imbalance leads to harm for man. So the scientist will not treat nature as a slave but, taking inspiration, perhaps, from the *Canticle of the Creatures* by St. Francis of Assisi, he will consider it rather as a sister called to cooperate with him to open new ways for the progress of humanity.

This way cannot be traversed, however, without the help of technique, of technology, which make scientific research efficient. Allow me to refer to my recent encyclical *Redemptor hominis,* where I recalled the necessity of a moral rule and ethics which enable man to take advantage of the practical applications of scientific research, where I spoke of the fundamental question of the deep disquiet of modern man. "Does this progress, which has man for its author and promoter, make human life on earth 'more human' in every aspect of that life? Does it make it more 'worthy of man?' " (cf. no. 15)

There is no doubt that from many points of view technical progress, born of scientific discoveries, helps man to solve very serious problems, such as food, energy, the struggle against certain diseases more than ever widespread in the third world countries. There are also these great European projects, with which your international seminar dealt, which cannot be solved without scientific and technical research. But it is also true that man, today, is the victim of great fear, as if he were threatened by what he produces, by the results of his work and the use made of it. In order to prevent science and technique from becoming slaves to the will for power of tyrannical forces, political as well as economic, and in order positively to ordain science and technique to the advantage of man, what is necessary, as is usually said, is a supplement of soul, a new breath of spirit, faithfulness to the moral norms that regulate man's life.

ABIDING BY MORAL NORMS

It is incumbent on scientists of the different disciplines, and particularly on you, physicists, who have discovered immense energies, to use all your prestige in order that scientific implications abide by moral norms in view of the protection and development of human life.

A scientific community such as yours, comprising scholars of all European countries and of all religious convictions, can cooperate in an extraordinary way in the cause of peace. As you have just said, science, in fact, transcends political frontiers and calls, especially today, for collaboration of a worldwide character. It offers specialists an ideal place for meetings and friendly exchanges which contribute to the service of peace.

In an increasingly higher conception of science, in which knowledge is put in the service of mankind in an ethical perspective, you will allow me to present to your reflection a new degree of spiritual ascesis.

There is a link between faith and science, as you were able to affirm, too. The Magisterium of the Church has always said so and one of the founders of modern science, Galileo, wrote that "Holy Scripture and Nature both proceed from the divine Word: one, as being dictated by the Holy Spirit, and the other, as the very faithful executor of God's orders"; so he wrote in his letter to B. Castelli in 1613 (*Edizione nazionale delle Opere di Galileo,* vol. V, p. 282).

If scientific research proceeds according to absolutely rigorous methods and remains faithful to its own object, and if the Scripture is read according to the wise directives of the Church, given in the conciliar Constitution *Dei Verbum,* which are, let us say, the most recent directives— previously there were other similar ones—there can be no opposition between faith and science. In cases in which history stresses such an opposition, the latter always derives from erroneous positions which the Council has openly rejected, deploring "certain attitudes (not unknown among Christians) deriving from a shortsighted view of the rightful autonomy of science: they have occasioned conflict and controversy and have misled many into opposing faith and science" (Pastoral Constitution *Gaudium et spes,* no. 36).

When scientists advance humbly in their search for the secrets of nature, God's hand leads them towards the summits of the mind, as was noted by my Predecessor, Pope Pius XI, in the *Motu proprio* which set up the Pontifical Academy of Sciences; the scientists called to be members of it "did not hesitate to declare, rightly, that science, in whatever branch it may be, opens and consolidates the way leading to Christian faith."

FAITH ENCOURAGES

Faith does not offer resources to scientific research as such, but it encourages the scientist to pursue his research knowing that he meets, in nature, the presence of the Creator. Some of you are walking along this way. All of you are concentrating your intellectual forces on your specialty, discovering every day, with the joy of knowledge, the indefinite possibilities that fundamental research opens for man, and the formidable questions that it sets him at the same time, sometimes even for his future.

I would like us to be able to continue this conversation in the future, finding the opportunity and methods of an indirect exchange—my occupations, like yours, do not leave any other possibility—which will enable me to get to know your concerns better and what you would like to hear from the Pope. I think that these few observations are, in a way, preliminary ones. I hope, ladies and gentlemen, that the blessing of the Almighty will descend on your work and on your persons, and will give you the comfort of contributing to the real progress of humanity, to physical and spiritual health, and to solidarity and peace among peoples. Thank you.

THE MORAL DIMENSION
OF STUDY AND RESEARCH

On Tuesday, April 1, 1980, the Holy Father received in audience about six thousand university students from forty-three countries, who had been taking part in the international congress "UNIV '80," organized by the Institute for University cooperation. John Paul II delivered the following address.

Beloved sons,

Welcome to Rome in . these days of Holy Week, during which you have wished to celebrate once more your congress on the situation of the university in the world. I greet you and thank you for your visit and for the meaning it takes on in the heart of each of you.

With this initiative of yours, you continue to bring into focus the reality, the problems and ideals of the university world, in which the consciences of so many young people, who are so dear to me, are formed—or can be warped. I know that, in your university commitment, you wish to serve man, with an industrious and constructive effort; therefore, you study and meditate to offer ideas and proposals that will open ever new spaces of hope in the difficult situation through which the university is passing at this end of the century.

PARTICULAR PROBLEM

1. This congress of yours in Rome has been preceded by a whole year of work. You have made surveys in over four hundred universities of the five continents and you have carried out many thorough discussions and meetings at the local level. In this way you have succeeded in distinguishing lights and shadows in the world panorama of university life more and more clearly.

Of the problems raised by this sector, I would like to dwell in particular on one: *that of the fragmentation of university culture, and its repercussions on human formation.* We are living at a time when scientific progress is accelerated in all areas. This expansion of knowledge is manifested today in the accumulation of an unimaginable quantity of data. It is not only the scientific and experimental disciplines that are involved in this fragmentation of knowledge, but also the humanistic ones, philosophical as well as historical, juridical, linguistic, etc. *Man cannot and must not halt these advances of scientific progress, since he is urged by God Himself to subdue the world* (cf. Gn. 1:28) with his own work. In this task, however, he must not forget the necessity of integrating his commitment of study and research in a wider framework of reference; otherwise, carrying out his scientific and cultural studies, he will run the risk of losing the very notion of his own being, the full and complete meaning of his own existence, and consequently he will act in lacerating disagreement with his own peculiar identity.

INVESTIGATING SELF

2. *In fact, when man loses sight of the interior unity of his being, he runs the risk of losing himself,* even if at the same time he can cling to many partial certainties about the world or marginal aspects of human reality. *For these reasons, we must stress that every member of a university, whether teacher or student, needs urgently to give space, within himself, to the investigation about himself, about his own concrete ontological status; he needs to reflect on the transcendent destiny, engraved in him as God's creature.* It is here, in this knowledge, that the thread is found which gives harmonious unity to man's whole activity.

I call upon you, therefore, to discover, in the complete and grandiose interior unity of man, the criterion by which scientific activity and study must be inspired, in order to be able to proceed in harmony with the deep reality of the person, and therefore in the service of the whole man and of all men. Scientific commitment is not an activity that concerns only the intellectual sphere. It involves the whole man. The latter, in fact, throws himself with all his strength into the pursuit of truth, precisely because truth appears to him as a good. *There exists, therefore, an inseparable correspondence between truth and good. This means that the whole of human operation possesses a moral dimension.* In other words:

in whatever we do—even our studies—we feel deep in our hearts a need of fullness and unity.

In order that science should not be presented as an end in itself, as an exclusively intellectual task, objectively and subjectively alien to the moral sphere, the Council recalled that "the moral order touches man in his total nature" (*Inter mirifica*, no. 6). *In the last analysis—and each of us knows this by experience—man either seeks himself, his own affirmation, personal utility, as the ultimate purpose of his existence, or he turns to God, the supreme Good and real ultimate Purpose, the only one able to unify, by subordinating them and directing to Himself, the many purposes that constitute the object of our aspirations and our work at different times.* Science and culture, therefore, take on a full, consistent and unified meaning, if they are ordained to reaching man's ultimate purpose, which is the glory of God.

To seek the truth and set out to attain the Supreme Good: this is the key to an intellectual commitment, which overcomes the risk of allowing the fragmentation of knowledge to divide the person interiorly, splitting up his life into a multitude of sectors independent of one another and, as a whole, indifferent to man's duty and destiny.

CHRIST'S GUIDANCE

3. The connection between intelligence and will seems explicit above all in the act of conscience, that is, in the act in which each one

evaluates the reason of good or evil inherent in a concrete action. To form one's own conscience appears, in this way, as a duty not to be postponed. To form one's conscience means discovering more and more clearly the light that starts man on the way to reaching in his own conduct the true fullness of his humanity. *It is only by obeying the divine law that man realizes himself fully as man:* "Man has in his heart"—I am again quoting the Council—"a law written by God. To obey it is the very dignity of man; according to it he will be judged" *(Gaudium et spes,* no. 16).

If the history of mankind, right from its first steps, is marked by the dramatic weakening produced by sin, it is also, however, and above all, the history of divine Love. The latter comes to us and, through the sacrifice of Christ, man's Redeemer, forgives our transgressions, illuminates consciences and reintegrates the capacity of will to aim at good. Christ is the Way, the Truth and the Life (cf. Jn. 14:6); Christ guides every man, enlightens him, and vivifies him. Only with the grace of Christ, with His light and His strength can man take his place at the supernatural level that belongs to him as a son of God. Furthermore, only with this grace does it become possible for him to realize also all the good proportionate to his human nature itself.

FORMATION OF CONSCIENCE

4. Beloved in Christ, in your commitment for man's dignity, for the defense of the interior

unity of those who operate on different fronts of knowledge, the formation of consciences occupies, therefore, a pre-eminent place. This formation is opposed by religious ignorance and, especially, by sin, which spread in man's conscience a darkness that prevents him from discerning the light offered to him by God (cf. Saint Augustine, *In Io. Ev.,* Tr. I, 19). Well, precisely because our weakness is obvious, Christ the Redeemer has come towards us as a Doctor who heals. Approach Him with living faith, receiving the sacraments frequently, and you will experience within yourself the power and light of the blood which was shed for us on the cross. Say to Him trustfully, like the blind man in the Gospel: *Domine, ut videam!* (Lk. 18:41) "Lord, let me receive my sight," and you will discover the deep meaning of what you are and of everything that you do.

These reflections bring us to the feet of a unique chair which, especially during these days of Holy Week, Christ invites us to approach in order to fill ourselves with a new wisdom: the chair of the cross, the lessons of which I already encouraged you last year to listen to. Let us stop in front of the Son of God, who dies to free us from our sins and restore life to us. *From the cross of Christ a light of extraordinary clarity passes into men's intelligence.* We are given the wisdom of God, and the highest meaning of our existence is manifested to us, since He who hangs from this tree is "the true light that enlightens every man" (Jn. 1:9). And our will receives from the cross new joy and strength, which enable us to walk "speaking the truth in love" (Eph. 4:15).

THE LIVING BOOK

The cross is the living book from which we learn definitively who we are and how we must act. This book is always open in front of us. Read, reflect, enjoy this new wisdom. Make it your own, and you will walk also along the paths of knowledge, culture and university life, spreading light in a service of love, worthy of children of God.

And look also to the Blessed Virgin, standing by the cross of Jesus (Jn. 19:25), where she is given to us as our mother: she is our hope, the seat of true Wisdom.

And may the Lord accompany you every day, sustain your witness and make your work fruitful.

On my part, I willingly grant you the apostolic blessing, which propitiates abundant heavenly favors; and I invite you to extend it to your friends and to all your dear ones.

STUDY THE WORLD
TO KNOW MAN

On Friday, September 28, 1979, the Holy Father received in audience participants in the conference on "The problem of the cosmos," promoted by the Institute of the Italian Encyclopedia to honor Albert Einstein on the first centenary of his birth.

John Paul II delivered the following address.

I am particularly happy to receive today the organizers, rapporteurs and participants in the international conference on *The Problem of the Cosmos.* The authority of the institute that promoted it, the competence of the illustrious rapporteurs, the interest of the subject for discussion, have rightly drawn the attention of a vast public, and also mine, to this important scientific initiative.

The Institute of the Italian Encyclopedia has, in fact, won wide esteem among men of culture of the whole world owing to its tradition of research, for more than fifty years now, in the most varied fields of culture. Solid and serious research, which aims at truth, animated by the moral incentive of an objectivity which will not let itself be deflected by passing fashions or party interests, and yet research which is quite aware of the continual progress of scientific knowledge, and present at frontiers of the fascinating adventure of 20th-century man, who is almost on the threshold of a new millennium.

EINSTEIN'S CENTENARY

Now this new fruit of the work of the Institute, the *Enciclopedia del Novecento* (Encyclopedia of the Twentieth Century), already expresses a program in its very title. In these two words there are conveyed, in fact, the determination to forge and express a culture present in our time and at the same time the inner tension towards the unity of this culture. Since in a work of such vast scope, attentive to all the ways through which man sincerely seeks the truth, there cannot be lacking space and an adequate prominence for religious subjects, I am happy in particular at the importance that has been given to these subjects, an eloquent sign of the depth and seriousness of the approach.

It was precisely from the wide research program that converges on this Encyclopedia, and then starts out from it again, that there arose, in the centenary year of the birth of Albert Einstein, your meeting on *The Problem of the Cosmos*. A subject rich in immense fascination for present-day man, as for the man of the past, for the man of always.

SCIENCE OF TOTALITY

What a stupendous science is yours, which, in the field of researches on nature, takes its place in a certain way at the summit of all the others, since its inquiry does not refer to a particular field of nature itself and its phenomena, but with a magnificent drive, which exalts and ennobles man's mind, even tries to embrace the immensity of the universe, to penetrate its structure and follow its evolution. Cosmology, a science of the totality of what exists as experimentally observable being, is therefore endowed with a special epistemological status of its own, which sets it more than any other, perhaps, at the borders with philosophy and with religion, since the science of totality leads spontaneously to the question about totality itself, a question which does not find its answers within this totality.

HIGHWAY TO WONDER

It is with deep emotion that I speak to you today, students of such a vast science, which unfolds before you the whole of creation. Your science is for man a highway to wonder. The contemplation of the firmament has always been for man a source of absolute amazement, from the most ancient times; but today you guide us, men of the 20th century, along the ways of a new wonder. They are ways that pass through the laborious and patient advance of reason, which has studied nature with wisdom and constancy, with an austere discipline which, in a certain way, has set aside delight in contemplation of the beauty of the sky in order to sound its abysses more and more deeply and systematically.

More and more powerful and ingenious instruments—telescopes, radiotelescopes, space probes—have made it possible to reveal to our astonished minds and eyes objects and phenomena that our imagination would never have dared to conceive—star-clusters, galaxies and groups of galaxies, quasars and pulsars.... They have expanded the frontiers of our knowledge to distances of milliards of light years; they have made it possible for us to go back in time to the most remote past, almost to the origins of that process of expansion of the universe which is one of the most extraordinary and unexpected discoveries of our time.

"GRATUITOUS" SCIENCE

So scientific reason, after a long journey, makes us discover things again with new wonder. It induces us to raise again with renewed intensity some of the great questions man always asks: where do we come from? where are we going? It leads us to pit ourselves once more against the frontiers of mystery, that mystery of which Einstein said that it is "the fundamental feeling, which is at the side of the cradle of true art and of true science" and, we add, of true metaphysics and true religion.

But I appreciate your science particularly also for another reason. Unlike so many other sciences of nature, which are cultivated and developed with particular solicitude today because they put in man's hands the power to change the world in which he lives, your science is, in a certain sense, a "gratuitous" science. It does not give man power to construct or to destroy, but it satisfies the pure desire, the deep ideal of knowing. And this, in a world strongly tempted by utilitarianism and thirst for command, is a value to bear witness to and to guard. I acknowlege that to you.

But, actually, to get to know the world is not a gratuitous or useless thing; on the contrary, it is supremely necessary in order to know who man is. Not for nothing has the view of the cosmos in different periods and different cultures always been closely connected with, and had a strong influence on, the view that the cultures themselves had of man. Now, if knowledge of the boundless dimensions of the cosmos has cancelled the illusion that our planet or our solar system is the physical center of the universe, not for this reason has man been diminished in his dignity. On the contrary, the adventure of science has made us discover and experience with new vividness the immensity and transcendence of man's spirit, capable of penetrating the abysses of the universe, of delving into its laws, of tracing its history, rising to a level incomparably higher than the other creatures that surround him.

MYSTERY OF MAN

So the words of the ancient Psalmist spring spontaneously again to the lips of the 20th century believer: "O Lord, our Lord.... When I look at your heavens, the work of your fingers, the moon and the stars which you have established, what is man that you are mindful of him, and the son of man that you care for him? Yet you have made him little less than the angels..." (Ps. 8:2, 4-5, 6a). As already before the sublimity of creation, so also before man, searching the universe and its laws, our spirit starts with amazement and wonder, since here, too, it touches the mystery.

Is it not a question, fundamentally, of one great mystery: the one that is at the root of all things, of the cosmos and its origin, as well as of man who is capable of studying it and understanding it? If the universe is, as it were, an immense word which, though with difficulty and slowly, can at last be deciphered and understood, who is it who says this word to man? The believer's voice and even his thought tremble after You have led him along the ways and into the depths of immensity, and yet I, a witness of the faith at the threshold of the third millennium, utter once more with fear and joy the blessed name: God, Creator of heaven and earth, whose love is revealed to us in Christ the Lord.

With these sentiments, I encourage you all to continue your austere studies, while I invoke on you, on your scientific labors, and on your dear ones, the riches of the gifts of the *Pantocrator,* the Lord of heaven and of earth.

CONNECTION BETWEEN SCIENTIFIC THOUGHT AND THE POWER OF FAITH IN THE SEARCH FOR TRUTH

In the early afternoon of Saturday, November 15, 1980, John Paul II met teachers and university students in Cologne Cathedral. During the meeting the Holy Father delivered the following address.

Venerable confrères in the Episcopate!
Beloved brothers and sisters!
Ladies and gentlemen!

1. I greet you with joy and gratitude, men and women scientists of the Federal Republic of Germany, students of the German universities, which have exercised such a lasting influence on the history of science in Europe. You are gathered here also as representatives of the many researchers, teachers, collaborators and students in the universities, academies and other research institutes. You also represent the numerous collaborators who, engaged in research in the public and private sectors, exercise a considerable influence on the development of science and technology, and consequently have a particular responsibility with regard to men.

SIGN OF READINESS
FOR DIALOGUE

2. Today's meeting must be understood as a sign of readiness for dialogue between science and the Church. The day itself, as well as the place, give this meeting special importance. Seven hundred years ago today, there died in a Dominican convent not far from this cathedral, at whose foundation he was probably present, Albert "the German," as his contemporaries called him, and on whom, alone among the Doctors of the Church, posterity conferred the title "the Great."

Albert carried out a multiple activity in his time as a religious and a preacher, as religious superior, as bishop and mediator of peace in his own city, Cologne. But his claim to fame in world history is as a researcher and scholar who mastered the knowledge of his time and made it his lifework to reorganize it. His contemporaries already recognized in him the *auctor,* the initiator and promoter of science. Posterity defined him as *doctor universalis.* The Church, which counts him among her saints, refers to him as one of her "doctors" and honors him in the liturgy under this title.

Our memory of Albert the Great, however, must not be just an act of due piety. It is more important to actualize again the essential meaning of his lifework, to which we must attribute a fundamental and abiding importance. Let us cast a brief glance at the historico-cultural situation of Albert's time. It is marked by the growing rediscovery of Aristotelian literature and of Arabic science. Up to then the Christian West had kept alive and scientifically developed the tradition of Christian antiquity.

Now it is met by a comprehensive non-Christian view of the world, based only on a profane rationality. Many Christian thinkers, including some very important ones, saw above all a danger in this claim. They thought they had to defend the historical identity of Christian tradition against it; for there were also radical individuals and groups who saw an unsolvable conflict between scientific rationality and the truth of faith, and made their choice in favor of this "scientific precedence."

Between these two extremes Albert takes the middle way: *The claim to truth of a science based on rationality is recognized; in fact, it is accepted in its contents, completed, corrected and developed in its independent rationality. And precisely in this way it becomes the property of the Christian world.* In this way the latter sees its own understanding of the world enormously enriched without having to give up any essential element of its tradition, far less the foundation of its faith. *For there can be no fundamental conflict between a reason which, in conformity with its own nature which comes from God, is geared to truth and is qualified to know truth, and a faith, which refers to the same divine source of all truth. Faith confirms, in fact, the specific rights of natural reason.* It presupposes them. In fact, its acceptance

presupposes that freedom which is characteristic only of a rational being. This shows at the
same time that faith and science belong to different orders of knowledge, which cannot be
transferred from one to the other. It is seen,
furthermore, that reason cannot do everything
alone; it is finite. It must proceed through a
multiplicity of separate branches of knowledge;
it is composed of a plurality of individual sciences. It can grasp the unity which binds the
world and truth with their origin only within partial ways of knowledge. Also philosophy and
theology are, as sciences, limited attempts which
can represent the complex unity of truth only in
diversity, that is, within an open system of com-
plementary items of knowledge.

Let us repeat: Albert recognizes the articu-
lation of rational science in a system of different
branches of knowledge in which it finds confirmation of its own peculiarity, and at the same
time remains geared to the goals of faith. In this
way Albert realizes the statute of a Christian
intellectuality, whose fundamental principles
are still to be considered valid today. We do
not diminish the importance of this achievement
if we affirm at the same time: Albert's work is
from the point of view of content bound to his
own time and, therefore, belongs to history. The
"synthesis" he made retains an exemplary
character, and we would do well to call to mind
its fundamental principles when we turn to the
present-day questions about science, faith, and
the Church.

IN FAVOR OF FREEDOM
OF RESEARCH

3. Many people see the core of these questions in the relationship between the Church and modern natural sciences, and they still feel the weight of those notorious conflicts which arose from the interference of religious authorities in the process of the development of scientific knowledge. The Church remembers this with regret, for today we realize the errors and shortcomings of these ways of proceeding. We can say today that they have been overcome: thanks to the power of persuasion of science, and thanks above all to the work of a scientific theology, which has deepened understanding of faith and freed it from the conditionings of time. The ecclesiastical Magisterium has, since the First Vatican Council, recalled those principles several times, most recently and explicitly in the Second Vatican Council (*Gaudium et spes,* no. 36), principles which are already recognizable in the work of Albert the Great. *It has explicitly affirmed the distinction of orders of knowledge between faith and reason; it has recognized the autonomy and independence of science, and has taken up a position in favor of freedom of research.* We do not fear, in fact we deny, that a science which is based on rational motives and proceeds with methodological seriousness, can arrive at knowledge which is in conflict with the truth of faith. This can happen only when the distinction of the orders of knowledge is neglected or denied.

This view, which should be ratified by scientists, could help to overcome the historical weight of the relationship between Church and science and facilitate a dialogue on an equal footing, as already often happens in practice. It is not just a question of overcoming the past, but of new problems, which derive from the role of sciences in universal culture today.

RADICAL TRANSFORMATION IN TECHNOLOGY

Scientific knowledge has led to a radical transformation of human technology. Consequently, the conditions of human life on this earth have changed enormously and have also considerably improved. The progress of scientific knowledge has become the driving power of general cultural progress. The transformation of the world at the technical level seemed to many people to be the meaning and purpose of science. In the meantime, it has been seen that the progress of civilization does not always improve living conditions. There are involuntary and unexpected consequences, which may become dangerous and harmful. I will recall only the ecological problem, which arose as a result of the progress of technico-scientific industrialization. In this way serious doubts arise as to whether progress, on the whole, serves man. These doubts have repercussions on science, understood in the technical sense. Its meaning, its aim, its human significance are questioned.

This question takes on particular weight with regard to the use of scientific thought regarding man. The so-called human sciences have supplied extremely important information concerning human activity and behavior. They run the risk, however, in a culture determined by technology, to be misused in order to manipulate man, for purposes of economic and political domination.

If science is understood essentially as "a technical fact," then it can be conceived as the pursuit of those processes that lead to technical success. What leads to success, therefore, is considered "knowledge." The world, at the level of a scientific datum, becomes a mere complex of phenomena that can be manipulated, and the object of science a functional connection, which is examined only with reference to its functionality. Such a science may conceive itself as a mere function. The concept of truth, therefore, becomes superfluous, and sometimes, in fact, it is explicitly renounced. Reason itself seems, when all is said and done, a mere function or an instrument of a being who finds the meaning of his existence in life outside knowledge and science.

FACING ITS OWN LIMITS

Our culture, in all its areas, is imbued with a science which proceeds in a way that is largely functionalistic. This applies also to the area of values and norms, of spiritual orientation in general. Precisely here science comes up against its own limits. There is talk of a crisis of legitimation of science, nay more, of a crisis of orientation of our whole scientific culture. What is its essence? *Science alone is not able to give a complete answer to the question of meanings, which is raised in the crisis. Scientific affirmations are always particular.* They are justified only in consideration of a given starting point, they are set in a process of development, and they can be corrected and left behind in this process. But above all: how could something constitute the result of a scientific starting point when it first justifies this starting point and, therefore, must already be presupposed by it?

Science alone is not capable of answering the question of meanings, in fact it cannot even set it in the framework of its starting point. And yet this question of meanings cannot tolerate indefinite postponement of its answer. *If widespread confidence in science is disappointed, then the state of mind easily changes into hostility to science. In this space that has remained empty, ideologies suddenly break in.* They sometimes behave as if they were "scientific" but they owe their power of persuasion to the urgent need for an answer to the question of meanings and to interest in social and political change. *Science that is purely functional, without values and alienated from truth, can enter the service of these ideologies; a reason that is only instrumental runs the risk of losing its freedom.* Finally there are new manifestations of superstition, sectarianism, and the so-called "new religions," whose appearance is closely connected with the crisis of orientation of culture.

These wrong ways can be detected and avoided by faith. But the common crisis concerns also the believing scientist. He will have to ask himself in what spirit, in what direction, he is pursuing his studies. He must assume the task, directly or indirectly, of examining, in a constantly renewed form, the procedure and aim of science from the standpoint of the question of meanings. We are jointly responsible for this culture and we are called upon to cooperate in overcoming the crisis.

4. In this situation the Church does not advocate prudence and restraint, but courage and decision.

There is no reason not to take up a position in favor of truth or to be afraid of it. The truth and everything that is true represents a great good to which we must turn with love and joy. Science too is a way to truth; for God's gift of reason, which according to its nature is destined not for error, but for the truth of knowledge, is developed in it.

This must apply also to science, orientated in a technico-functional direction. It is reductive to understand knowledge only as a "method for success," while on the contrary it is legitimate to judge as a proof of knowledge the outcome it obtains. *We cannot consider the technical world, the work of man, as a kingdom completely estranged from truth.* Then, too, this world is anything but meaningless: it is true that it has decisively improved living conditions, and the difficulties caused by the harmful effects of the development of technical civilization do not justify forgetting the goods that this same progress has brought.

There is no reason to consider technico-scientific culture as opposed to the world of God's creation. It is clear beyond all doubt that technical knowledge can be used for good as well as for evil. Anyone who studies the effects of poisons can use this knowledge to cure as well as to kill. But there can be no doubt in what direction we must look to distinguish good from evil.

Technical science, aimed at the transformation of the world, is justified on the basis of the service it renders man and humanity.

It cannot be said that progress has gone too far as long as many people, in fact whole peoples, still live in distressing conditions, unworthy of man, which could be improved with the help of technico-scientific knowledge. Enormous tasks still lie before us, which we cannot shirk. To carry them out represents a brotherly service for our neighbor, to whom we owe this commitment, just as we owe the man in need the work of charity, which helps his necessity.

We render our neighbor a brotherly service because we recognize in him that dignity characteristic of a moral being; we are speaking of personal dignity. *Faith teaches us that man's fundamental prerogative consists in being the image of God. Christian tradition adds that man is of value for his own sake, and is not a means for any other end.* Therefore man's personal dignity represents the criterion by which all cultural application of technico-scientific knowledge must be judged.

REPERCUSSIONS IN PRIVATE AND PUBLIC LIFE

This is of particular importance at a time when man is becoming more and more the object of research and of human technologies. It is not yet a question of an unlawful way of proceeding, because man is also "nature." Certainly, dangers and problems arise here, which, due to the worldwide effects of technical civilization, raise completely new tasks for most peoples today. These dangers and problems have been for a long time the subject of discussion at the international level. It is a proof of the high sense of responsibility of modern science that it takes charge of these fundamental problems, and endeavors to solve them with scientific means.

The human and social sciences, but also the sciences of culture, not least of all philosophy and theology, have stimulated in multiple ways the reflection of modern man about himself and his existence in a world dominated by science and technology. The spirit of modern consciousness, which accelerates the development of the modern natural sciences, has also set for itself as its purpose the scientific analysis of man and of the world in which he lives, at the social and cultural level. An absolutely incalculable mass of knowledge has thereby come to light, which has repercussions on both public and private life. The social system of modern states, the health and educational system, economic processes and cultural activities are all marked in many ways by the influence of these sciences. But it is important that science should not keep man under its thumb. *Also in the culture of technology, man, in conformity with his dignity, must remain free; in fact, it must be the meaning of this culture to give him greater freedom.*

It is not only faith that offers the perception of man's personal dignity and of its decisive importance. Natural reason, too, can have access to it, since it is able to distinguish truth from falsehood, good from evil, and recognizes freedom as the fundamental condition of human existence. It is an encouraging sign, which is spreading all over the world. *The concept of human rights does not mean anything else,* and not even those who, in actual fact, oppose it with their actions, can escape it. There is hope, and we want to encourage this hope.

More and more voices are raised that refuse to be content with the immanent limitation of sciences and ask about a complete truth in which human life is fulfilled. It is as if knowledge and scientific research stretched out towards the infinite, only to snap back to their origins: the old problem of the connection between science and faith has not become outdated with the development of modern sciences; on the contrary, in a world more and more imbued with science, it manifests its full vital importance.

KNOWLEDGE OF TRUTH
HAS ITS MEANING

5. We have spoken so far mainly of the science that is in the service of culture and consequently of man. It would be too little, however, to limit ourselves to this aspect. Precisely with regard to the crisis, we must remember that science is not only service for other purposes. *Knowledge of truth has its meaning in itself. It is an accomplishment of human and personal character, an outstanding human good.* Pure "theory" is itself a kind of human "praxis," and the believer is waiting for a supreme "praxis," which will unite him forever with God: that "praxis" which is vision, and therefore also "theory."

We have spoken of the "crisis of the legitimation of science." Certainly, science has a meaning of its own and a justification when it is recognized as being capable of knowing truth, and when truth is recognized as a human good. Then also the demand for the freedom of science is justified; in what way, in fact, could a human good be realized if not through freedom? *Science must be free also in the sense that its implementation must not be determined by direct purposes of social utility or economic interest.* That does not mean, however, that on principle it must be separated from "praxis." But to be able to influence praxis, it must first be determined by truth; and therefore be free for truth.

A free science, bound only to truth, does not let itself be reduced to the model of functionalism or any other, which limits understanding of scientific rationality. Science must be open, in fact it must also be multiform, and we need not fear the loss of a unified approach. This is given by the trinomial of personal reason, freedom and truth, in which the multiplicity of concrete realizations is founded and confirmed.

I do not hesitate at all to see also the science of faith on the horizon of rationality understood in this way. *The Church wants independent theological research, which is not identified with the ecclesiastical Magisterium, but which knows it is committed with regard to it in common service of the truth of faith and the People of God.* It cannot be ignored that tensions and even conflicts may arise. But this cannot be ignored either as regards the relationship between Church and science. The reason is to be sought in the finiteness of our reason, limited in its extension and, therefore, exposed to error. Nevertheless we can always hope for a solution of reconciliation, if we take our stand on the ability of this same reason to attain truth.

CHURCH MUST TAKE UP DEFENSE

In the past, precursors of modern science fought against the Church with the slogans: reason, freedom and progress. Today, in view of the crisis with regard to the meaning of science, the multiple threats to its freedom and the doubt about progress, the battle fronts have been inverted. Today it is the Church that takes up the defense:

—for reason and science, which she recognizes as having the ability to attain truth, which legitimizes it as a human realization;

—for the freedom of science, through which the latter possesses its dignity as a human and personal good;

—for progress in the service of a humanity which needs it to safeguard its life and its dignity.

With this task, the Church and all Christians are at the center of the debate of these times of ours. *An adequate solution of the pressing questions about the meaning of human existence, norms of action, and the prospects of a more far-reaching hope, is possible only in the renewed connection between scientific thought and the power of faith in man in search of truth.* The pursuit of a new humanism, on which the future of the third millennium can be based, will be successful only on condition that scientific knowledge again enters upon a living relationship with the truth revealed to man as God's gift. *Man's reason is a grand instrument for knowledge and structuring of the world. It needs, however, in order to realize the whole wealth of human possibilities, to open to the Word of eternal Truth, which became man in Christ.*

OBJECTIVELY
AND PERSEVERINGLY

I said at the beginning that our meeting today was to be a sign of the readiness for dialogue between science and the Church. Has it not emerged clearly from these reflections how urgent this dialogue is? Both parties must continue it objectively, listening to each other, and perseveringly. We need each other.

In this cathedral there have been kept and venerated for centuries the bones of the Wise Men, who at the beginning of the new age which dawned with the Incarnation of God, set out to pay homage to the true Lord of the world. These men, in whom the knowledge of their time was summed up, become therefore the model of every man in search of truth. The knowledge which reason attains finds its completion in the adoration of divine truth. The man who sets out towards this truth does not suffer any loss of his freedom: on the contrary, in trusting dedication to the Spirit whom we have been promised through Jesus Christ's redeeming work, he is led to complete freedom and to the fullness of a truly human existence.

I appeal to the scientists, students, and all of you gathered here today, and ask you always to keep before your eyes, in your striving for scientific knowledge, the ultimate aim of your work and of your whole life. For this purpose I recommend to you particularly the virtues of courage, which defends science in a world marked by doubt, alienated from truth, and in need of meaning; and humility, through which we recognize the finiteness of reason before Truth which transcends it. These are the virtues of Albert the Great.

UNDENIABLE DIALOGUE BETWEEN THEOLOGY AND MAGISTERIUM

On Tuesday evening, November 18, 1980, the Holy Father met with German theologians in the Capuchin Convent of Kloster San Konrad *in Altötting. The Pope delivered the following address.*

Dear professors, dear brothers,

It is a special pleasure for me to meet you here this evening. It was my personal wish to see theologians of your country, for theological science is today especially one of the most important expressions and tasks of ecclesiastical life. I most cordially greet you, and in you all theologians. You are following a great tradition as manifest in the works of St. Albert the Great, Nikolaus von Kues, Möhler and Scheeben, Guardini and Przywara, to mention only a few. I name these distinguished theologians as representatives of many others who, both past and present, have enriched and are still enriching not only the Church in countries where German is spoken, but the theology and the life of the Church as a whole.

For this reason I wish to express my sincere thanks to this work, to you and to all those you represent. *Scientific study nearly always involves self-denial and quiet perseverance.* This applies particularly to the task of providing reliable texts and exploring the sources of theology. Many patristic, medieval and modern text editions are the result of the selfless work of scholars from your country. The wider the range of theological knowledge, the more urgent the task of establishing a synthesis. In numerous glossaries, commentaries and handbooks, you have provided very helpful surveys on the state of developments in nearly all fields of study. Especially in the post-Conciliar period such fundamental guidance is very important. These works inform us about the legacy of the past with the insight of the present. In the field of biblical interpretation the cooperation among exegesis scholars has been very gratifying. It has also given strong impulses for ecumenical work and will no doubt give more. May I request all of you to continue this well-founded theological research. In doing so, be very exact in your consideration of the problems and cares of the people. But do not let yourselves be led astray by chance and short-lived currents of human thought. Scientific and especially theological discernment calls for courage to venture forth and the patience of maturity. It has its own laws which it should not allow to be imposed upon from outside.

One reason why theological research is one of the real treasures of the Church in your country is no doubt the fact that the faculty of theology has a place in the state universities. The relationship between the freedom of scientific theology and its link with the Church, as embodied in the concordats, has time and again proved to be a successful model in spite of some conflicts. This relationship affords you the opportunity to study philosophy and theology in the context of, and in cooperation with, all the science faculties of a modern university. This situation has also enhanced the quality of the colleges of philosophy and theology of the dioceses and orders, of the comprehensive universities and teacher-training colleges, and of the ecclesiastical research institutes. *Moreover, the publication of theological findings would not be possible without efficient Catholic publishing companies.* My thanks go to all those who in their various ways help to foster the science of theology.

Those with exceptional intellectual gifts also have great responsibility, especially in the present situation which at times appears critical. I wish, therefore, to take this opportunity to draw your attention to three perspectives which I deem particularly important.

FOSTER ANEW
THE UNDERSTANDING OF GOD

1. The complexity and specialization of today have produced an abundance of tasks and queries, methods and disciplines. They have produced valuable findings and new appraisals. But there is a danger of the sheer quantity in any one branch of learning blurring the meaning and purpose of theology from time to time. *As God's*

tracks have in any case been largely covered up in this secularized world, the concentration on the divine Trinity as the origin and lasting foundation of our life and of the whole world is the foremost task of theology today. All the passion of theological perception must ultimately lead to God Himself. As late as during the Second Vatican Council it was still believed that the answer to the question of God's existence could be taken for granted. In the meantime it has been seen that the very relationship between man and God has become shaky and needs to be strengthened. May I, therefore, ask you to work with all your strength to foster anew the understanding of God, and *here I would emphasize the Trinity of God and the concept of creation.*

This concentration on God and the salvation He brings for mankind implies an inner system of theological truths. God the Father, Jesus Christ, and the Holy Spirit are the fulcrum of that system. The Scriptures, the Church and the sacraments remain the great historical institutions of the salvation of the world. But the "hierarchy of truths" demanded by the Second Vatican Council (Ecumenical Decree, no. 11) does not imply a simple reduction of comprehensive Catholic Faith to a few basic truths, as some people thought. The more deeply and the more radically we grasp the center of things, the more distinct and the more convincing also are the lines of communication from the divine center of things to those truths which appear to be on the periphery. The depth of that concentration also reveals itself in the fact that it extends to all branches of theology. The theologian's work in the service of teaching about God is, in the view of St. Thomas Aquinas, at the same time an act of love towards man (cf. *Summ. Theol.,* II-II, qq. 181, a. 3c; 182, 1. 2c; I, q. 1, a. 7c). *By making him as deeply and as abundantly aware as possible that He is the thou of all divine utterances and is the object of all divine action, it explains and illustrates to him his own ultimate and eternal dimension which transcends all finite limits.*

2. *Every theology is based on Holy Scripture. All theological traditions derive from Holy Scripture and lead back to it.* Remain, therefore, faithful to the twofold task entailed in any interpretation of Scripture. Preserve the incomparable Gospel of God which was, not made by man, and at the same time have the courage to carry it out again into the world in this purity. The study of the whole Scripture therefore remains, as the Constitution on Divine Revelation of the Second Vatican Council says, "the soul of theology" (no. 24). It nourishes and rejuvenates our theological searching ever anew. Let us live our lives from the Scripture; then, whatever differences may remain, we shall still come closer to our separated brethren.

The Catholic theologian cannot build a bridge between Scripture and the problems of the present without the mediation of Tradition. *That Tradition is not a substitute for the Word of God in the Bible;* rather it testifies to it through the ages and new interpretations. Maintain your dialogue with the living Tradition of the Church. Learn from its treasures, many of which are still undiscovered. Show the people of the Church that in this process you do not rely on the relics of the past, but that our great legacy from the Apostles down to the present day is a huge reservoir from which to draw the answers to some of the questions as to the meaning of life today. We shall be better able to pass on the Word of God if we heed the Holy Scripture and its response in the living Tradition of the Church. We shall also become more critical of and sensitive to our own present. It is not the sole nor the ultimate measure of theological perception.

Explaining the great Tradition of our Faith is not easy. To be able to open it up we need foreign languages, the knowledge of which is today unfortunately declining in many respects. It is essential not only to open up the sources historically but to allow them to address us in our age. *The Catholic Church, which embraces all ages of civilization, is convinced that every epoch has acquired some knowledge of the truth which is of value to us as well.* Theology includes prophetic renewal from these sources, which at the same time imply an awakening and continuity. Have the courage to lead the young people, your students of philosophy and theology, to these treasures of our Faith.

FAITH AS THE BASIS

3. Theology is a science with all possibilities of human perception. It is free in the application of methods and analyses. Nevertheless, theolo-

gians must see where they stand in relation to the Faith of the Church. The credit for our Faith goes not to ourselves; indeed it is "built upon the foundation of the Apostles and prophets, Jesus Christ himself being the chief cornerstone" (Eph. 2:20). Theologians, too, must take faith as the basis. They can throw light on it and promote it, but they cannot produce it. They, too, have always stood on the shoulders of the Fathers in the Faith. They know that their specialized field does not consist of purely historical objects in an artificial test tube, but that it is a question of the faith of the Church as experienced in life. The theologian, therefore, teaches not least in the name and on behalf of the religious community. *He should and must make new proposals to contribute to the understanding of the Faith, but they are only an offer to the whole Church.* Much of what he says must be corrected and expanded in a fraternal dialogue until the Church as a whole can accept it. Theology is very much a selfless service for the community of the faithful. That is why objective disputation, fraternal dialogue, openness and the willingness to modify one's own views, are essential elements of it.

THE RIGHT TO KNOW

The believer has a right to know what he can rely on in practicing his faith. Theologians must show him the means of final support. For this reason in particular the Church has been blessed with the Spirit of Truth. *The sole object of teaching is to determine the truth of the Word of God, especially where there is a danger of distor-*

tion and misunderstanding. The infallibility of the Church's Magisterium must also be seen in this context. I should like to repeat what I wrote on May 15th in my letter to the members of the German Bishops' Conference: "The Church must...be very humble and certain that it remains within that very truth, that very doctrine of faith and morals, which it has received from Jesus Christ who has bestowed upon it in this field the gift of a special 'infallibility.' " It is true that infallibility is not of such central importance in the hierarchy of truths, but it is "to some extent the key to that certainty with which the faith becomes known and is preached, and also to the life and conduct of the faithful. For if one shakes or destroys that essential foundation, the most elementary truths of our faith also begin to disintegrate."

TWO DIFFERENT TASKS

Love for the physical Church, which also includes belief in the testimony of faith and the Magisterium of the Church, does not estrange the theologian from his work and does not deprive that work of any of its indispensable self-reliance. The Magisterium and theology have two different tasks to perform. That is why neither can be reduced to the other. Yet they serve the one whole. But precisely on account of this configuration they must remain in consultation with one another. In the years since the Council you have furnished many examples of good cooperation between theology and the

Magisterium. Let us deepen this basis. And whenever conflicts arise, apply your common efforts in the spirit of the common faith, of the same hope, and of the love that forms the bond between all of them.

I wanted to meet you this evening in order to confirm you in your work so far and to encourage you to pursue further achievements. Do not forget your great mission for the Church of our time. Work with care and untiringly. And while being meticulous, let your research have not only reason but also feeling. It was St. Albert the Great in particular, the 700th anniversary of whose death brought me to Germany, who constantly pointed to the need to bring science and piety, intellectual judgment and the whole individual, into harmony. Be also models of practicing faith for the many students of theology in your country, precisely at this time. Be inventive in faith so that all of us together can bring Christ and His Church nearer again, with a new language, to the many people who no longer participate in the life of the Church. *Never forget your responsibility for all members of the Church, and remember in particular the important task of teaching the Faith which falls to missionaries all over the world.*

Before I meet each one of you personally, please accept my fraternal greetings and God's blessing for all your colleagues, associates, and students. "The grace of our Lord Jesus Christ and the love of God and the fellowship of the Holy Spirit be with you all" (2 Cor. 13:13).

VI. Addresses to Roman Ecclesiastical Universities

1) Address on the Philosophy of Thomas Aquinas to the Angelicum University. November 17, 1979.

2) Address to the Gregorian University. December 15, 1979.

3) Address to the Lateran University. February 16, 1980.

4) Address to the Eighth International Thomistic Congress. September 13, 1980.

PERENNIAL PHILOSOPHY OF ST. THOMAS FOR THE YOUTH OF OUR TIMES

On Saturday, November 17, 1979, John Paul II returned as Pope to his Alma Mater, the "Angelicum," where he had been a student from 1946-1948. He went there to speak at the conclusion of an international congress, organized by the International Society of St. Thomas Aquinas, to commemorate the hundredth anniversary of the publication of Pope Leo XIII's encyclical Aeterni Patris.

Among those present were Cardinals Parente, Ciappi, Philippe, Knox and Garrone. After an address of homage by Father Vincent de Couesnongle, Master of the Dominican Order, the Holy Father spoke as follows:

Esteemed professors and very dear students!

1. It is with a feeling of deep joy that I find myself once more, after no short space of time, in this hall. It is well known to me because I entered it so many times as a student in the years of my youth when I also came from far away to the Pontifical Athenaeum "Angelicum" to deepen my knowledge of the teaching of the Common Doctor, St. Thomas of Aquin.

Since then the Athenaeum has grown significantly. It has been raised to the rank of a Pontifical University by my venerated Predecessor, Pope John XXIII; it has been enriched by two new Institutes: to the already existing Faculties of Theology, Canon Law and Philosophy there have been added those of Social Sciences and the Institute *Mater Ecclesiae* which has the aim of preparing future "Teachers of the Religious Sciences." I take note with pleasure of these signs of vitality in the old stock which shows that fresh streams of sap flow through it. Thanks to these it can satisfy, through its new scientific institutions, the cultural needs as they gradually show themselves.

The joy of today's encounter is notably increased by the presence of a select group of learned exponents of Thomistic thought who have come here from many places to celebrate the first centenary of the Encyclical *Aeterni Patris,* published on the fourth of August, 1879, by the great Pontiff, Leo XIII. This gathering, promoted by the "International Society of Saint Thomas of Aquin," links up ideally with that held recently near Cordoba in Argentina, on the initiative of the Catholic Argentinian Association of Philosophy, in order to commemorate the same event by inviting leading representatives of present-day Christian thought to exchange views on the theme: "The Philosophy of the Christian Today." This present meeting, more directly concerned with the figure and the work of St. Thomas, while doing honor to this celebrated Roman center of Thomistic studies where one can say that Aquinas lives "as in his own home," is an act of recognition due to the immortal Pontiff who played so great a part in reviving interest in the philosophical and theological work of the Angelic Doctor.

2. I would like, therefore, to extend my respectful and cordial greeting to those who have organized this meeting: in the first place to you, Reverend Father Vincent de Couesnongle, Master of the Dominican Order and President of the "International Society of St. Thomas of Aquin"; with you I greet also the Rector of this Pontifical University, Reverend Father Joseph Salguero, the distinguished members of the Academic Staff, and all those speakers, noted for their competence in Thomistic studies, who have honored this meeting with their presence and enlivened its sessions by sharing their store of knowledge.

I would also like to offer my affectionate greetings to you, students of this University, who give yourselves, with eager generosity, to the study of philosophy and theology as well as of the other useful auxiliary sciences, taking as your guide St. Thomas to whose thought you are introduced by the enlightened and earnest efforts of your professors. The youthful enthusiasm with which you approach Aquinas with the questions which your sensitivity towards the problems of the modern world suggest to you, and the impression of luminous clarity which you gain from the answers which he gives to you in his own clear, calm and sober way, afford the most convincing proof of the inspired wisdom which moved Pope Leo XIII to promulgate the encyclical whose centenary we are celebrating this year.

3. It cannot be doubted that the chief aim which the great Pontiff had in mind in taking

that step of historic importance was to take up again and to develop the teaching of the First Vatican Council on the relations between faith and reason. As Bishop of Perugia he had played a most active role in that Council. In the Dogmatic Constitution *Dei Filius,* in fact, the Conciliar Fathers had given special attention to this theme of burning actuality. When treating of "faith and reason" they were united in opposing those philosophical and theological trends which had been infected by the then rampant rationalism. Taking their stand on Divine Revelation, as passed on and faithfully interpreted by preceding ecumenical councils, as clarified and defended by the Holy Fathers and Doctors of both East and West, they had declared that faith and reason, far from being opposed, could and should meet in a friendly way (cf. *Ench. Symb.* DS: 3015-3020; 3041-3043).

The persistent and violent attacks of those who were hostile to the Catholic Faith and to right reason induced Leo XIII to reaffirm and to develop the teaching of Vatican I in his encyclical. Here, having recalled the gradual and ever growing contribution made by the leading lights of the Church, both in the East and in the West, to the defense and progress of philosophical and theological thought, the Pope turns to what St. Thomas did by way of deep penetration and of synthesis. In words which should be quoted in their flowing classical Latin, he has no hesitation in pointing to the Angelic Doctor as the one who carried rational research into what faith makes known towards results which have proved to be

of lasting value: "Thomas gathered their doctrines together—they had long lain dispersed like
the scattered limbs of a body—and knitted them
into one whole. He disposed them in marvelous
order and increased them to such an extent that
he is rightly and deservedly considered the pre-
eminent guardian and glory of the Catholic
Church.... Again, beginning by establishing, as is
only right, the distinction between reason and
faith, while still linking each to the other in a
bond of friendly harmony, he maintained the
legitimate rights of both, and preserved their
respective dignities in such a way that human
reason soared to the loftiest heights on the wings
of Thomas and can scarcely rise any higher,
while faith can expect no further or more reliable
assistance than such as it has already received
from Thomas" (*Leonis XIII, Acta,* vol. I, pp. 274-
275; English translation, J. F. Scanlan, in:
St. Thomas Aquinas, Angel of the Schools,
by J. Maritain, London, 1933, Appendix I,
pp. 204-206).

4. Statements as weighty as these call to
commitment. To us, heeding them a century
later, they above all offer practical or pedagogical guidance; for, in so speaking, Leo XIII
wanted to set before teachers and students of
philosophy and theology the highest ideal of a
Christian dedicated to research.

Well then, what are the qualities which won
for Aquinas such titles as: "Doctor of the
Church," and "Angelic Doctor," awarded him by
St. Pius V; "Heavenly Patron of the Highest
Studies," conferred by Leo XIII in the Apostolic

Letter *Cum hoc sit* of August 4, 1880, that is, on the first anniversary of the encyclical we are celebrating (cf. *Leonis XIII, Acta,* vol. II, pp. 108-113)?

The first quality is without doubt his complete submission of mind and heart to divine revelation, one which he renewed on his deathbed, in the Abbey of Fossanova, on the seventh of March, 1274. How beneficial it would be for the Church of God if also today all Catholic philosophers and theologians followed the wonderful example of the "*Doctor communis Ecclesiae!*" Aquinas treated the Holy Fathers and Doctors with the same reverence, insofar as they bear common witness to the revealed Word, so much so that Cardinal Cajetan did not hesitate to write—and his words are quoted in the encyclical: "St. Thomas, because he had the utmost reverence for the Doctors of antiquity, seems to have inherited in a way the intellect of all" (*In Sum. Theol.* II-II, q. 148, a. 4 c; *Leonis XIII, Acta,* vol. 1, p. 273; Scanlan, loc. cit., p. 204).

The second quality, one which has to do with his excellence as a teacher, is that *he had a great respect for the visible world because it is the work, and hence also the imprint and image, of God the Creator.* Those, therefore, who sought to accuse St. Thomas of naturalism and empiricism were mistaken. "The Angelic Doctor," we read in the encyclical, "considered philosophical conclusions in the reasons and principles of things, which, as they are infinite in extent, so also contain the seeds of almost infinite truths for succeeding masters to cultivate in the appropriate season and bring forth an abundant harvest of truth" (*Leonis XIII, Acta,* vol. I, p. 273; Scanlan, p. 205).

Lastly, the third quality which moved Leo XIII to offer Aquinas to professors and students as a model of "the highest studies" is his sincere, total and life-long acceptance of the teaching office of the Church, to whose judgment he submitted all his works both during his life and at the point of death. Who does not recall the moving profession of faith which he wished to make in that cell at Fossanova as he knelt before the Blessed Eucharist before receiving it as his Viaticum of eternal life! "The works of the Angelic Doctor," writes Leo XIII once more, "contain the doctrine which is most in conformity with what the Church teaches" (*ibid.,* p. 280). His writings make it clear that this reverential assent was not confined only to the solemn and infallible teaching of the Councils and of the Supreme Pontiffs. An attitude, as truly edifying as this, deserves to be imitated by all who wish to be guided by the Dogmatic Constitution *Lumen gentium* (no. 25).

5. These three qualities mark the entire speculative effort of St. Thomas and make sure that its results are orthodox. It is for this reason that Pope Leo XIII, wishing to treat "of the method of teaching philosophical studies in such a way as shall most fitly correspond with the blessing of faith and be consonant with the respect due to the human sciences themselves" (*Leonis XIII Acta,* vol. 1, p. 256; Scanlan, p. 190),

looked principally to St. Thomas as "leader and master of all the Doctors of the Schools" (*ibid.*, p. 272).

The immortal Pontiff recalled that the method, the principles and the teaching of Aquinas had, down the centuries, been especially favored not only by learned men but by the supreme teaching authority of the Church (cf. encycl. *Aeterni Patris,* loc., cit., pp. 274-277). If today also, he insisted, philosophical and theological reflection is not to rest on an "unstable foundation" which would make it "wavering and superficial" (*ibid.,* p. 278), it will have to draw inspiration from the "golden wisdom" of St. Thomas in order to draw from it the light and vigor it needs to enter deeply into the meaning of what is revealed and to further the due progress of scientific endeavor (cf. *ibid.,* p. 282).

Now that a hundred years of the history of thought have passed we are able to appreciate how balanced and wise these appraisals were. With good reason, therefore, the Supreme Pontiffs who succeeded Leo XIII, and the Code of Canon Law itself (cf. can. 1366, par. 2) have repeated them and made them their own. The Second Vatican Council also, as we know, recommends the study and the teaching of the perennial philosophical heritage, of which the thought of the Angelic Doctor forms a notable part. (In this connection I would like to recall that Paul VI wanted an invitation to attend the Council to be sent to Jacques Maritain, one of the best known interpreters of Thomistic thought, intending also in this way to signify his high regard for the the Master of the Thirteenth Century and for a way of "doing philosophy" that is in keeping with the "signs of the times.") The Decree on priestly formation (*Optatam totius*), before it speaks of the need for teaching to take account of modern trends in philosophy, especially of "those which are most influential in the homeland of the candidates," requires that "philosophical subjects should be taught in such a way as to lead the students gradually to a solid and consistent knowledge of man, the world and God. The students should rely on that philosophical patrimony which is forever valid" (no. 15; *Vatican Council II,* ed. A. Flannery, O.P., Dublin, 1975, p. 718). In the Declaration on Christian Education (*Gravissimum educationis*) we read: "By a careful attention to the current problems of these changing times and to the research being undertaken, the convergence of faith and reason in the one truth may be seen more clearly. This method follows the tradition of the Doctors of the Church and especially St. Thomas Aquinas" (no. 10; Flannery, p. 735). The words of the Council are clear: the Fathers saw that it is fundamental for the adequate formation of the clergy and of Christian youth that it preserve a close link with the cultural heritage of the past, and in particular with the thought of St. Thomas; and that this, in the long run, is a necessary condition for the longed-for renewal of the Church.

There is no need for me to reaffirm here my intention to carry out fully what the Council has laid down, since I made this quite clear already in the homily which I delivered on October 17, 1978, shortly after my election to the Chair of Peter (cf. *AAS*, 70, 1978, pp. 921-923) and several times afterwards.

6. I am very pleased, then, to find myself this evening among you, who fill the halls of the Pontifical University of St. Thomas, drawn by his philosophical and theological teaching, just as great numbers of students from various nations surrounded the chair of the Dominican friar in the thirteenth century when he taught in the universities of Paris or of Naples or in the "Studium Curiae," or in the House of Studies of the Priory of Santa Sabina in Rome.

The philosophy of St. Thomas deserves to be attentively studied and accepted with conviction by the youth of our day by reason of its spirit of openness *and of universalism, characteristics which are hard to find in many trends of contemporary thought.* What is meant is an *openness* to the whole of reality in all its parts and dimensions, without either reducing reality or confining thought to particular forms or aspects (and without turning singular aspects into absolutes), as intelligence demands in the name of objective and integral truth about what is real. Such *openness* is also a significant and distinctive mark of the Christian faith, whose specific countermark is its catholicity. *The basis and source of this openness lie in the fact that the philosophy of St. Thomas is a philosophy of* being, *that is, of the "act of existing" (actus essendi)*[1] *whose transcendental value paves the most direct way to rise to the knowledge of subsisting Being and pure Act, namely to God.* On account of this we can even call this philosophy: the philosophy of the proclamation of being, a chant in praise of what exists.

It is from this proclamation of being that the philosophy of St. Thomas derives its ability to grasp and to "affirm" all that shows itself to the human intellect (what is given by experience, in the widest sense) as a determinate existing being in all the inexhaustible richness of its content; that it derives its ability, in particular, to grasp and to "affirm" that "being" which is able to know itself, to be filled with wonder in itself, and above all to decide for itself and to fashion its own unrepeatable history.... St. Thomas is thinking of this "being" and of its dignity when he speaks of man as that which is "the most perfect thing in the whole of nature" *(perfectissimum in tota natura: S. Th.* I, q. 29, a. 3), a "person," requiring that it must be given exceptional and specific attention. This says all that is essential with regard to the dignity of the human being, even though much more still remains to be investigated in this field, one where the contribution of modern trends of philosophy can be helpful.

It is also from this affirmation of being that the philosophy of St. Thomas draws its power to justify itself from the methodological point of view, as a branch of knowledge that cannot be reduced to any other science whatever, and as one that transcends them all by establishing itself as independent of them and at the same time as bringing them to completion in regard to their true nature.

Moreover, it is by reason of this affirmation of being that the philosophy of St. Thomas is able to, and indeed must, go beyond all that presents itself directly in knowledge as an existing thing (given through experience) in order to reach "that which subsists as sheer Existing" *(ipsum Esse subsistens)* and also creative Love; for it is this which provides the ultimate (and therefore necessary) explanation of the fact that "it is preferable to be than not to be" *(potius est esse quam non esse)* and, in particular, of the fact that we exist. "This existing itself," Aquinas tells us, "is the most common effect of all, prior and more intimate than any other effect; that is why such an effect is due to a power that, of itself, belongs to God alone" *(Ipsum enim esse est communissimus effectus, primus et intimior omnibus aliis effectibus; et ideo soli Deo competit secundum virtutem propriam talis effectus: QQ. DD. De Potentia,* q. 3, a. 7, c).

St. Thomas puts philosophy moving along lines set by this intuition, showing at the same time that only in this way does the intellect feel at ease (as it were "at home") and that, therefore, it can never abandon this way without abandoning itself.

By maintaining that the proper object of metaphysics is reality "in so far as it is being" (sub ratione entis) *St. Thomas pointed to that analogy which accompanies being as such, finding there the justification of the method for forming propositions dealing with the whole of reality and with the Absolute itself.* In so far as methodology is concerned it would be hard to exaggerate the importance of this discovery for philosophical research, as indeed also for human knowledge in general.

There is no need to stress the debt owed to this philosophy by theology itself, since it is nothing other than "faith seeking understanding" *(Fides quaerens intellectum)* or the "understanding of faith" *(intellectus fidei)*. Not even theology, then, can abandon the philosophy of St. Thomas.

7. Is it to be feared that by favoring the philosophy of St. Thomas one will undermine the right to exist that is enjoyed by different cultures or hinder the progress of human thought? Such a fear would clearly be groundless because the methodological principle invoked above implies that whatever is real has its source in the "act of existing" *(actus essendi)*[2]; and because the perennial philosophy, by reason of that principle, can claim in advance, so to speak, all that is true in regard to reality. *By the same token, every understanding of reality—which does in fact correspond to reality—has every right to be accepted by the "philosophy of being," no matter who is to be credited with such progress in understanding or to what philosophical school that person belongs.* Hence, the other trends in philosophy, if regarded from this point of view, can and indeed should be treated as natural allies of the philosophy of St. Thomas, and as *partners* worthy of attention and respect in the dialogue that is carried on in the presence of reality. This is needed if truth is to be more than partial or one-sided. That is why the advice given by Saint

Thomas to his followers in his "Letter on how to study" where he said: "look rather to what was said than to who it was that said it" *(Ne respicias a quo sed quod dicitur)*, is so much in keeping with the spirit of his philosophy. That is also why I am so pleased that the program of studies in the Faculty of Philosophy in this university offers, besides the theoretical courses dealing with the thought of Aristotle and of St. Thomas, other courses such as: Science and Philosophy, Philosophical Anthropology, Physics and Philosophy, History of Modern Philosophy, the Phenomenological Movement, as required by the recent Apostolic Constitution *Sapientia Christiana* for Universities and Ecclesiastical Faculties *(AAS* 71, 1979, pp. 495-496).

8. *There is still one more reason why the philosophy of St. Thomas has enduring value: its prevailing characteristic is that it is always in search of the truth.* In his commentary on Aristotle, his favorite philosopher, he writes: "Philosophy is not studied in order to find out what people may have thought but in order to discover what is true" *(De Coelo et Mundo,* I, lect. 22; ed. R. Spiazzi, no. 228: *"Studium philosophiae non est ad hoc quod sciatur quid homines senserint, sed qualiter se habeat veritas).* The reason why the philosophy of St. Thomas is pre-eminent is to be found in its realism and its objectivity: it is a philosophy "of what is, not of what appears," *(de l'etre et non du paraitre).* What makes the philosophy of the Angelic Doctor so wonderfully apt to be the "handmaid of faith" *(ancilla fidei)* is that it has gained possession of truths of the

natural order, which have their origin in God the Creator, just as truths of the divine order have their source in God as revealing.

This does not lessen the value of philosophy or unduly restrict its field of research; on the contrary, it allows it to develop in ways that human reason alone could not have discovered. Hence the Supreme Pontiff Pius XI of holy memory, issuing the Encyclical *Studiorum ducem* on the occasion of the sixth centenary of the canonization of St. Thomas, did not hesitate to declare: "In honoring St. Thomas something greater is involved than the reputation of St. Thomas, and that is the authority of the teaching Church" *(In Thoma honorando maius quiddam quam Thomae ipsius existimatio vertitur, id est Ecclesiae docentis auctoritas; AAS* 15; 1923, p. 324; English trans. Scanlan. *loc. cit.,* p. 238).

9. St. Thomas, because his "reason was enlightened by faith" (Vatican Council I, Dogmatic Constitution *Dei Filius,* ch. 4: *DS.* 3016), was in fact able to throw light also on problems concerning the Incarnate Word, "Savior of all men" (Prologue to Part III of the *Summa Theologiae).* These are the problems to which I referred in my first Encyclical *Redemptor hominis,* in which I spoke about Christ as "Redeemer of man and of the world, center of the universe and of history..., the chief way for the Church" for our return "to the Father's house" (nos. 1, 8, 13). This is a theme of the highest importance for the life of the Church and for Christian science. Is not Christology perhaps the basis and the first condition for working out a more complete anthropology

such as is required by the needs of our day? *We must not forget that, in fact, it is Christ alone who "reveals man fully to himself"* (cf. Pastoral Constitution *Gaudium et spes,* no. 22).

St. Thomas has, moreover, shed the light of reason, purified and elevated by faith, on problems concerning man: *on his nature as created to the image and likeness of God, on his personality as worthy of respect from the first moment of his conception, on his supernatural destiny as found in the beatific vision of God, One and Three.* On this point we are indebted to St. Thomas for a precise and ever valid definition of that which constitutes man's essential greatness: "he has charge of himself" *(ipse est sibi providens;* cf. *Contra Gentiles,* III, 81).

Man is master of himself. He can make provision for himself and form projects towards fulfilling his destiny. This fact, however, taken by itself, does not settle the question of man's greatness, nor does it guarantee that he will be able, by himself, to reach the full perfection of personality. *The only decisive factor here is that man should let himself be guided, in his actions, by the* truth; *and truth is not made by man; he can only discover it in the nature that is given to him along with existence.* It is God who, as Creator, calls reality into being and, as Revealer, shows it forth ever more fully in Jesus Christ and in His Church. The Second Vatican Council, when it speaks of this self-providence of man "insofar as it involves knowing what is true" *(sub ratione veri)* as a "kingly ministry" *(munus regale),* goes to the heart of this intuition.

This is the teaching which I set out to call to mind and bring up to date in the Encyclical *Redemptor hominis,* by drawing attention to man as "the primary and fundamental way for the Church" (no. 14).

10. I must add one last word at the end of these reflections which, of necessity, have to be brief. It concerns the thought with which Leo XIII ends his *Aeterni Patris.* "Let us follow the example of the Angelic Doctor" *(Leonis XIII, Acta, loc. cit.,* p. 283) is what he advises. That is what I also repeat this evening. This advice is indeed fully justified by the witness which he gave by his manner of living and which gave force to what he said as a teacher. He had indeed the technical mastery befitting a teacher, but, prior to this, his manner of teaching was that of a saint who lives the Gospel fully, of one for whom love is everything: love of God, the primal source of all truth; love of one's neighbor, God's masterpiece; love of all created things, for these also are precious caskets full of the treasures which God has poured into them.

If we look for the driving force behind his commitment to a life of study, the secret urge which led him to consecrate himself through a total dedication, we find it in his own words: "All things issue from charity as from a principle, and all things are ordered towards charity as to an end" *(A caritate omnia procedunt sicut a principio et in caritatem omnia ordinantur sicut in finem: In John, XV, 2).* And in fact the huge intellectual effort of this master of thought was stimulated, sustained and given direction by a heart full of the love of God and of his neighbor. "The knowledge of what is true is given by the fervor of love" *(Per ardorem caritatis datur cognitio veritatis: ibid., V, 6)*. These words could be taken as his motto. They allow us to perceive, behind the thinker able to rise to the loftiest heights of speculation, the mystic accustomed to going straight to the very fountain of all truth to find the answer to the deepest questionings of the human spirit. Did not he himself tell us that he never wrote anything nor gave class unless he had first had recourse to prayer?

One who approaches St. Thomas cannot set aside this witness which comes from his life; he must rather follow courageously the path traced out by him and bind himself to follow his example if he would wish to taste the most secret and savory fruits of his teaching. This is the burden of the prayer which the liturgy places on our lips on his feastday: "O God, since it was by Your gift that St. Thomas became so great a saint and theologian, give us the grace to understand his teaching and follow his way of life."

This is also what we ask from the Lord this evening, as we entrust our prayer to the intercession of "Master Thomas" himself, a master who was deeply human because he was deeply Christian, and precisely because he was so deeply Christian was so deeply human.

FOOTNOTES

1. *(Translator's note)*. No literal English rendering could convey the meaning which this technical Latin expression—

or its equivalent *esse ut actus*—had for Saint Thomas, and presumably retains for Pope John Paul. It does not refer to the mere fact of existing, of "being there," especially if this is taken in a spatial or temporal sense. The meaning of the Latin *esse* is not properly expressed by the infinitive "to be," for this may refer only to the function of the copula in a proposition. Nor is the abstract term "existence" adequate, for we are dealing with the most concrete of all realities. "Actual existing," or "actual be-ing," come closer to the meaning intended; but to avoid the connotation either of "existence" or of "being" which can be taken in a substantive sense, it might be advisable to coin the active and concrete word "is-ing." What St. Thomas has in mind is the most actual of all actualities, the most perfect of all perfections, the inmost principle and source of all the actuality, perfection, reality, and indeed also of the know-ability of anything that is. It is *esse* in this metaphysical sense which makes anything be, and be real; it is the immediate source of the reality and perfection of all things. This may help the reader to appreciate the Pope's insistence on this insight, so central in the thought of St. Thomas, and the implications which he draws from it in nos. 6 and 7 of his discourse.

2. *Ibid.*

THEOLOGY DYNAMICALLY INVOLVED IN THE PROPHETIC MISSION OF THE CHURCH

During his visit to the Pontifical Gregorian University on Saturday afternoon, December 15, 1979, the Holy Father delivered the following address.

Venerable brothers and dearest sons and daughters:

1. Tonight I am in your midst with a deep sense of joy for this solemn, yet informal meeting which officially allows me to meet the teaching staff of this illustrious center of ecclesiastical studies, the students who receive their intellectual formation here, as well as both its officials and workers whose competence keeps it running smoothly.

I willingly accepted the invitation your authorities made a while ago, not only because I recognize it as a praiseworthy sign of devotion and fidelity to the Successor of St. Peter, but also because it affords me the opportunity, in this the fiftieth anniversary of your being in your new campus at Piazza della Pilotta, to make a concrete gesture of the esteem in which I hold this university and its sister institutes.

So I greet with fraternal affection their Eminences Cardinal Gabriel M. Garrone, the Chancellor; the former Rector of this Atheneum, Pablo Muñoz Vega; the Superior General of the Society of Jesus and Vice Chancellor of the University, Fr. Pedro Arrupe; the Rector, Fr. Carlo Martini; and its distinguished professors, some of whom I have the pleasure of knowing personally, while others I have been able to meet and appreciate through their published books and articles.

I greet you with deepest feelings, dear young people who have come to this *Alma Mater* from every part of the world, impelled by the desire to enrich your minds with treasures of Catholic doctrine and to strengthen your hearts through a prolonged stay in the places made holy by the blood of the Apostles and martyrs and made illustrious by the remarkable monuments of traditions glorious in both the Christian and humanistic realms.

I would also like to greet in a particularly warm way the rector, the professors and students of the Pontifical Institute of Oriental Studies whose function in the Church has played no small part in recent developments in ecumenical dialogue, and of the Pontifical Biblical Institute which celebrates the seventieth anniversary of its foundation in the happy awareness of both having rendered and continuing to render an important service to the Church in performing the duty set for it according to the Apostolic Letter *Vinea electa* of Pope St. Pius X in far off 1909, on May 7th.

In the meantime, the Biblicum has truly become a "center of higher studies for Holy Writ," able to promote "in a proper way the doctrine of the Bible and all the studies which attend it in a way which is more efficacious and follows the sense of the Catholic Church," according to the express wishes of the Holy Pontiff (cf. *AAS* 1, 1909, pp. 447f.). In these decades very many students have "trained and perfected themselves" there, submitting to the disciplines necessary to develop the study of the Word of God done "so that what is accomplished both in public and in private in writing or teaching..., be performed with due seriousness and with wholesome doctrine" (*ibid.*, p. 448). Further, if one adds up the large and distinguished series of scientific publications "published in the name and with the authority of the Institute" (cf. *ibid.*, p. 448) in the course of these seventy years, one should not be surprised that the Biblicum is held in such high esteem in the world of scientific scholarship throughout the world. The Pope is happy to say "well done!" to your administrators and professors on this anniversary.

2. My very presence in your midst, dear members of the Pontifical Gregorian University, expresses and bears witness to the interest with which I follow your activities, and of the trust I place in your work; also of the hope with which I await the fruits of your toil, from which the Church ought to benefit greatly.

In fact, the Christian community awaits a sound contribution from you: that reasoned and systematic reflection on the Faith which is the specific function of theology. Moreover, this has been the task which has qualified the "Roman College" practically from its inception, more than four centuries ago, when it was begun providentially through the apostolic zeal of St. Ignatius of Loyola and then gradually developed until it reached the imposing dimensions of the present university with its variety of faculties and specializations.

What a noble line of professors, often at the highest level, has brought honor to your institution over the many years of its history! Their constant desire has been to pour over the depths of the revealed Word of God and the Church's living tradition with understanding and love. And I am pleased to emphasize as a legitimate cause of pride for your university that they did all this, engaging in the twofold work which is of fundamental importance to every piece of theological research. Firstly and above all, they had a constant openness which bespoke loyalty and docility to the directions of the Magisterium; and this harmonizes with the spirit proper to the Society of Jesus which animates this center of learning. And, secondly, they have always been open to scientific advancements which have import for theology.

This last point deserves to be dwelled on a little. In effect, the history of your university shows that here theology was never seen as an isolated discipline. It has always been connected with other disciplines, as it was designed in the old *Ratio Studiorum* which proposed to assume the integration of research and theological knowledge in a way in which one's knowledge was thus stamped with modernity. In this way one tends towards a construct which is "Christian Wisdom." The recent apostolic constitution on the universities and ecclesiastical faculties describes this as a reality which stimulates one "to gather events and human activities into a single living synthesis together with religious values, under whose guidance all things are coordinated one with the other for the glory of God and the holistic development of humankind; which development embraces the goods of both body and spirit" (Apostolic Constitution *Sapientia Christiana,* Foreword, I).

3. There is a point here on which I would like to dwell. In its millennial history, theology has always sought out "allies" which would aid it in penetrating all the riches of the divine plan as it reveals itself in human history and as one reflects on the magnificence of the cosmos. These "allies" have shown up in the sciences and other academic disciplines, which have continued to emerge under the impulse of a desire to know more deeply the mystery of humankind and its history and the ambience of human life.

The heads of the Roman College showed an awareness of this from its very beginning. It amazes one who examines the story of this center of learning to see how, alongside theology, not only philosophy and literature, but also arts, archeology and the study of the heritage and cultures of ancient times were studied, as well as the physical sciences, mathematics, astronomy and astrophysics. Evidently they sensed a need to be in close contact with all the studies which, with the passage of the years, made up the changing vision which man had of himself and of the world which surrounded him. And if one would only realize that students of that time were conditioned by their cultural ambience, one could accept that there were brilliant forerunners and freer spirits, like St. Robert Bellarmine in the case of Galileo Galilei, who wished to avoid useless tensions and harmful rigidities between faith and science.

The natural sciences treated in those days have become ever more specialized, and many have gone beyond the scope of work proper to an ecclesiastical university. However, the fundamental urge to take into account all the progress made by science in things pertaining to man and the context of his life still remains a valid one for us. *To be precise, in view of this, it is still desirable to have a rapport between an ecclesiastical university and state universities, together with the research centers run in a modern society.* In fact, "the gap between faith and culture constitutes an impediment to evangelization, while, on the contrary, a culture in which the Christian spirit breathes life is a valid instrument for the diffusion of the Gospel" (Apostolic Constitution *Sapientia Christiana,* Foreword, I).

4. From the institutional and organizational point of view, your university has provided strong "allies" for theology by the creation of a series of chairs in the emerging disciplines, which have developed into institutes and faculties absorbed into the university juridically.

They exist at the side of theology, and of these the oldest—as old as the faculty of theology itself—is that of philosophy.

I would like to say something specific at this point on philosophical studies in general, to which I am linked by long experience of teaching and research. In an ecclesiastical university, it is important that philosophy fulfill its traditional mandate, which is the methodical investigation of the problems native to it and the search for their solution based on our ever valid philosophical patrimony, using the light of reason as its guide (cf. Apostolic Constitution *Sapientia Christiana,* Special Norms, art. 79, par. 1).

But it is also important to notice that the relationship to our past patrimony ought not to be construed as a foreclosure of the possibility of a study which would endow modern and contemporary currents with value. What I said at the beginning of my pastoral ministry on the Chair of Peter was a cry to all not to fear to throw open the doors to Christ; and it bears repetition with regard to the great movements of contemporary thought, endowing with value their capacity for and inclination towards the whole truth.

There is no time now to rehearse the list of faculties, recalling the time of their institution. I cannot do more than note that at the institution of each there was an awareness on the part of the officials of the university of an increasing differentiation in the field of religious studies and the necessity of a constant focus on the most recent research on humankind. Each faculty and

institute represents a new stage in the development of the ecclesiastical sciences which surround theology.

5. Tonight, my dear friends, I am happy to
encourage you to follow this way. You will do it,
obviously, with the prudence and discernment
which should attend the enterprise. In fact,
theology ought to choose its "allies" according
to the criteria supplied by its own methodology.
There are currents of thought which, either because of their foundations or because of the
developments made of them by their promoters,
do not offer the requisites necessary for a useful
collaboration with theological research. In such
a case it will be indispensable to offer clear
proofs, arrived at critically, in evaluating the
contributions offered by one or the other philosophical or scientific system, and to choose
what will prove useful in advancing theological
knowledge and to reject what impedes that advance. The instruction of St. Paul has its point
here: "Test everything, hold on to what is good"
(1 Thes. 5:21).

*In fact, there are perspectives, points of view
and philosophical languages decidedly lacking
in usefulness. There are scientific systems so
poor or so closed as to render any translation and
interpretation of the Word of God impossible.* To
take on these systems as allies in an acritical
way would mean theological suicide and cause
irreparable damage. The story of some theological trends which have gone astray in the past
decades is instructive.

Therefore, it is necessary to cultivate in yourselves the capacity "to discern." This calls for a solid theological formation by virtue of which the student who has mastered a method and controls the instruments of theological research can probe the richness hidden in the Word of God. So this tool will become in his hands "sharper than any two-edged blade," able to "penetrate up to the point where soul separates from spirit, bones from marrow, and to search the feelings and thoughts of the heart" (Heb. 4:12).

If one presupposes this firm base, the meeting with the other disciplines will prove fruitful, fostering a creative exchange without risking a hybrid mixture or dangerous distortion. Thus, to use the language of St. Paul, one will not find oneself in the situation of "children tossed about on every wave, borne here and there by every wind of doctrine, according to the deceits of men, with which tricks they wish to lead one into error" (Eph. 4:14).

6. In speaking of the openness theology ought to cultivate in relation to the other disciplines, it comes to me immediately to recall another openness which is even more essential: the openness to the concrete problems of human beings, the openness which is in the service of the ecclesial community.

Theology is an ecclesial science because it grows in the Church and works on the Church. Therefore *theology is never the private affair of a specialist, cut off in a kind of ivory tower. It is a service of the Church and, therefore, ought to feel itself dynamically involved in the mission of the Church, particularly in its prophetic mission.*

It is not that theology ought to be a substitute for preaching, but by deepening and extending one's knowledge of Revelation, theology is an important aid to the ecclesial office of preaching and, in a certain way, becomes the base for our liturgical and pastoral activity.

Dear friends, this pastoral aspect ought to stand in the forefront of your work in the university and ought not to deter you from its seriousness, but rather should be a stimulus for generosity in your work in view of the relevance which your hard work has in bringing to life the salvific plan of God. Theological thought and pastoral action are not at loggerheads with each other; rather they foster one another. Scientific investigation and evangelization go together; the one bears and sustains the other.

My dear friends, we ought to serve the men and women of our time. We ought to serve them in their thirst for total truth, evolved in them by Christ the Redeemer of humankind: a thirst for human rights and justice, for morality and spirituality; a thirst for ultimate and definitive truths; a thirst for the Word of God; a thirst for unity among Christians.

Mark it well, dear professors and students, and also your co-workers here in the university: the realities which you come here to probe, the pedagogic and formative service which you render here, the doctrines which you disseminate from here, are not something peripheral, as if they were luxuries over and above the real problems of our world. Rather, they touch on the most profound aspects of existence which Christ Himself came to illumine with His life, death and resurrection. *They are the realities which all men and women of our time need in order to open themselves to love and hope.* Humanity could not survive without this love, without this hope.

7. I have referred to the pedagogic and formative function of the university. This leads me to turn to you men and women from all over the world who study here. I deeply feel your presence as a force for life in the Church and I detect in you, as I wrote in the Encyclical *Redemptor hominis,* the desire to "come closer to Christ and to 'appropriate' and assimilate all the reality of the incarnation and redemption in order to find yourselves" (cf. no. 10). And I confirm here the conviction that if you satisfy this desire and activate this deep process, then each one of you "will bear fruit not only of adoration of God, but also of deep wonder at himself" and there will be born in each "that deep amazement at man's worth and dignity, which is the Gospel, or better, the Good News" (cf. *ibid.,* no. 10).

To this end it is necessary that each of you become an active part of the thought process which goes on in a university so that this "deep wonder" might mature in you in your reasoned reflection and your scientifically validated conclusions. Therefore, I wish to stimulate an active, full and joyous participation in all of you as you penetrate the revealed mystery and the realities connected with it. You must be engaged in it yourselves in order to collaborate responsibly in the cognitive process. You do not merely assimilate ideas; you are researchers called to bring about your own contribution to the progress of theological knowledge; all this not only under the direction of your professors, but together with them.

Therefore, it is important that you not limit yourselves to study; you must, above all, master a method which shapes the way you conduct your study, so as to be able to follow the road by yourselves and at your own pace. Academic degrees are really only official recognition of scientific maturity already acquired. Besides, it is obvious that one's theological reflections will have pastoral import because of this maturity. It makes you able to enter into dialogue almost at once with the mentality, the desires, the expectations and the language of men and women of our time.

It is evident that such an active participation in the cognitive process which happens in the university ought to be fulfilled gradually. It should adapt itself to the nature of the cycles on which your curriculum of study is based. The first cycle, in fact, is designed to provide general information through a well modulated exposition of all the prime disciplines; this, together with an introduction into the use of a scientific method. In the cycles which follow, however, one embarks on the study of a particular segment of the disciplines at the same time as one is introduced to a more complicated experience of doing scientific research according to a method. This takes one gradually to a level of scientific maturity (cf. Apostolic Constitution *Sapientia Christiana*, General Norms, art. 40).

Here it is important that I recall something which ought to be one of the chief characteristics of a university: namely, the necessity to "fulfill one's teaching office especially in the institutional cycle where above all those doctrines should be communicated which deal with the patrimony of the Church" (*ibid.*, Special Norms, art. 70). In fact, it is only on the basis of a responsible assimilation of such a patrimony that one can stimulate creativity and the spirit of research among one's students done in a union of minds and aims and given support by its very movement towards the one truth.

In this way one will bring about a great cognitive drive in which all will faithfully contribute. This includes the university whole and entire, employing all its components in the penetration of revealed truth, and employing all the methods of research.

8. Who does not see the fundamental importance which this cognitive drive has for the Church's life and, in particular, for its unity? Furthermore, St. Ignatius was thinking of this when he founded the Roman College. He conceived of it as "a university for all peoples" which was to be sited in Rome close to the Vicar of Christ and linked to him firmly with fidelity; and it was to be a service for the churches from around the world which would foster a preaching of the Gospel...with both accuracy and a lively sense of Catholic unity; and all this in the midst of a profound theological reflection on the

Faith. In this way he made a noteworthy contribution toward maintaining the unity of the Christian world derived from the depths of his vision of it.

Since its inception, students and professors of different nations and cultures have lived and collaborated in harmony within the structures of this center of learning as they learned to know one another, mutually, and matured on a foundation of a commonly held Faith, which is the permanent bond of unity. It is this Catholic unity which has been vigorously proclaimed throughout the whole world through the doctrine, life and frequent martyrdoms of your alumni, of whom nineteen have been canonized and twenty-four beatified by the Church. This same Catholic unity has been served by sixteen Popes, innumberable Cardinals, bishops, priests and—for some time now in ever increasing numbers—religious women and lay people. All of these have deepened their faith in the lecture halls of this university.

In the light of such a noble tradition, I say to all you who hear me: a great mission awaits you in the service of all the Churches. Here you are learning to value yourselves and to be brothers and sisters in a common work and in a disciplined search for unique truth. The knowledge which you acquire here, and the experiences you have, you will put at the service of the Churches of the whole world. In fact, it is necessary that each local Church develop its peculiar strengths of expression and exploit its own religious and cultural traditions. But to do this it is equally necessary that you face among yourselves, weigh and exchange such experiences in an atmosphere of common understanding and mutual openness so that the communion of minds and hearts might be preserved.

This is the most important function of a center which is a "university for all peoples" in the heart of Rome and close to the Pope. In making use of the age-old tradition of collaboration at the level both of students and of teachers, among peoples of different cultures, languages and mentalities, this can and should contribute to the maintenance and growth of a sense of fraternity, to mutual sensitivity and to the ability to understand oneself, without which one can neither safeguard unity nor tend towards having it.

The Pope counts on you to follow in this tradition of service for unity. When you men and women return to your churches, you ought to take on various responsibilities of ministry and service. You know how to keep alive amidst all these responsibilities and amidst your many contacts this sense of catholicity and openness to all people and things, which is as the very life breath of the Church. You are the promoters of unity and brotherhood, upholding openness and dialogue among the diverse languages and cultures. Make your own contribution to the harmonious fusion of every culture's individual characteristics with all those elements which are the permanent fonts of Catholic unity.

9. And I encourage you professors and offer my grateful acknowledgement of the fact that

you labor in a situation which demands a particular sacrifice and a constant focusing of your attention and openness to whatever comes from not only every part of the Catholic world but also from the entire human family.

I want you to do your work for truth courageously and openly, free from every prejudice and pinching narrowness of mind. Fix your gaze on our central mystery which is the Christ who is at work and reveals Himself in His Church and has wished to place in the Church of Rome the visible sign of the unity of His body, entrusting to Peter and his Successors the work of guaranteeing the integral proclamation of Catholic truth at the service of the Church and of the whole human race.

With your study let your love for Christ grow so that your teaching can convey to the young a living experience of Him. Do not forget that the fundamental scope of your work is the formation of Christians, and in particular of priests, capable of making in the future a real contribution of pastoral activity by the witness of their word but above all by their lives.

My dear professors, the Pope has also been a man dedicated to the life of study in the university, and he understands the difficulties of your work very well. He understands the irksome weight of the task and the sharpness of the obstacles to your work and your ideals. Do not give way to discouragement brought on by the day's tensions. Realize that each day is to be creative; and do not content yourselves too easily with what was useful in the past. Have the courage to explore new ways; but be prudent about it. The Apostolic Constitution *Sapientia Christiana* recognizes that there is "a real freedom to do research and to teach, in order that one can grow in one's knowledge and comprehension of divine truth" (General Norms, art. 39 and 1, 1).

Especially to bring this about it is necessary that you have an interior balance, strength of mind and spirit and, above all, a profound humility of heart which will make you disciples attentive to the truth and docile hearers of God's Word which is authentically interpreted by the Magisterium. St. Thomas warns us that the proud "cannot stomach the excellence of truth, but delight in their own excellence" *(S. Theol., II-II, q. 162, a. 3, ad 1).*

10. My dear professors, students and co-workers, providence has made this meeting the sweeter by the nearness of the feast of the Nativity. Within a few days we will relive the ineffable mystery of the birth of the eternal Word of God in time. For one who is searching, God has given Himself the features, the voice, the gestures of a human being. The invisible God has become, in Christ, Emmanuel, God with us.

The words of the Christmas preface come to mind: "In the mystery of the Word Incarnate a new light of your glory has appeared to the eyes of our mind, because by knowing God in a visible way we are seized with a love of invisible realities." Do we not find the deep meaning of your work in the university synthesized in these words? Christ is the true "method" of every theological research because He is "the Way" (Jn. 14:6) through which God has come to us and through whom we can reach God. He it is who sustains your studies. He is the center of your life and of your prayer. Follow this "way" with enthusiasm, sustained by faith and love!

In calling down on you and your work an abundance of celestial light, I place your university and its allied institutes under the watchful protection of her who is the Mother of Wisdom, because she is the Mother of Christ. May Mary be at your side as you do your daily work.

I offer you my apostolic blessing with my most cordial wishes for a joyful and holy Christmas.

FAITHFULNESS,
SENSE OF CATHOLICITY

On February 16, 1980, the Holy Father visited the Pontifical Lateran University and delivered the following address.

1. After my recent visits to the University of St. Thomas Aquinas and to the Gregorian University, there could not but be a meeting with you, beloved brothers and sons, superiors, teachers, pupils and former pupils of the Pontifical Lateran University. It is a meeting equally appreciated and significant owing to the importance that this outstanding center of studies takes on before the Catholic world and to the close bond which, by the desire of the Sovereign Pontiffs, has always united and unites it with the Apostolic See. Near as it is to the Patriarchal Basilica of St. John—the Pope's cathedral—it expresses vividly, I would say, with its very topographical position, an eminent position of dignity and responsible commitment in the field of sacred sciences, in relation to the spiritual needs of the diocese of Rome, which has also its major seminary nearby, and of the other particular Churches which send their students to you.

But it is my desire, first and foremost, to express a fervent and special greeting to all the representatives and members of academic life.

I affectionately greet the Cardinal Vicar in his capacity as Grand Chancellor and, with him, together with the Cardinals and prelates surrounding him, I greet the Commissioner Mons. Pangrazio and the Rector, his collaborators and then, according to the order of the various Faculties and Institutes, all those who work in them: the deans and heads of departments, the teachers and the students. The greeting is then extended to those who belong to the various centers of study which are connected, by means of affiliation, with the Lateran University itself, to guarantee a suitable didactic level and the necessary continuity in scientific research: even if these communities are distant physically, this afternoon I consider them present in our midst, as vital and flourishing offshoots of a fruitful plant. I am happy to address, at the very beginning, a word of due praise for the initiative of these affiliations which, if they bear witness essentially to assistance, desire for collaboration and—I would almost say—a marked sense of "cultural communion," also recall in a way that relationship which the Holy Lateran Church *tamquam mater et caput* has with the Churches scattered throughout the world.

2. You, therefore, by special title are called the *University of the Pope:* a title that is certainly an honorary one, but no less onerous *(honoronus)* for that reason. Shall we reflect then on what this title implies, in actual fact?

Already the term Catholic University—as the Second Vatican Council teaches—*designates a school of higher learning which "effects" a public, constant and universal presence of Christian thought, and proves how Faith and Reason converge in the one truth* (cf. Decree *Gravissimum Educationis,* no. 10). And by the term *Ecclesiastical University*—as I recalled in the recent Apostolic Constitution *Sapientia Christiana* (III)—is meant one of "those concerned particularly with Christian revelation and questions connected therewith and which are therefore more closely connected with her mission of evangelization."

What should be meant, in addition, by the term *Pontifical University*? You understand very well that these three adjectives are not disconnected, but are rather arranged "in crescendo" on the basis, already so noble and worthy in itself, of the very existence of a University, which is the chosen dwelling-place of knowledge as such, and a place methodologically appropriate and equipped for the researches necessary to reach it. A Pontifical University appears as at the summit in its indispensable educational and teaching task in the service of Christian faith. That service, in the case of this university, can be defined as the specific duty of supplying an adequate pastoral and doctrinal preparation for seminarians and priests, in support of their ministry in the respective dioceses. Those who go down from the Lateran are called, precisely on account of what they have received here, to tasks of particular responsibility for the animation of the People of God and for the ongoing formation of the clergy.

This convergence of attributions and titles cannot but have a rigorous premise, by way of an obligatory starting point: unfailing faithfulness to the true content of the Creed and, therefore, to the organ that proposes and interprets it, that is, to the living Magisterium of the legitimate Pastors of the Church, beginning with that of the Roman Pontiff. In this way, then, in a university such as this, the natural rigor of the scientific procedure is deeply connected with absolute respect for divine Revelation, which is entrusted to Peter's See. These are fundamental elements, they are the unavoidable poles of reference, from which it will never be lawful to deviate or break away, under penalty of losing one's identity. In fact, if one were to be lacking, the university would descend to the level of a second-rate school, where, for obvious reasons, there cannot be either research or discovery or creativity; in the absence of the other—I mean, adherence to revelation—it would be on its way to an inevitable decadence as regards that very high "ministry of magisterium" which the Church herself, as the first recipient of the *Euntes...docete* of the Risen Christ (Mt. 28:19), entrusted to it when she erected it. In either case, it could not avoid a serious danger: that of not corresponding to the reasons of knowledge or to those of faith!

3. Are these severe words? Certainly not, if we consider how exacting the cultural context is today and how urgent and necessary, at the same time, is a fruitful and stimulating circulation of Catholic thought in it. Ours, beloved Brothers and Sons, are not times of ordinary administration, in which it is lawful to sink passively

into a rut, or to be content with a practically mechanical repetition of concepts and formulae. *The men of our time, far more than those of past generations, have a highly developed critical sense. They want to see, they want to know, they want to realize and touch with their hands, as it were. And they are right!* Now, if that holds good for secular disciplines, how much more does it hold good for sacred sciences, for dogmatic theology and moral theology above all, in which what is learned does not remain suspended in a void, but has, must have, an application which is practical and—note well—literally personal. You will tell me that also the laws of chemistry, physics, biology, etc., involve similar applications. That is true, but how different is the meaning and how much more binding is the significance of certain religious dogmas and certain moral laws, ascertained in the light of divine Revelation. In these areas, in fact, there is a direct involvement of persons, because it is a question of *vital truths*, which touch the conscience of everyone and concern his present and future life.

I will not repeat, however, what I already stated at the Gregorian University. I will merely say that, if every University must be an active mine of scientific knowledge, the Pontifical University must function—thanks to the generous and coordinated effort of all its members—as a center of propulsion of a theological science that is certain and abundant, open and dynamic, fresh and bubbling—like pure spring water— from tireless reflection on the Word of God. This is precisely its task, because on it, too—as on every Christian—there is incumbent the duty of always being ready to answer anyone who calls us to account for the hope that is in us (cf. 1 Pt. 3:15).

ITS PECULIAR FEATURES

4. But keeping in mind the peculiar features and characteristics of the Lateran University—such as its direct dependence on the Pope, the role that the secular clergy play in it, its primary purpose in favor of the ministerial priesthood—it seems to me that its testimony will be all the more clear and convincing and credible, the more and the better the teaching imparted in it and the research carried out in it, correspond to certain criteria. I wish, therefore, to recall them and recommend them.

a) The first criterion—as I have already mentioned—is *faithfulness,* to be understood not in a generic sense, far less in the reductive sense of only just keeping within the limits of orthodoxy, avoiding deviations and positions in conflict with the statements of the Apostles' Creed, the Ecumenical Councils, and the ordinary and extraordinary Magisterium. Not in this way! Faithfulness means, must be, a resolute and stable orientation, which inspires research and follows it closely: it means putting the Word of God, which the Church "listens to religiously" (cf. Dogmatic Constitution *Dei verbum,* no. 1), at the very origin of the theological process and referring to it all the acquired knowledge and conclusions gradually reached; it implies careful and permanent confrontation with what the Church believes and professes. Faithfulness does not mean shirking responsibility; it is not a falsely prudential attitude, causing one to renounce deep study and reflection. Rather it stimulates to investigating, illustrating, defining—as far as possible —the truth in all the riches with which God endowed it; it is concerned about its most suitable and plausible presentation. Faithfulness is the exercise of obedience: it is a reflection of that "obedience of faith," of which St. Paul writes (Rom. 1:5; 16:26; cf. 10:16).

b) The second criterion is that of *exemplarity,* which this university must exercise before others, particularly before the affiliated universities. This means that, aware of its position of prestige and of the delicate function delegated to it by the Church, for the Church and in the Church, it must be able to offer itself as a model to others: through the high quality of teaching; the fervor of research; the exquisitely ecclesial education it can guarantee pupils; the level of spiritual and cultural preparation which it ensures the latter, especially if they are destined for the priesthood; and, in a word, through full correspondence to its own institutional purposes. A university such as this—I will say with the attractive evangelical image—is like a city set on a hill, which cannot be hidden; it is like a lamp, which must not be put under a bushel, but on a stand, so that its flame may expand and give light to all in the house (cf. Mt. 5:14-16). The Lord's admonition "You are the light of the world" (*ibid.*) can and must find an original and substantial fulfillment in it.

c) I will recall, further, as the third criterion, the sense of *catholicity*. The Second Vatican Council accustomed us to hearing other voices in the Church. From the various nations of Christian Europe, as from the countries of Latin America, new approaches and new problems came, which—in the name, of course, of a wholesome and defined pluralism, and without detriment to the dogmatic unity of faith—can enjoy the right of citizenship in the framework of theological reflection and elaboration. Not being able here to go into the individual positions (for some of them, moreover, the necessary clarifications have been made, as I myself did in Puebla last year, in the message to the Latin-American Episcopate), I will say only that the emergence of this fact cannot but call forth the duty of discernment and synthesis. Now what better place is there to carry out this work of critical evaluation and positive integration, than this university, Roman twice over? It is its eminently Catholic sense, congenial to it, and the fact that it is grounded on the Magisterium, that creates the best conditions for it. In this connection, the necessary careful consideration is intertwined with the Apostle's precept: "Do not quench the Spirit, do not despise prophesying, but test everything; hold fast what is good" (1 Thes. 5:19-21).

A select area, in which such work can be carried out, is certainly that of ecclesiological doctrine, and in this connection I wish to bestow well-deserved praise on you, because I know that this study is cultivated with particular assiduity here. Continue with perseverance, because the field is a vast one and so rich in fruitful seeds. It would suffice just to recall the major pontifical and conciliar documents, which immediately come to one's mind, and contain in abundance matter for analysis, explanation and deeper study: Pius XII's encyclical *Mystici Corporis* and Paul VI's *Ecclesiam suam,* the Constitutions *Lumen gentium* and *Gaudium et spes* of the recent Council, form, as it were, an ideal quadrilateral, within which study is to be carried out, without forgetting obviously the precious heritage that patristic and scholastic tradition offers us about the true "Ecclesia Christi."

d) A last criterion springs from that type of research, for which the Lateran University is called to carry out a really promotional activity: I mean pastoral theology. I wish, therefore, to mention the *Pontifical Pastoral Institute,* erected in 1957 by His Holiness, Pius XII, with the series of ancient and modern, human and religious disciplines presented in its various courses, and with the specialization in pastoral theology. In fact, while the Roman Ecclesiastical Universities have especially the high responsibility of forming for the Church teachers who will then ensure, in the local schools of the dioceses, adequate teaching of the sacred sciences, and avail themselves for this purpose of persons and structures of outstanding religious orders, this university, on the other hand, though it is capable of giving us excellent teachers (it has done so in the past and still does), is specially qualified for the preparation of learned and zealous priests, who will have to nourish the pastoral vitality of ecclesial communities. In a word, it aims at supplying experts in that "art of arts," which is, according to St. Gregory the Great, the direction of souls (cf. *Regula Pastoralis* I, 1; PL t. 77, col. 14). Owing to the level reached thanks to this Institute, it can contribute effectively to the formation not only of the laity, but also of priests, through the priests that come out of this school. The fundamental aim is, in fact, education to faith with action differentiated according to needs, circumstances and ages. Listening to the voices that rise today from men, believers and unbelievers, doubtful and indifferent, a study is made of the ways of the proclamation, the techniques of catechesis, sacramental service, the animation of groups and communities, religious presence in the schools, charitable and welfare works, in order that Christian life may, as the occasion arises, be established or increase or mature its fruits in *sanctitate et iustitia* (Lk. 1:75). As for ecclesiology, for this field, too, I will indicate to you two documents, the importance of which is equal to their topicality: the Apostolic Exhortations *Evangelii nuntiandi* and *Catechesi tradendae,* as texts to be studied, meditated upon and expressed in ministerial praxis.

THE INSTITUTE "UTRIUSQUE IURIS"

5. I have spoken until now mainly of theological doctrine and pastoral art, because these are

disciplines of great importance at the Lateran University. I am not forgetting, however—I could not and would not do so—the other teachings imparted here, of a philosophical, biblical, patristic, juridical character, etc. How could I fail to refer, even if only rapidly, to the *Pontificium Institutum Utriusque Iuris* and to the two Faculties that compose it? You know it: in the scientific world it represents an "unicum" of unquestioned prestige, and not just today. It meets real requirements, because the Church will always need good canonists and jurists at all levels: from government to the administration of justice, from teaching to relations with the political authorities. Promoting the study of both systems of law, it bears witness to the interdependence, in depth, of both canon and civil law, confirming, in fact, that law, in its absolute aspect, insofar as it is synonymous with justice, is one.

But, having recalled the function of the original *Institutum,* I would like to mention the possibilities of active presence, very wide ones, which I consider are opening up to it, especially at this moment. There are at least three spheres in which it will be able to offer a valuable contribution: in the preparation and subsequent study of the new *Codex Iuris Canonici;* in deeper study of those rights of the person which, precisely because they are so often trampled upon in modern society, must be all the more considered and safeguarded by the Church, for which man will always remain the first and fundamental way (cf. Enc. *Redemptor hominis,* no. 14); in the great cause of European unity, a cause that is so dear to the Holy See, and in which juridical institutions—if well-prepared Christians are present—will be able to exercise a salutary influence, contributing to make the human and Christian features of the continent shine forth more brightly. The function of our *Institutum* can be very useful, further, in research aimed at establishing new international relations, inspired by justice, brotherhood and solidarity.

6. The range of subjects taught leads me to point out, on the other hand, that, in spite of their multiplicity, their sacred character remains unquestioned in an overall view, while what I would call the religious profile of all those—priests and laity—who, by mandate of the Church, are its legitimate teachers, appears in a very precise and clear way. That prompts me also to stress an element which is of decisive importance, in the perspective of the life of the Lateran University. I take it from section II of the aforesaid Constitution *Sapientia Christiana,* concerning the academic community and its government. Art. 11 says: "Since the university (...) forms a sort of community, all the people in it (...) must feel, each according to his or her own status, coresponsible for the common good and must strive to work for the institution's goals."

This is a really precious indication: since the Academic Body of this university consists both of members of the secular clergy of various dioceses and nationalities, and of religious belonging to different orders and congregations, as well as of lay people, this situation shows even more clearly the *necessity of deep communion* between members of the same Body, in order to find, even in the very context of the teaching, an increasingly strong and organic link for a real unity of policy, in relation to the aims to be reached.

This communion, understood as a serious and thorough effort of research for the development of the sacred sciences taught, will serve to stimulate in the students the formation of a sound mentality on the doctrinal plane, which will then have an easier and almost natural pastoral projection. But for that very reason communion will have to involve also the students who, already started on their way and edified by the example of their teachers, will be called to collaborate in the first place with diligence in academic commitments and then with the undertaking and implementation of particular tasks. If the whole community of teachers is able to show a strong spirit of ecclesial communion, the result will be a witness from which the students especially will benefit. The latter will then be able to return to their dioceses, well trained to guide the brethren with certainty of doctrine and with zeal for the sacred ministry, and the more firmly they are attached to the rock that is Peter (cf. Mt. 16:18) and imbued with an ecclesial sense, the more available they will be for a courageous pastoral service. If this is the goal envisaged, mark it well, illustrious and dear professors, how important and delicate is the function, or rather, the pedagogical mission entrusted to each of you. It is a question of a real ecclesial service, in which the act of confidence carried out by the Church, the office of trust conferred by her, must be met, on your part, by sincere and constant loyalty in discharging it.

7. And now we speak directly to you, beloved students. To you, too, the Constitution on Ecclesiastical Universities and Faculties dedicates a special section, the fourth. It determines the criteria to judge your fitness in moral conduct and in the studies carried out previously (art. 31); it recommends to you, in addition to respect for norms and discipline, participation in the community life of the university (art. 33-34). But I would like to add, on a general and preliminary plane, that a certain awareness is required of you, sons: that of finding yourselves here in a very special place where, as a result of a happy and providential combination of circumstances, you can benefit from the most suitable means to ensure and reach really complete formation. The formation, I say, that is best adapted to your personality, and that the Church confidently expects.

You who are called to the priesthood, reflect on what and how many opportunities you find here to meet the intrinsic and indispensable requirements of your vocation. The years you are passing now are really a *tempus acceptabile:* I would even say that they are—in the perspective of adult life and of your future priestly ministry—*dies salutis* (cf. 2 Cor. 6:2) for your souls and for the brothers whom you already meet and whom you will meet in greater numbers one day. May this thought serve to sustain your commitment and your youthful enthusiasm; stimulate you in application to study and in the sacrifices it necessarily entails; strengthen your will, tempering it to the whip of discipline and to the exercise of obedience. Learn to take advantage in a holy way from this period, in order to arrive at the priesthood with due preparation. Let doctrine, indeed, be sound (cf. 2 Tm. 4:3) and abundant in you, but with it there must also and above all be an ardent love for souls, since—as a great Doctor of the Church says—*est (...) tantum lucere vanum; tantum ardere parum; ardere et lucere perfectum* (St. Bernard, *Sermo in nativitate S. Ioannis Baptistae,* Par. 3 PL 183, Col. 399 [983]).

8. When, in November of 1958, less than a month after his elevation to the pontificate, my venerated predecessor John XXIII wished to visit the then Lateran Athenaeum, which he had attended as a young student at the beginning of the century and at which he had later taught, he uttered some inspiring words which I wish to recall now: "From the nearby altar of our Lateran Basilica to these sacred halls of our Pontifical Athenaeum, the same current of light and heavenly grace passes. In fact, the main occupation of university study at ecclesiastical schools consists in research and expounding of divine science (...) not just to contemplate religious truth..., but also to derive practical guidance for the apostolate of souls."

A few months afterwards, there followed, as you well know, the attribution of the title of university, conferred with the Motu Proprio *Cum inde,* which, from the first lines, confirms the bond of affection that the lovable Pontiff preserved with it and which he considered to have grown still more when he assumed the supreme ministry in the Church: *ad Petri Cathedram evecti.... Nos exinde artioribus vinculis illi iuventutis nostrae veluti sacrario devinciri sentimus* (cf. *AAS* LI [1959], pp. 401-403).

I would now like, if I may, to make my own these heartfelt sentiments and thoughts to tell you, to assure you, brothers and sons who are listening to me, of the deep interest, composed of esteem, expectation, consideration and predilection, which I feel for this "Alma Mater Studiorum," so famous and so well deserving.

For the glory of Christ the Lord, for the honor of His Church, in the service of science and faith, I wish it continual and abundant development, while, as a token of heavenly favors, I willingly bless you all, who are the protagonists and the creators of the life that pulsates in it.

METHOD AND DOCTRINE OF ST. THOMAS IN DIALOGUE WITH MODERN CULTURE

On Saturday, September 13, 1980, the Holy Father received in audience the participants in the Eighth International Thomistic Congress, dedicated to the study of the origin and contents of the encyclical "Aeterni Patris," of its implementation by the successors of Leo XIII, and of the Thomistic renewal that brought the pontifical document to maturity at the turn of the century.

The Pope delivered the following message after an address by Cardinal Luigi Ciappi, President of the Pontifical Roman Academy of St. Thomas Aquinas.

Venerated and very dear brothers!

I am truly glad to be able to welcome in a cordial meeting today the participants in the Eighth International Thomistic Congress held on the occasion of the centenary of the encyclical *Aeterni Patris* of Leo XIII, and likewise of the foundation at the bidding of the same Supreme Pontiff of the "Pontifical Roman Academy of St. Thomas Aquinas."

I greet those present with all my affection, and in particular the venerated brother Cardinal Luigi Ciappi, President of the Academy, and Monsignor Antonio Piolanti, Vice-President.

CONCLUDING THE CENTENARY

1. The holding of the Eighth International Thomistic Congress, organized by the Pontifical Roman Academy of St. Thomas Aquinas and of Catholic Religion, concludes the commemorative celebration of the centenary of the encyclical *Aeterni Patris,* issued August 4, 1879, and the foundation of the academy itself by the great pontiff Leo XIII, which occurred on October 13, 1879.

From the first meeting held in the University of St. Thomas Aquinas in November of last year up to today, the celebrations multiplied in Europe and other continents. These closing academic sessions, which saw illustrious qualified teachers meeting in Rome from every part of the world in the name of Pope Leo XIII and St. Thomas Aquinas, were able simultaneously to strike a balance between the celebrations held this year and those of the centenary of the encyclical.

Since the beginning of my Pontificate I have not let pass a *propitious occasion without recalling the sublime figure of St. Thomas,* as, for example, on my visits to the Pontifical Angelicum University and the Catholic Institute in Paris, in the address to UNESCO, in an explicit and implicit manner, in my meetings with the Superiors, Lecturers and students of the Pontifical Gregorian and Lateran Universities.

ENCYCLICAL'S PRINCIPLES

2. The hundred years of the encyclical *Aeterni Patris* have not passed in vain, nor has that

celebrated document of pontifical teaching gone out of date. The encyclical is based on a fundamental principle which lends it a profound inner organic unity: *it is the principle of harmony between the truths of reason and those of faith.* It is this that was uppermost in the heart of Leo XIII. This principle, always consequential and relevant, has made considerable progress in the last hundred years. Suffice it to consider the consistent Magisterium of the Church from Pope Leo XIII to Paul VI and what was completed in Vatican Council II, especially in the documents *Optatam totius, Gravissimum educationis, Gaudium et spes.*

In light of Vatican Council II, we see, perhaps better than a century ago, the unity and continuity between authentic humanism and authentic Christianity, between reason and faith, thanks to the directives of *Aeterni Patris* of Leo XIII, who with this document, subtitled *De philosophia christiana...ad mentem Sancti Thomae...in scholis catholicis instauranda,*[1] showed awareness that a crisis, a rupture, a conflict, or at least an obscuration in the relationship between reason and faith had occurred.

Within the culture of the 19th century two extreme attitudes in fact can be singled out: rationalism (reason without faith) and fideism (faith without reason). Christian culture moves between these two extremes, swinging from one part or the other. Vatican Council I had already had its say on the matter. It was then time to mark out a new course in the internal studies of the Church. Leo XIII farsightedly prepared for this task, presenting again—in the sense of establishing—the perennial thought of the Church in the clear, deep methodology of the Angelic Doctor.

The dualism setting reason and faith in opposition, not at all modern, constituted a renewal of the medieval doctrine of the "double truth," which threatened from within "the intimate unity of the man-Christian" (cf. Paul VI, *Lumen ecclesiae,* no. 12). It was the great scholastic doctors of the 13th century that put Christian culture on the right road again. As Paul VI stated, "In accomplishing the work signaling the culmination of medieval Christian thought, St. Thomas was not alone. Before and after him many other illustrious doctors worked toward the same goal: among whom St. Bonaventure and St. Albert the Great, Alexander of Hales and Duns Scotus are to be recalled. But without a doubt St. Thomas, as willed by divine Providence, reached the height of all 'scholastic' theology and philosophy, as it is usually called, and set the central pivot in the Church around which, at that time and since, Christian thought could be developed with sure progress" (*Lumen Ecclesiae,* no. 13).

It is for this reason that the Church has given preference to the method and doctrine of the Angelic Doctor. Quite other than exclusive preference, this deals with an exemplary preference that permitted Leo XIII to declare it to be *"inter Scholasticos Doctores, omnium princeps et magister"* (*Aeterni Patris,* no. 13).[2] And truly such is St. Thomas Aquinas, not only for the completeness, balance, depth, and clarity of his style, but still more for his keen sense of fidelity to the truth, which can also be called realism. *Fidelity to the voice of created things so as to construct the edifice of philosophy: fidelity to the voice of the Church so as to construct the edifice of theology.*

LISTEN TO AND QUESTION THINGS

3. In philosophic scholarship, before listening to what humanity's sages say, St. Thomas' opinion is that *it is necessary to listen to and question things.* "*Tunc homo creaturas interrogat, quando eas diligenter considerat; sed tunc interrogata respondent*" *(Super Job. II, Lect. I).*[3] True philosophy should faithfully mirror the order of things themselves, otherwise it ends by being reduced to an arbitrary subjective opinion. "*Ordo principalius invenitur in ipsis rebus et ex eis derivatur ad cognitionem nostram*" *(S. Theol., II-IIae, q. 26, a. 1. ad 2).*[4] Philosophy does not consist in a subjective system put together at the pleasure of the philosopher, but must be the faithful reflection of the order of things in the human mind.

In this sense St. Thomas can be considered a true pioneer of modern *scientific realism, which has things speak by means of empirical test, even if its interest is limited to having them speak from the philosophical point of view. It is rather to be questioned if it is not precisely philosophical realism that historically has stimulated the realism of the empirical sciences in all their branches.*

This realism, far from excluding the historic meaning, creates bases for the historicity of knowledge without letting it decline into the fragile circumstance of historicism, widespread today. Therefore, after having given precedence to the voice of *things,* St. Thomas takes an attitude of paying respectful attention to what the philosophers have said and say in order to evaluate it, comparing them with the concrete reality. *"Ut videatur quid veritatis sit in singulis opinionibus et in quo deficiant. Omnes enim opiniones secundum quid aliquid verum dicunt"* (I Dist. 23, q. 1, a. 3).[5] It is impossible to think that *human knowledge and the opinion of men are completely without every truth.* It is a principle that St. Thomas borrows from St. Augustine and makes his own: *"Nulla est falsa doctrina quae non vera falsis intermisceat"* (S. Theol. I-IIae, q. 102, a. 5, ad 4). *"Impossibile est aliquam cognitionem esse totaliter falsam, sine alique veritate"* (S. Theol. II-IIae, q. 172, a. 6; cf. also S. Theol. I, q. II, a. 2, ad 1).[6]

TRUTH IS LIKE A BRIDGE

This presence of truth, even if it be incomplete and imperfect and at times distorted, is a bridge uniting every man to other men and makes understanding possible when there is good will.

In this view, St. Thomas has always given respectful attention to all authors, even when he could not entirely share their opinions; even when pre-Christian and non-Christian authors are concerned, as for example the Arab commentators on Greek philosophy. This leads to his invitation to approach with human optimism even the early Greek philosophers whose language is not always clear and precise, trying to go beyond linguistic expression, still rudimentary, in order to scrutinize their deep intentions and spirit, not heeding *"ad ea quae exterius ex eorum verbis apparet"* but the *"inentio" (De Coelo et mundo, III, lect. 2, no. 552),*[7] that guides and encourages him. When it comes to the great Fathers and Doctors of the Church, he then always tries to find a point of agreement, more in the completeness of truth that they possess as Christians, than in the way, apparently different from his, with which they express themselves. *It is well known, for example, that he tries to attenuate and almost make every divergence with St. Augustine disappear as long as the right method is used: "profundius intentionem Augustini scrutari" (De spirit. creaturis, a. 10 ad 8).*[8]

Furthermore, the basis of his attitude, sympathetic towards everyone, but without failing to be openly critical every time he felt he had to— and he did it courageously in many cases—is in the very concept of truth. *"Licet sint multae veritates participatae, est una sapientia absoluta supra omnia elevata, scilicet sapientia divina, per cuius participationem omnes sapientes sunt sapientes" (Super Job, I, lect. 1, n. 33).*[9] *This supreme wisdom, which glows in creation, does not always find the human mind disposed to receive it, for very many reasons. "Licet enim aliquae mentes sint tenebrosae, id est sapida et lucida sapientia privatae, nulla tamen adeo tenebrosa est quin ali-*

quid divinae lucis participet...quia omne verum, a quocumque dicatur, a Spiritu Sancto est" (ibid., lect. 3, no. 103).[10] *Hence the hope of conversion for every man, however intellectually and morally misled.*

This realistic and historic method, fundamentally optimistic and open, makes St. Thomas not only the *Doctor Communis Ecclesiae,* as Paul VI calls him in his beautiful letter *Lumen ecclesiae,* but the *Doctor Humanitatis,* because he is always ready and available to receive the human values of all cultures. The Angelic One can rightly state: *"Veritas in seipsa fortis est et nulla impugnatione convellitur" (Contra Gentiles,* III, c. 10, n. 3460-b).*[11] Truth, like Jesus Christ, can be denied, persecuted, fought, wounded, martyred, crucified; but it always comes back to life and rises again and can never be uprooted from the human heart.* St. Thomas put all the strength of his genius at the exclusive service of the truth, behind which he seems to want to disappear almost for fear of disturbing its brightness so that truth and not he may shine in all its brilliance.

EXEMPLARY MODEL
OF THEOLOGICAL RESEARCH

4. Faithfulness to the voice of things, in philosophy, corresponds, according to Saint Thomas, to faithfulness to the voice of the Word of God transmitted by the Church in theology. And its rule, which never fails, is the principle: *"Magis standum est auctoritati Ecclesiae...quam*

cuiuscumque Doctoris" (S. Theol. II-IIae, q. 10, a. 12).[12] *Truth, suggested by the authority of the Church assisted by the Holy Spirit, is therefore the measure of truth as expressed by all the theologians and doctors—past, present and future.* The authority of St. Thomas' doctrine is here resolved and replenished in the authority of the Church's Doctrine. That is why the Church has proposed it as an exemplary model of theological research.

In theology, too, St. Thomas therefore prefers not the voice of the Doctors or his own voice, but that of the Universal Church, almost anticipating what Vatican II says: "The totality of the faithful who have received the unction of the Holy Spirit cannot be mistaken in believing" *(Lumen gentium,* no. 12); "When both the Roman Pontiff and the body of the bishops with him define a doctrinal point, they do it in accordance with revelation itself, which everyone must stay with and conform to" *(Lumen gentium,* no. 25).

It is not possible to review all the reasons that induced the Magisterium of the Church to choose St. Thomas as a sure guide in theological and philosophical disciplines; but one is doubtless this: his having set the principles of universal value which bear out the relationship between reason and faith. *Faith contains the values of human wisdom in a superior, different, and eminent way: therefore it is impossible for reason to be in disagreement with faith, and if in disagreement, it is necessary to look at and reconsider the conclusions of philosophy: In this* sense faith itself becomes a priceless aid for philosophy.

The recommendation of Leo XIII is still valid: *"Quapropter qui philosophiae studium cum obsequio fidei christianae coniungunt, ii optime philosophantur: quandoquidem divinarum veritatum splendor, animo exceptus, ipsam juvat intelligentiam; cui non modo nihil de dignitate detrahit, sed nobilitatis, acuminis, firmitatis plurimum addit"* (Aeterni Patris, no. 13).[13]

Philosophical and theological truth converge into a single truth. Truth of reason goes back from creatures to God; *truth of faith descends directly from God to man.* But this diversity of method and origin does not take away their fundamental oneness, because there is a single identical Author of truth manifested through creation, and truth communicated personally to man by means of His Word. Philosophical research and theological research are two different directions of movement of a single truth, destined to meet, but not collide, on the same road, in order to help each other. Thus reason, illuminated, strengthened, and guaranteed by faith, becomes a faithful companion of faith itself, and faith immensely widens the limited horizon of human reason. On this point Saint Thomas is truly an enlightening teacher: *"Quia vero naturalis ratio per creaturas in Deo cognitionem ascendit; fidei vero in nos, e converso, divina revelatione descendit, est autem eadem via ascensus et descensus, oportet eadem via procedere in his quae supra rationem credentur, qua in superioribus processum est circa ea quae ratione investigantur de Deo" (Contra Gentiles,* IV, 1, no. 3349).[14]

The difference in the method and instruments of research greatly differentiates philosophical knowledge from theological. Even the best philosophy, which is of the Thomist style, which Paul VI has so well defined as "natural philosophy of the human mind," flexible in listening and faithful in expressing the truth of things, is always conditioned by the limits of intelligence and human language. However, the Angelic One does not hesitate to declare: *"Locus ab auctoritate quae fundatur super ratione humana est infirmissimus" (S. Theol,* I, q. 1, a. 8, ad 2).[15] Any philosophy, in that it is a product of man, has man's limits. On the contrary, *"locus ab auctoritate quae fundatur super revelatione divina est efficacissimus" (ibid).*[16] Divine authority is absolute; therefore, faith enjoys the solidity and security of God Himself; human science always has man's weakness, to the extent that it is founded upon man. *Yet, even in philosophy there is something absolutely true, unfailing and necessary: its first principles, the foundation of every knowledge.*

LOVE OF TRUTH AND OF GOOD GO TOGETHER

A correct or honest philosophy raises man to God, as Revelation brings God closer to man. For St. Augustine: *"verus philosophus est amator Dei" (S. Augustinus, De Civ. Dei,* VIII, 1: Pl. 41, 225).[17] St. Thomas in echoing him says the same thing in other words: *"Fere totius philosophiae consideratio ad Dei cognitionem ordinatur" (Contra Gentiles, I, c. 4, no. 23). "Sapientia est veritatem praecipue de primo principio meditari" (Contra Gentiles, I, c. 1, no. 6).*[18] *When they are authentic, love of truth and love of good go together always.* The idea of St. Thomas as a cold intellectual, advanced by some, is disproved by the fact that the Angelic One reduces knowledge itself to love of truth when he puts as a principle of every knowledge: *"verum est bonum intellectus" (Ethic. I, lect. 12, no. 139; cf. also Ethic. VI, no. 1143; S. Theol. q. 5, a. 1; ad 4; I-IIae, q. 8, a. 1).*[19] Hence the intellect is made for truth and loves it as its innate good. *And when the intellect is not satisfied by any partial truth acquired but always reaches beyond it, the intellect reaches beyond every particular truth and is naturally extended to total and absolute Truth which can really be none other than God. Desire for truth is transfigured into a natural desire for God and finds its clarification only in the light of Christ, Truth made Man.*

Thus all of St. Thomas' philosophy and theology are not posited without, but within, St. Augustine's famous aphorism: *"fecisti nos ad te; et inquietum est cor nostrum, donec requiescat in te" (S. Augustinus, Conf. I, 1).*[20] And when St. Thomas passed from the inherent tendency of man towards the truth and the good to the order of grace and redemption, he is transformed, not less than St. Augustine, St. Bonaventure and St. Bernard, into a supreme poet of charity: *"Charitas est mater et radix omnium virtutum in quantum est omnium virtutum forma" (S. Theol.*

I-IIae, q. 62, a. 4, cf. also I-IIae, q. 65, a. 2; I-IIae, q. 65, a. 3; I-IIae, q. 68, a. 5).[21]

MAN—THE NOBLE CREATURE

5. There are still other reasons that make St. Thomas timely: his very deep sense of man, *"tam nobilis creatura" (Contra Gentiles, IV, 1, no. 3337).*[22] The idea he has of this *"nobilis creatura,"* the image of God, is easy to observe every time he begins to talk of the Incarnation and redemption. From his first great youthful work, the Comment on the Judgments of Pier Lombardo in the prologue to the Third Book, in which he starts to deal with the Incarnation of the Word, he does not hesitate to compare man to the "sea," in that he collects, unifies, and elevates in himself the less than human world, as the sea collects all the waters of the rivers which flow into it.

In the same prologue he defines man as the horizon of creation in which sky and land join, like a link between time and eternity, like a synthesis of creation. In the last years of his life, when beginning the treatise on Incarnation in the third part of the *Summa Theologica,* still inspired by St. Augustine, he affirms that by merely taking on human nature, the Word could show *"quanta sit dignitas humanae naturae ne eam inquinemus peccando" (S. Theol.* III, q. 1, a. 2).[23] And right after that he adds: by being incarnated and taking on human nature, God was able to show *"quam excelsum locum inter creaturas habeat humana natura" (ibid.).*[24]

UPDATING ST. THOMAS

6. Among other things, in the meetings of your Congress it has been observed that the principles of the philosophy and theology of St. Thomas were not perhaps utilized in the moral area, such as is demanded by the times and which it is possible to obtain from the great principles set forth by St. Thomas to be firmly connected to metaphysical bases for a greater organic unity and vigor. More has been done in the social area, but there is still a great gap to be bridged so as to meet the deepest and most urgent problems of man today.

It is possible that this is something to be taken up by the Pontifical Roman Academy of St. Thomas Aquinas for the immediate future, staying alert to the signs of the times, to the demands of greater organic unity and penetration, in accordance with the directives of Vatican II (cf. *Optatam totius*, no. 16; *Gravissimum educationis*, no. 10), and the currents of thought of the contemporary world, for not a few aspects differing from those of St. Thomas' times and also from the period in which the Encyclical *Aeterni Patris* was issued by Leo XIII.

St. Thomas has pointed out a path that can and should be followed and updated without betraying its spirit and fundamental principles, but also keeping in mind modern scientific conquests. *Science's true progress can never contradict philosophy, just as philosophy can never contradict faith.* The new scientific contributions can have a cleansing and liberating function in the face of the limits imposed on philosophical research by medieval backwardness, not to speak of the non-existence of a science such as we possess today. Light can never be dimmed but only strengthened by light. Science and philosophy can and should work together so that both remain faithful to their own method. Philosophy can illuminate science and free it from its limits, as in its turn science can throw new light on philosophy itself and open new roads to it. This is the teaching of the Master of Aquinas, but still before that is the Word of Truth itself, Jesus Christ, who assures us: *"Veritas liberabit vos"* (Jn. 8:32).[25]

AN OUTSTANDING PONTIFICAL ACADEMY

7. As is well known, Leo XIII, rich in wisdom and pastoral experience, did not content himself with issuing theoretical directives. He exhorted the bishops to create academies and Thomistic study centers, and he himself gave them the first example by establishing here in Rome the Pontifical Academy of St. Thomas Aquinas to which was then joined in 1934 the older Academy of Catholic Religion. The Congress meeting in these days also had the purpose of celebrating the centenary of your own Academy—and with good reason, because famous personages, illustrious Cardinals, many of the best talents and teachers of the sacred sciences of Rome and the world are its members as presidents and

associates. It is an Academy that was always especially dear to all my Predecessors up to Paul VI, who received it twice in audience on the occasion of the previous congresses, addressing them and giving memorable directives.

It is impossible to pass over in silence the principal characteristics that have permitted your Academy to be faithful to the commitments assigned to it from time to time by the Supreme Pontiffs: its Catholic universality because of which it has always had among its associates personalities residing in Rome and outside of Rome—how can Jacques Maritain and Etienne Gilson not be remembered? Members of the diocesan clergy and religious of every order and congregation; its timeliness in making the study of contemporary problems the subjects of analysis in the light of Church doctrine: *"Ecclesiae Doctorum, praesertim Sancti Thomae vestigia premendo" (Gravissimum educationis,* no. 10).[26] almost as a prelude to Vatican Council II.

The most convincing evidence is the works of the Academy: the numerous cycles of conferences, the publications, the periodic congresses requested by Pope Pius XI and carried out with exemplary precision and great profit to Catholic studies.

Nor can I fail to recall among the students who obtained their degrees from the Pontifical Roman Academy of St. Thomas Aquinas two of my illustrious Predecessors: Pius XI and Paul VI.

WITH GREAT COMMITMENT AND SERIOUSNESS

Dear venerated brothers!

Vatican Council II, which gave new impetus to Catholic studies with its decree on priestly training and Catholic education along the lines of the teaching of St. Thomas (S. Thoma magistro: cf. Optatam totius, no. 16), serves as a stimulus and omen for a renewed life and more abundant fruits in the near future for the good of the Church!

In expressing to you my deep pleasure in the International Thomistic Congress, that in these days has truly made a notable scientific contribution both because of the qualifications of its participants and rapporteurs, and the careful preparation of the various historical and philosophical problems, I urge you to continue, with great commitment and seriousness, to accomplish the goals of your Academy so that it can be a living, pulsing, modern center in which the method and doctrine of St. Thomas can be put into continuous contact and serene dialogue with the complex leavens of contemporary culture in which we live and are immersed.

With these wishes, I renew my sincere kind feelings and heartily bestow my apostolic blessing.

FOOTNOTES

1. Subtitled "On Christian Philosophy...according to the mind of Saint Thomas...to be established in the Catholic schools."

2. To declare it to be "...among the Scholastic Doctors, the first and teacher of all" (*Aeterni Patris,* no. 13).

3. "Then man, when he attentively considers creatures, questions them; but once questioned, creatures give the answer" (*Super Job. II. Lect. I*).

4. "Order is to be found in things themselves, and flows from them into our knowlege" (*S. Theol.* II-IIae, q. 26, a, 1, ad 2).

5. "...to see how much truth there is in each opinion and in what each is defective. For in a certain respect every opinion contains some truth" (*1 Dist. 23, q. 1. a. 3*).

6. "There is no false doctrine that does not contain some admixture of truth" (*S. Theol.* I-IIae, p. 102, a.).

"It is impossible for any knowledge to be wholly false, without some mixture of truth" (*S. Theol.* II-IIae q. 172, a. 6; cf. also *S. Theol,* I, q. 11 a. 2, ad 1).

7. "What their words seem to express on the surface" but the "intention" (*de Caelo et mundo, III, lect. 2,* no. 552).

8. "examine more deeply what St. Augustine really means" (*de spir. creaturis, a. 10 ad 8*).

9. "Granted that there are many participated truths, there is one absolute wisdom which transcends all, namely the divine wisdom, through whose participation all the wise are wise" (*Super Job, I, lect. 1,* no. 33).

10. "Although some minds are enwrapped in darkness; that is, deprived of clear and meaningful knowledge, yet there is no human mind in such darkness as not to participate in some of the divine light...because all that is true, by whomsoever it is uttered, comes from the Holy Spirit" (*ibid., Lect. 3,* no. 103).

Doctor Communis Ecclesiae—The Common Doctor of the Church

Doctor humanitatis—The Doctor of Mankind

11. "Truth in itself is strong and cannot be destroyed by any attack" (*Contra Gentiles, III, c. 10,* no. 3460-b).

12. "We ought to abide by the authority of the Church rather than by that...of any doctor whatever" (*S. Theol.* II-IIae, q. 10, a. 12).

13. "Those, therefore, who to the study of philosophy unite obedience to the Christian faith are philosophers indeed; for the splendor of the divine truths, received into the mind, helps the understanding, and not only detracts in nowise from its dignity, but adds greatly to its nobility, keenness, and stability" (*Aeterni Patris,* no. 13).

14. "But, since natural reason ascends to a knowledge of God through creatures and, conversely, the knowledge of faith descends from God to us by a divine Revelation—since the way of ascent and descent is still the same—we must proceed in the same way in the things above reason which are believed as we proceed in the foregoing with the investigation of God by reason" *(Contra Gentiles, IV, I, 3349)*.

15. "the argument from authority based on human reason is the weakest" *(S. Theol. I, q. 1, a. 8, ad 2)*.

16. "the argument from authority based on divine Revelation is the strongest" *(ibid.)*.

17. "the true philosopher is a lover of God."

18. "Almost all of philosophy is directed towards the knowledge of God" *(Contra Gentiles, I, c. 4, no. 23)*. "It is wisdom especially to meditate on the truth of the first principle" *(Contra Gentiles, I, c. 1, no. 6)*.

19. "truth is the good of the intellect" *(Ethic 1, lect. 12)*.

20. "You have made us for Yourself, and our hearts are restless till they rest in You" (St. Augustine; *Conf. I, 1)*.

21. "Charity is the mother and the root of all the virtues, inasmuch as it is the form of them all" *(S. Theol. I-IIae, q. 62, a. 4, cf. also I-IIae, q. 65, a. 2; I-IIae, q. 65, a. 3; I-IIae, q. 68, a. 5)*.

22. "such a noble creature" *(Contra Gentiles, IV, 1, no. 3337)*.

23. The word could show "how great is man's dignity, lest we should sully it with sin" *(S. Theol., q. 1, a. 2)*.

24. "what an exalted position human nature holds among creatures" *(ibid.)*.

25. "the truth will set you free" (Jn. 8:32).

26. "according to the example of the Doctors of the Church and especially of St. Thomas Aquinas" *(Gravissimum educationis, no. 10)*.

VII. A Papal Doctrinal Homily
On Seeking the Lord

March 20, 1980

LET US SEEK
THE LORD,
FOR HE IS NEAR!

On Thursday, March 20, 1980, John Paul II celebrated in St. Peter's the Mass for university students preparing for Easter. At least ten thousand were present, including many teachers and researchers of the Roman universities.

The Holy Father delivered the following homily.

1. *"Quaerite Dominum dum inveniri potest. Invocate eum, dum prope est."*

"Seek the Lord while he may be found, call upon him while he is near" (Is. 55:6).

If we meet again today, in St. Peter's Basilica, teachers and students of the University and of the other colleges of Rome, it is certainly Lent that brings us here. The forty-day period of preparation for Easter was established by the Church in ancient times, in order that the invitation to seek the Lord: "Quaerite Dominum!" might be realized in it. We can never neglect seeking Him: there exist periods, however, which make it necessary to do so more intensely, because in them the Lord is particularly near, and it is, therefore, easier to find Him and meet Him. This nearness is the Lord's answer to the invocation of the Church, which is expressed continually by means of the liturgy. It is precisely the liturgy, in fact, that brings about the nearness of the Lord.

Hence the invocation: seek, *quaerite!*

Lent, as the forty-day period of preparation for Easter, has its precise history in the Church, through which it is inscribed in the history of hearts and human consciences.

As you know, the origin of Lent seems to go back to the fourth century; but already in the second and third centuries—before the fixed period of forty days was established—the faithful prepared for Easter with special fasting and prayers (cf. Tertullian, *Traditio Apostolica* of Hippolytus, St. Irenaeus). In this period, public penitents prepared for reconciliation, and catechumens for Baptism.

Lent is a period of repentance, conversion and change of heart *(metanoia),* which springs from various reasons, but above all from meditation on the passion and death of Jesus Christ. Precisely from this meditation there begins that turning of one's glance to the Lord, that "waiting for the God of salvation," of which the prophet Micah speaks today: "I will look to the Lord, I will wait for the God of my salvation; my God will hear me" (Mi. 7:7).

It is well, therefore, that we should gather here in this period, and it is a good thing, too, that in Rome, precisely in your University and academic environments, there has been no lack of initiatives suitable for meditation, prayer and lenten life in depth. These initiatives have not, perhaps, the "mass" character they once had, which they still have in some places today. It is necessary, however, always to take into account the factors that facilitate these initiatives or make them difficult and that determine their "social" extension. Sometimes it will be sufficient to continue them in the conditions already created in the past, sometimes these conditions will have to be created anew, sought in the way most suited to the circumstances. Nevertheless, the Church can never stop encouraging these initiatives. The presence of the Lord in this period of the liturgical year is so deep, so eloquent, so powerful, that we cannot fail to commit ourselves to go to meet Him.

MEETING THE LIGHT
THAT ILLUMINATES

2. Even in Lent, perhaps, there are few days in which the liturgy highlights so clearly as today the truth that the meeting with Christ is a meeting with the Light that illuminates, in a radical and salvific way, the ways of human life: radical because it goes down to the foundations of being; salvific because it shows the full perspective of good.

"The Lord is my light and my salvation; / whom shall I fear? / The Lord is the stronghold of my life; / of whom shall I be afraid?" (Ps. 27:1)

All this finds confirmation in the event that the apostle-evangelist John has handed down in an exceptionally precise and detailed way; Jesus gives sight to a man blind from birth (cf. Jn. 9:1-41).

First of all, Jesus answers the question of the disciples about the origin of the blindness of the wretched man: an answer which says a great deal. Then, having made clay with His spittle, Jesus anoints the blind man's eyes and orders him to wash in the pool of Siloam. Having carried out the order, the blind man receives sight.

Let us examine carefully the circumstances of this gift. The man, blind from birth, has never seen anything or anyone. At the moment when he acquired sight, the whole world, which we see every day, was manifested to him for the first time, as something absolutely new. Up to then he had managed with the help of touch, perhaps with the help of the white stick, like blind men in our times, or perhaps a dog-guide helped him. These aids, however, barely enabled him to move with difficulty, his life limited to the narrow circle of objects. What did he feel when he acquired sight? How was he to live now? In what perspective was he to feel liberated? Liberated because he could see!

And finally: what feelings did he nourish with regard to the One who, on that memorable day, spread mud on his eyelids and ordered him to go and wash in the pool of Siloam? What did he think of Him?

It happened that, for some more days, Christ remained unknown to him. He had not seen Him when He put the mud on his eyes; he had only heard Him say: "Go, wash in the pool of Siloam." At the moment of his meeting with Jesus, which took place only after a certain time, the following conversation took place: "Do you believe in the

Son of man?..."; "And who is he, sir, that I may believe in him?..."; "You have seen him, and it is he who speaks to you." He answered: "...Lord, I believe."

The gift of sight has touched not only the sense of the body, but has reached the depths of the soul.

A NEW CREATION

3. This passage of the Gospel has its particular historical motivation in the fourth week of Lent. In the first centuries the period of Lent was, in the Church, the time of particularly intensive preparation for Baptism. It was the time dedicated particularly to the catechumenate. Thus there was carried out, in it, that process of conversion which must be considered as the first and most fundamental: the conversion to God which gives us new life in Christ. We must, in fact, be immersed in His death in order to become, then, in the sacrament of Baptism—participating, at the cost of this death, in His resurrection—the new creature. To become the living subject of the mystery in which God renews, in each of us, the old man, creating him, anew, by means of grace, in the image of His only begotten Son.

Those who were preparing, in this way, for Baptism in the night of the resurrection, bore the name of catechumens. They were surrounded by the special solicitude of the whole community of the Church, because each of them was to become, on Easter Night, now near, the subject

of the greatest mystery. The resurrection of the
Lord was to be repeated in him, in a sacramen-
tal way. Each was to become the subject of the
Pasch, that is, the passing from death to life.

To reach the way that leads to that passing—
to the Pasch—to persevere in it to the end, each
of the catechumens had to meet the light of the
Lord. The Lord had to open his eyes, as He had
opened the eyes of that man blind from birth, of
whom today's liturgy speaks; blind through no
fault of his parents. Blind, "that the works of
God might be made manifest in him" (Jn. 9:3),
"the mighty works of God"—"magnalia Dei"!
(Acts 2:11)

For this purpose the catechumen passed
through the various teachings. He became
acquainted with the articles of faith. He had to
know them in their human expression. But
knowledge alone was not enough. He had to
receive the light, the inner light that comes from
Christ Himself. This light makes· man see
everything, the world and himself, in a radically
new way. It makes him see in a completely new
way: from the foundations, from the beginning. It
makes him become the subject of a new knowledge, since he participates in the knowledge with
which God Himself knows, and which He has
handed down to us in His Son. So man becomes
the subject of new knowledge, in order to be able
to become, in a fully conscious way, the subject
of new life.

4. The liturgy of today, therefore, is linked in
a special way with the liturgy of the paschal
night. The catechumens—those who, thanks to

Christ, have become participants in the new knowledge, those who have (like the man blind from birth) acquired sight—walk through this liturgy with their singing: with the singing of men, to whom God has revealed Himself, and, together with God, the world and man have been revealed in a new way.

"The Lord is my light and my salvation; / whom shall I fear? / The Lord is the stronghold of my life; / of whom shall I be afraid? ...Hear, O Lord, when I cry aloud, / be gracious to me and answer me! / You have said, 'Seek my face.' / My heart says to you, / 'Your face, Lord, do I seek.' Hide not your face from me. / Turn not your servant away in anger, / you who have been my help. / Cast me not off, forsake me not, / O God of my salvation!... / I believe that I shall see the goodness of the Lord in the land of the living! Wait for the Lord; / be strong, and let your heart take courage; yes, wait for the Lord!" (Ps. 26, 27:1, 7-9, 13-14)

At the prospect of Baptism, now close, the catechumens express the joy of the spiritual sight they have received, in which they have become participants. They have found themselves on the way that leads to the sight of God "face to face" (1 Cor. 13:12). The search for the "face of God" has become the way of the man aware of his definitive fulfillment. And this is the way of faith.

SECOND CATECHUMENATE

5. We, too, are on the way. It is no longer the way of the catechumens. It is the way of faith.

Therefore, we have already carried out, in a way, this experience to which today's liturgy wishes to bring us. Or, perhaps, we do not know it at all.

Receiving Baptism in infancy, we arrive at faith by means of the community of our family, which wishes to open up to us the riches of the Church as soon as possible, assuming all the consequent duties.

The Church decided, a long time ago, that this is the way to take, considering both the circumstance that the moment of grace in a man's life cannot be delayed, and the fact that, through the baptism of the children, it is necessary to help the construction of the family understood as "the domestic church," conferring on it, particularly, the possibilities of the "second catechumenate, so to speak." And in this way in the course of so many generations, instead of the "primary education to faith," there has been formed and ripened a rich experience of education "in faith." While in the first case the grace of Baptism was the point of arrival, in the second case, it is the basis: It is the starting point of all that as a result of which we are Christians and as a result of which we behave as Christians.

And it is also the starting point of this Lenten meeting of ours today.

MEETING A CATECHUMEN

6. It is a good thing that in the framework of this meeting we can consider the problem of the catechumenate. For the catechumenate must always be, somehow, the foundation of our

Christian being and our behavior as Christians, since it is for us, precisely, the basis and the starting point.

It is a good thing, therefore, that in today's liturgy, we meet a catechumen—that is, the man for whom Christ became light, the man who received the sight of faith, who found himself on the way to the new knowledge:

Let us look attentively at the behavior of this man. Immediately after acquiring sight, he becomes the object of interrogations and investigations. He is first questioned by acquaintances and neighbors. Then the latter take him to the scribes and Pharisees. Here the character of the questions changes. They do not merely marvel at the fact that the man blind from birth has acquired sight. Nor do they limit themselves to accepting—like the neighbors and acquaintances —what he declares, that is, that he has acquired sight thanks to a man who is called Jesus. On the contrary, they try to weaken this certainty in him and to make him deny this very truth. Not being able to deny the fact, which is evident—it was evident that the man blind from birth could now see—they try to deny the circumstances and the meaning of the event. *The circumstances:* "This man is not from God, for he does not keep the sabbath"..."we know that this man is a sinner." *And the meaning of the fact,* which is precisely the most important thing for them: "What do you say about him, since he has opened your eyes?" He answers: "He is a prophet." The answer disturbs them. It might be dangerous if it spread among men (men must consider Jesus of

Nazareth as a sinner who breaks the law of the sabbath). The Pharisees try to influence him through his parents. In vain. All the efforts that aim at discrediting the performer of miracles in the eyes of the cured man end in failure. Pressed by their questions, he keeps his presence of mind. He reasons in a logical and incontrovertible way and ends with the words: "If this man were not from God, he could do nothing." The Pharisees can do nothing but show their resentment and anger: "You were born in utter sin, and would you teach us?" "And they cast him out."

Thus ends the first practical examination of the catechumen's faith.

EXAMINING OUR FAITH

7. Let us examine this problem exactly. Along the way of faith in Christ, we will be repeatedly called to an examination of faith. Perhaps we think, wrongly, that if the examination were to take place in the same way as for the man blind from birth, we, too, would certainly pass it, just like him.

On the contrary, our examination of faith in Christ is not the same. It is never like that of the blind man. Every examination of faith is different.

What is it?

What is this examination of faith—examination of knowledge of Jesus Christ, examination about our Christian convictions—which must be made by each of you, modern men, representatives of university circles in Rome, in the city which has been for two thousand years the capital of Christianity and, at the same time, the capital of European culture...?

What is this examination?

I will not try to answer this question. It would be a vain effort. The answers must be as numerous as yourselves, present in this basilica.

However, I raise this question. And I ask you to try to give it an answer. Precisely in this Lent. Let this be the testimony of that "second catechumenate," to which Lent always refers, in a way, for each of us baptized. For each of us, mature Christians.

Do not think even for a moment that any of us can escape being questioned, in his life, about Christ.

Do not think that our times do not demand, from each of us, that examination of knowledge regarding Christ and membership of Christ in His Church!

Our times impose it, and how deeply!

They impose it with different methods, on the basis of a different list of questions. Sometimes the latter seem very dissimilar. Yet we are questioned. Yet the examination takes place. And it is a very deep examination. A very radical one.

8. Thus Lent is the time of a special meeting with Christ, who does not cease to speak about Himself: "I am the light of the world; he who follows me...will have the light of life" (Jn. 8:12).

Thus it was a long time ago—at the time of the early catechumenate. And thus it is today—at the time of the "second catechumenate."

Lent is that blessed time in which each one of us can, in a particular way, pass through the area of light. A powerful light, an intense light comes from the Upper Room, from Gethsemane, from Calvary, and finally from the Sunday of the resurrection.

It is necessary to cross this area of light so as to find life in oneself again.

Is the light in me? Is life in me? This life that Christ grafted?

Together with the light of faith, Christ grafted in each of us the life of grace.

Is the life of grace in me?

Or has sin, perhaps, prevailed in me?

In the paschal light, in the light of the passion and the cross, sin stands out more clearly. In the paschal light, in the light of the resurrection, the way to overcome sin and arrive at expiation, repentance and remission, opens up more clearly. "He who follows me will have the light of life"! (Jn. 8:12)

May each of you, dear friends, spend this Lent in such a way as to become penetrated by the light of life.

Man is born again to life in Christ—for the first time, in the sacrament of Baptism.

Man, with Baptism, is born again to life in Christ, to the grace he had lost, because of sin, and every time he is born again by means of the sacrament of Penance.

Be born again to life in Christ. Amen.

VIII. Pastoral Addresses to University Faculty and Students About Christianity and Intelligence

BUILD YOUR FUTURE
ON THE FOUNDATION
OF CHRIST!

About 11:30 a.m. on July 1, 1980, John Paul II arrived at Belo Horizonte. He drove in an open car across the city and was given a rapturous welcome by the population. On arrival at the Praca Israel Pinheiro on the outskirts of the city, he celebrated Mass there for youth and for students. The following is the text of his homily.

Dear young people and my friends,

1. Do not be surprised if the Pope begins this homily with a confession. I had read many times that half of the population of your country is under twenty-five years of age. Contemplating from my arrival at Brasilia, wherever I went, an infinity of young faces; passing amid multitudes of young people, on reaching this city; seeing you young people in such large numbers round this altar, I confess that I have understood better, from this concrete sight, what I had learned in an abstract way. I think that I have also understood better why the bishops of Puebla speak of a preferential option—not an exclusive one, certainly, but a priority one—for the young.

This option means that the Church assumes the commitment of continually proclaiming a message of full liberation to the young.

It is the message of salvation that she hears from the mouth of the Savior Himself and that she must transmit with absolute faithfulness.

YOU MUST BEAR WITNESS

2. At this Mass that I have the joy of celebrating in your midst and for your intentions, this message appears in its essential content from the readings we have just heard.

"Keep justice and do righteousness," the Prophet Isaiah exhorts us, with a forcefulness that is not exhausted 2,500 years afterwards (Is. 56:1). And he adds: it is important above all to "hold fast my covenant," the covenant that God sealed with man. It is an invitation to consistency and faithfulness, an invitation that concerns the young very closely.

In Paul's letter to the Christians of Corinth, we heard strong and convincing words as those of the great Apostle usually are: whoever wishes to construct his life must not lay a foundation other than that which has already been laid: Christ Jesus (cf. 1 Cor. 3:10). Paul knew very well what he was saying. As an adolescent, he had persecuted the Church. But one fine day on the way to Damascus there was that unexpected meeting with Jesus in person. And it is the testimony of his own life that makes him say: there is no other foundation possible. It is urgent to place Jesus as the foundation of existence.

In the Gospel of St. Matthew, there is that page that no one can reread without emotion. Jesus asks the Apostles: "Who do men say that the Son of man is?" After they have reported a series of opinions, the fundamental question comes: "But who do you say that I am?" *We all know this moment, in which it is no longer sufficient to speak about Jesus repeating what others have said. You must say what you think, and not quote an opinion.* You must bear witness, feel committed by the witness you have borne and carry this commitment to its extreme consequences. The best friends, followers and apostles of Christ have always been those who heard within them one day the definitive, unescapable question, before which all others become secondary and derivative: "For you, who am I?" *The life, the destiny, the present and future history of a young person depends on the clear and sincere answer, without rhetoric or subterfuges, that he gives to this question.* It has already changed the lives of many young people.

THE CHURCH LOOKS TO YOU

3. It is from these messages offered by the Word of God that I would like to draw a simple and straightforward message to leave to you at this meeting, which enables me to feel the seriousness with which you are facing up to your lives.

The greatest wealth of this country, which is immensely rich, is you. The real future of this "Country of the future" is enclosed in the present of you young people. Therefore, this country, and with it the Church, looks to you with expectation and hope.

Open to the social dimensions of man, you do not conceal your determination to change radically the social structures that you consider unjust. You say, rightly, that it is impossible to be happy when you see a multitude of brothers who lack the minimum required for a life worthy of man. You also say that it is not right that some people should waste what is lacking on the table of others. You are resolved to construct a just, free and prosperous society, in which one and all will be able to enjoy the benefits of progress.

TREMENDOUS EXPERIENCE

4. *In my youth I lived these same convictions.*
As a young student, I proclaimed them with the voice of literature and art.

God willed that they should be tempered in the fire of a war whose atrocity did not spare my family. I saw these convictions trampled upon in many ways. I feared for them, seeing them exposed to the tempest. *One day I decided to confront them with Jesus Christ: I realized that He was the only One who revealed to me their real content and value and that in this way I could protect them against the inevitable wear and tear of time, in its mysterious workings.*

All this, this tremendous and precious experience, taught me that social justice is true only if it is based on the rights of the individual. *And that these rights will be really recognized only if we recognize the transcendent dimension of man, created in the image and likeness of God, called to be His son and the brother of other men, and destined to eternal life.* To deny this transcendency is to reduce man to an instrument of domination, whose fate is subject to the selfishness and ambition of other men, or to the omnipotence of the totalitarian state, erected as the supreme value.

In the same interior movement that led me to the discovery of Jesus Christ and drew me irresistibly to Him, I perceived something that the Second Vatican Council expressed clearly much later. I realized that "the Gospel (of Christ) announces and proclaims the freedom of the sons of God; it rejects all bondage resulting from sin; it scrupulously respects the dignity of conscience and its freedom of choice; it never ceases to encourage the employment of human talents in the service of God and man; and, finally, it commends everyone to the charity of all. This is nothing other than the basic law of the Christian scheme of things" (Const. *Gaudium et spes,* no. 41).

HOLDING TO CONVICTIONS

5. *I learned that a young Christian ceases to be young, and has no longer been a Christian for a long time, when he lets himself be won over by doctrines or ideologies that preach hatred and violence.* For a just society cannot be constructed on injustice. It is not possible to construct a society that deserves to be called human without respecting and, worse still, by destroying human freedom, denying individuals the most fundamental freedoms.

Sharing as a priest, bishop and Cardinal the lives of innumerable young people at universities, in youth groups, in excursions in the mountains, in clubs for reflection and prayer, *I learned that a youth begins to grow old in a dangerous way, when he lets himself be deceived by the facile and convenient principle that "the end justifies the means"; when he adopts the belief that the only hope of improving society is to promote struggle and hatred between social groups, that it is to be found in the utopia of a classless society, which very soon reveals itself as the creator of new classes.* I became convinced that only love draws closer things that are different, and brings about union in diversity. Christ's words: "A new commandment I give to you, that you love one another, even as I have loved you" (Jn. 13:34), then appeared to me, in addition to their incomparable theological depth, as the seed and principle of the one transformation radical enough to be appreciated by the young. The seed and principle of the one revolution that does not betray man. Only true love constructs.

KNOW WHAT YOU WANT

6. *If a young man such as I was, called to live his youth at a crucial moment of history, can say something to young people like you, I think he would say to them: Do not let yourselves be used!*

Try to be clearly aware of what you want and what you do. But I see that this is just what the bishops of Latin America said to you, when they were gathered in Puebla last year: "There will be formed in the young a critical sense before...the cultural countervalues that the various ideologies try to transmit to them" (Puebla Document, no. 1197), particularly ideologies of a materialistic character, so that they will not be manipulated by them. And the Second Vatican Council: "The social order requires constant improvement: it must be founded in truth, built on justice and enlivened by love: it should grow in freedom towards a more *humane equilibrium*" (Const. *Gaudium et spes,* no. 26).

A great Predecessor of mine, Pope Pius XII, took as his motto: "To construct peace in justice." I think it is a motto and above all a commitment worthy of you, young Brazilians!

OVERCOME TEMPTATIONS

7. I am afraid that many good desires to construct a just society founder on the lack of authenticity and burst like a bubble when they are not sustained by a serious commitment of austerity and frugality. In other words, it is necessary to overcome the temptation of the so-called "consumer society," the temptation of the ambition to *have* more and more, instead of trying to *be* more and more; the ambition to have more and more, while others have less and less. In this connection, I think that the beatitude of the poor in spirit should take on concrete meaning and power in your lives: in the rich young man, so that he will understand that the superfluous things he has are nearly always what others lack, and that he may not go away

sorrowfully (cf. Mt. 19:22) if he hears in the depths of his conscience a call of the Lord to fuller detachment; in the young man who is living the hard experience of uncertainty of the future, who may even suffer the pangs of hunger, so that, seeking to improve, as is right, the living standards of his family and of himself, he may be attracted by human dignity, not by ambition, greed, and the fascination of the superfluous.

My friends, you are also responsible for the preservation of the real values that have always done honor to the Brazilian people. Do not let yourselves be swept away by the provocation of sex, which compromises the authenticity of human love and leads to the disintegration of the family. "Do you not know that you are God's temple and that God's Spirit dwells in you?" Saint Paul wrote in the text we have heard read to us.

Let girls try to find true *feminism,* the real fulfillment of woman as a human person, as an integral part of the family and as a member of society, in conscious participation, according to her characteristics.

BUILD ON JESUS CHRIST

8. In conclusion, I take up again the key words we have gathered from the readings of this Mass: do what you should do and practice righteousness; do not build on any foundation other than Jesus Christ; have an answer to give the Lord when He asks: "for you, who am I?"

This is the sincere and trustful message of a friend. My desire would be to shake hands with each of you and speak to each one.

In any case, I say to one and all: young people of Belo Horizonte and of the whole of Brazil, the Pope loves you! The Pope will never forget you! The Pope takes away from here a great yearning for you!

Receive, dear friends, the apostolic blessing that I shall give you at the end of this Mass, as a sign of my friendship, of my confidence in you, and in all the young people of this country.

Before going on to the Eucharistic liturgy properly speaking, just one more word: only love builds, only love brings close, only love unites men in their diversity.

Recently I was in France, and there the young people I met asked me spontaneously to bring you some messages of friendship, which I was very happy to do. May this gesture of the outstretched hand serve as a symbol and stimulus to construct human, Christian and ecclesial brotherhood more and more in the world.

"Where are you going?" With you I ask this question; with you, dear young people, I am about to offer also all that is noble in your hearts, all the beautiful experience we are living here together, for the success of the Eucharistic Congress of Fortaleza, to which I am going as a pilgrim, together with the Church in Brazil.

"Where are you going?" Amen.

PROCLAIM MAN
RENEWED IN CHRIST

On Sunday afternoon, May 4, 1980, John Paul II returned to the vast square in front of the People's Palace and there he met thousands of university students and a group of intellectuals. He was welcomed by Most Reverend Tshibangu Tshishiku, Rector of the National University of Zaire and Auxiliary Bishop of Kinshasa, and also by the Minister of Education. The Holy Father gave the following address.

Most Reverend Rector,
Ladies and gentlemen of the teaching staff,
Dear students,

1. I am deeply touched by the words of welcome that have just been addressed to me, and I thank you warmly. Is it necessary to tell you my joy at being able to contact the African university world this afternoon? In the tribute you have paid to me, I see not only the honor done to the first Pastor of the Catholic Church; I also perceive an expression of gratitude to the Church, for the role she has played in the course of history and which she still plays in the promotion of knowledge and science.

CONCEPT OF UNIVERSITY

2. *Historically, the universities had their origin in the Church.*

For centuries, she developed a conception of the world in which the knowledge of the period was set in the wider view of a world created by God and redeemed by our Lord Jesus Christ. Thus, a great many of her sons dedicated themselves to teaching and research, to initiate generations of students into the different stages of knowledge in a complete view of man, integrating, in particular, consideration of the ultimate reasons of his existence.

However, the very concept of university, universal by definition in its project, does not imply that it is set, in a way, outside the realities of the country in which it is implanted. On the contrary, history shows how universities have been instruments of formation and dissemination of a culture peculiar to their country, contributing a great deal to forging awareness of national identity. Thereby, the university is naturally part of the cultural heritage of a people. In this sense, it could be said that it belongs to the people.

This way of seeing the university in its essential aim, to reach as much knowledge as possible, and in its concrete roots within a nation, is of great importance. It manifests in particular the legitimacy of the plurality of cultures, recognized by the Second Vatican Council (cf. *Gaudium et spes,* no. 53), and it makes it possible to discern the criteria of true cultural pluralism, connected with the way in which each people moves towards the one truth. *It shows, too, that a university faithful to the ideal of complete truth about man cannot ignore, even on the pretext of realism or the autonomy of sciences, the study of the superior realities of ethics, metaphysics and religion.* It was from this standpoint that the Church took a special interest in the world of culture, and made important contributions to it. *For her, the divine revelation about man, about the meaning of his life and his effort for the construction of the world, is essential for complete knowledge of man and in order that progress may always be completely human.* Such is the aim of the missionary activity of the Church: to bring it about, as the Council again recalls, that everything that is good in the hearts of men, in their thought and in their culture, may be raised and reach its completion for the glory of God and the happiness of man (cf. *Lumen gentium,* no. 17).

TWENTY-FIFTH ANNIVERSARY

3. The University of Kinshasa takes its place in a remarkable way in this historical collaboration between the Church and the world of culture. The centenary of the evangelization of Zaire coincides, in fact, with the twenty-fifth anniversary of the National University of the country. How could we fail to rejoice together at the clearsightedness of those who founded this university? It shows plainly the place that man's cultural and spiritual advancement has in evangelization. It is the proof that the Church, and particularly the famous Catholic University of Louvain, had been right in their view and had confidence in the future of your people and your country! Even now, the importance of the Cath-

olic community in your country makes it desirable that the university should remain open to trusting relations with the Church!

Thus, paying tribute today in your presence to the National University of Zaire and to the Zairean University community, I do so looking towards the whole African university world. It plays and will play to an ever increasing extent an outstanding role, irreplaceable and essential, in order that your continent may fully develop all the promise it bears for itself and for the world as a whole.

THE UNIVERSITY'S ROLE

4. You will allow, I am sure, a former university professor, who dedicated long and happy years to university teaching in his native land, to talk to you for a few moments of what I consider to be the two essential aims of all complete and authentic university formation: *knowledge* and *conscience;* in other words, access to knowledge and the formation of conscience, as is clearly expressed in the very motto of the National University of Zaire: *Scientia splendet et conscientia.*

The first role of a university is the teaching of *knowledge* and scientific research. Of this vast field, I will deal here only with one point: knowledge means truth. So there would be no true university spirit if there were not the joy of seeking and knowing, inspired by ardent love of truth. This pursuit of truth is the grandeur of scientific knowledge, as I recalled on last November 10, addressing the Pontifical Academy of Sciences:

"Pure science is a good worthy of being loved, for it is knowledge and, therefore, perfection of man in his intelligence. Even before its technical applications, it must be honored for its own sake, as an integral part of culture. Basic science is a universal good, which every people must be able to cultivate in full freedom from any form of international constraint or intellectual colonialism" (*L'Osservatore Romano*, French edition, November 20, 1979).

Those who dedicate their lives to science can, therefore, feel a legitimate pride, and also those who, like you students, may spend several years of their lives being trained in a scientific discipline, for nothing is finer, in spite of the work and the trouble it demands, than to be able to engage in the pursuit of truth about nature and about man.

THE TRUTH ABOUT MAN

5. How can we fail to draw your attention briefly here to love of the truth about man? Human sciences have, as I have already stressed several times, an increasing place in our knowledge. They are indispensable to arrive at a harmonious organization of life in common, in a world in which exchanges are becoming more and more numerous and complex. *But at the same time, it is only in a very special sense, radically different from the usual one, that we can speak of "sciences" of man, precisely because there is a truth about man that transcends all attempts of reduction to any particular aspects whatever.* In

this field, a really complete researcher cannot disregard in the elaboration of knowledge, as in its applications, spiritual and moral realities which are essential to human existence, or the values that are derived from them. *For the fundamental truth is that man's life has a meaning, on which the value of personal existence depends as well as a correct conception of life in society.*

FORMATION OF CONSCIENCE

6. These rapid considerations on love of truth, which I would like to be able to develop at length, dialoguing with you, will have already shown you what I mean when I speak of the role of the university and of your studies for the formation of *conscience.* Certainly, the university has in the first place a pedagogical role of formation of its students, in order that they will be capable of reaching the level of knowledge required and of exercising their profession effectively in the world in which they will later be called to work. But beyond the different branches of knowledge which it has the function of transmitting, the university cannot ignore another duty: that of permitting and facilitating the integration of knowledge in a wider, fundamental context, in a fully human conception of existence. In this way, the thoughtful student will avoid succumbing to the temptation of ideologies, deceptive because they are always simplified, and will be made capable of seeking at a higher degree the truth about himself and his role in society.

7. Dear friends, teachers and students, I would like to be able to express personally to each of you and to each of those you represent: the whole student world, the world of culture and of science in Zaire and in Africa, all my encouragement to accept fully, each one of you, his responsibilities. They are heavy ones; they demand the best of oneself, for the university has not as its aim in the first place the pursuit of degrees, diplomas or well paid posts: it has an important role for man's formation and service of the country. That is why it entails great requirements with regard to the work to be carried out, with regard to oneself and with regard to society.

If all university research calls for real freedom, without which it cannot exist, it also requires on the part of students hard work, qualities of objectivity, method and discipline, in short, competence. This, as you well know, opens onto the two other aspects. One of the characteristics of university work and of the intellectual world is that, more than elsewhere perhaps, each one is constantly referred to his own responsibility in the direction he gives to his work. On this last point, I am happy to repeat to you the greatness of your role and to encourage you to face up to it with your whole soul. You are not just working for yourselves, for your advancement. You take part, by the very fact that you are university students, in research concerning the truth about man, in pursuit of his good, with the care of cooperating in the exploitation of nature for a real service of man, in promotion of the cultural and spiritual values of mankind.

Concretely, this participation in the good of humanity is realized through the services you render and which you will be called to render for your country: for the physical and moral health of your fellow-citizens, and for the improved economic and social condition of your nation. *For the privileged education that the community offers you is not given to you in the first place for your personal profit.* Tomorrow, it is the whole community, with its material and spiritual needs, which will have the right to turn to you, which will need you. You will be sensitive to the appeals of your fellow countrymen. A difficult but exalting task, worthy of the sentiment of solidarity, which you possess so strongly: you will have to serve man, to serve the African in his deepest and most precious aspect—his humanity.

THE PRIMACY OF TRUTH AND MAN

8. The perspectives which I merely sketch before you this afternoon, dear friends, imply a fundamental reality: *that ethics, morality, spiritual realities, should be perceived as elements that make up the complete man, understood both in his personal life and in the role he must play in society, and therefore as essential elements of all society.* The primacy of truth and the primacy of man, far from conflicting with each other, unite and are harmoniously coordinated in a spirit that is anxious to reach and respect reality in all its fullness.

It follows further that, just as there is a wrong way of conceiving technical progress, by making it everything for man, by making it serve entirely the satisfaction of his most superficial desires—falsely identified with success and happiness—there is also a wrong way of conceiving the progress of our thought about the truth concerning man. In this field, as you can clearly feel, progress takes place through deep investigation, through integration. Errors are corrected, but they have always been errors, whereas *there is no truth about man, about the meaning of his personal and community life, that can be "outdated" or become an error.* This is important for you who, in a rapidly changing society, must work at its human and social progress by integrating the truth that comes to you from the past with that which will enable you to cope with new prospects.

9. It is in accordance with the truth about man, in fact, that materialism, in all its forms, must be rejected, for it is always a source of subjection: either subjection to a soul-less pursuit of material goods, or, far worse, the subjection of man, body and soul, to atheistic ideologies, always, when all is said and done, the subjection of man to man. That is why the Catholic Church has wished to proclaim solemnly the right to religious freedom in loyal pursuit of spiritual and religious values; that is also why she prays that all men may find, in faithfulness to the religious sense that God has put in their hearts, the way to the whole truth.

10. I would like to add here a short word particularly for my brothers and sisters in our Lord Jesus Christ. You believe in the message of the

Gospel; you wish to live by it. For us, the Lord Jesus Christ is our Way, our Truth and our Life (cf. Jn. 14:6). I have already developed, especially in the first Encyclical, *Redemptor hominis,* which I addressed to the world at the beginning of my pontifical ministry, and also in my message on January first on "truth, the power of peace," how, for us Christians, Christ our Lord, through His Incarnation—that is, through the reality of our humanity which He assumed for our salvation— revealed to us the most complete truth that exists about man, about ourselves, about our existence. He is, in all truth, man's way, yours. That is why evangelization, which responds to a command of the Lord, also finds its place in your collaboration in the future of your people, for it is collaboration in faith in divine plans for the world and for mankind, and, in short, collaboration in the history of salvation.

PROCLAIMING GOD'S WORD

11. At the moment when the centenary of the proclamation of the Word of God is being celebrated in Zaire, and at the moment when a new African world is being formed in the service of a richer humanity for Africa, you are called to participate fully, while being at the same time witnesses to Christ in your university and professional life. Give proof of your competence, of your African wisdom, but be at the same time men and women who bring the testimony of your Christian conception of the world and of man. Let your whole life be for those around you; and

beyond them, for your whole country, a proclamation of the truth about man renewed in
Christ, a message of salvation in the risen Lord. I
count on you, Catholic university students, dear
boys and girls; I count on your faithful commitment to service of your country, of the Church, of
the whole of mankind, and I thank you for it.

12. Dear friends, teachers and students, at
the beginning of its existence, your university
had as its motto: *Lumen requirunt lumine:* by its
light, they seek the light! I hope that your
studies, your research, your wisdom will be for
you all a way towards the supreme Light, the
God of truth, whom I pray to bless you.

THE WHOLE GOSPEL
IS A DIALOGUE
WITH MAN

*Before the Pope's journey to Paris the youth of that city con-
ducted a poll to draw up a list of questions to be submitted to
the Pope in order that he might answer them in his address to
them. The following is the full list of the 21 questions arrived at,
and three of these were eventually chosen as the subject of the
Holy Father's discourse in Parc des Princes.*

QUESTIONS ADDRESSED
TO THE POPE
BY THE YOUTH OF PARIS

1. In every country that you visited you
wished to meet the youth. Why?

2. In each country you visited you wished to
meet the rulers. Why? What did you say to them?

3. What do you expect to do for the unity of
Christians? How do you see this unity?

4. How does one pray as Pope?

5. You have taken pretty severe measures in
regard to some theologians. Why?

6. Two years have passed since your election:
at this point, how do you see your ministry?

7. Tell us about your own country. What can
we learn from Poland? And what can Poland
learn from France?

8. You have been in Latin America and in Africa: how do you view the relations between the Third World and countries such as France?

9. Can the Gospel provide an answer for the problems of today?

10. Before being a bishop and Pope you were a simple priest. How do you view the priest of today?

11. People frequently speak of a Third World War. What can we young people do to prevent it?

12. We wish to be happy. Is it possible to be so in the present-day world?

13. Speak to us simply about Jesus Christ. Who is Jesus Christ for you?

14. Is it necessary to continue the work of Vatican II?

15. What can the Catholic Church do for peace and justice in the world?

16. The Catholic Church is ruled by men. Will women always have a secondary role?

17. As regards sexuality, the Catholic Church always adopts decisions which are rather restrictive. Why? Do you not fear that the youth will gradually become estranged from the Church?

18. How can one be a witness of Christ today?

19. What is the role of the laity, and especially of the young, in the Church?

20. The Church is Western. Can it be really African or Asiatic?

21. If we had not submitted these questions to you, what would you have said to us?

The three questions addressed to the Pope in Parc des Princes were: If we had not submitted these questions to you, what would you have said to us?

Speak to us simply about Jesus Christ. Who is Jesus Christ for you?

People frequently speak of a Third World War. What can we young people do to prevent it?

In the course of his address, the Holy Father wished to give a complete reply to all twenty-one questions.

In the evening of Sunday, June 1, 1980, the Holy Father met over ninety thousand young Parisians gathered at Parc des Princes, the largest stadium in the French capital, for a prayer vigil.

The address that the Holy Father delivered to the young people during the meeting was not the one originally prepared for the occasion. The reason for this change was explained to the young people by the Pope himself who, before ending the meeting, said: "Before concluding I must tell you how I prepared this dialogue, this address-dialogue. I was sent the program and I was told that I had to speak to the young. So then I prepared a speech. Later the organizers sent me 'your' program and the questions you wished to ask the Pope. So it was necessary to change the address I had prepared and prepare the one you have just heard. But the 'monologue' address, the message, still remains and I would like to leave it with you so that you can read it and meditate on it. I think the organizers will willingly distribute it to you."

Dear young people of France,

1. I thank you for this meeting which you wished to organize as a kind of dialogue. *You wanted to speak to the Pope.* And that is very important for two reasons.

The first reason is that this way of acting refers us directly to Christ: in Him, there is continually unfolded a dialogue: God's conversation with man and man's with God.

Christ—you have heard—is the Word, the Word of God. He is the eternal Word. This Word of God, like man, is not the word of a "great monologue," but the *Word* of the "incessant dialogue" which takes place in the Holy Spirit. *I know that this sentence is difficult to understand, but I say it all the same, and I leave it to you so that you can meditate on it.* Did we not celebrate this morning the mystery of the Holy Trinity?

The second reason is the following: the dialogue corresponds to my personal conviction that, to be the servant of the Word, means "proclaiming" in the sense of "answering." *To answer, it is necessary to know the questions. So it is a good thing that you asked them; otherwise, I would have had to guess in order to be able to speak to you, to answer you!* (That is your question no. 21.)

I have arrived at this conviction, not only because of my experience in the past as a teacher, through lectures or working groups, but above all through my experience as a preacher—giving the homily, and above all preaching retreats. Most of the time I was addressing young people; they were young people whom I was helping to meet the Lord, to listen to Him, and also to reply to Him.

2. Addressing you now, I would like to do so in such a way as to be able to *answer all your questions, at least indirectly.*

It is for this reason that I cannot do so, taking them one after the other. In that case my answers would necessarily be only schematic!

So allow me to choose the question that seems to me the most important, the most central one, and to start with it. In this way, I hope that your other questions will appear gradually.

Your central question concerns Jesus Christ. You want to hear me speak of Jesus Christ, and you ask me who Jesus Christ is for me (it is your 13th question).

Allow me to return the question also and say to you: *Who is Jesus Christ for you?* In this way, and without evading the question, I shall also give you my answer, telling you what He is for me.

3. The whole of the Gospel is a dialogue with man, with the different generations, with nations, with different traditions...*but it is always and continually a dialogue with man, with every man: one, unique, absolutely individual.*

At the same time, we find many dialogues in the Gospel. Among the latter, I choose as particularly eloquent Christ's dialogue with the young man.

I will read you the text, because perhaps you do not remember it very well. It is in chapter 19 of the Gospel of Matthew.

"And behold, one came up to him, saying, 'Teacher, what good deed must I do, to have eternal life?' And he said to him, 'Why do you ask me about what is good? One there is who is good. If you would enter life, keep the commandments.' He said to him, 'Which?' And Jesus said, 'You shall not kill. You shall not commit adultery, You shall not steal, You shall not bear false witness, Honor your father and mother, and, You shall love your neighbor as yourself.' The young man said to him, 'All these I have observed; what do I still lack?' Jesus said to him, 'If you would be perfect, go, sell what you possess and give it to the poor, and you will have treasure in heaven; and come, follow me.' When the young man heard this he went away sorrowful; for he had great possessions."

Why does Christ dialogue with this young man? The answer is found in the Gospel narrative. *And you, you ask me why, wherever I go, I want to meet the young* (it is even your first question).

And I answer you: because "a young man" indicates a man who, in a special way, in a decisive way, is in the act of "forming himself." That does not mean that man does not form himself for the whole of his life: it is said that "education begins already before birth" and lasts to the last day. From the point of view of formation, however, youth is a particularly important, rich and decisive period. If you reflect on Christ's dialogue with the young man, you will find confirmation of what I have just said.

The young man's questions are essential ones. So are the answers.

4. These questions and these answers are not only essential for the young man concerned, important for his situation at that time; they are also of prime importance and essential for today. That is why, to the question whether the Gospel

can answer the problems of modern men (it is your 9th question), I answer: not only "is it capable of doing so," but we must go even further: it alone gives them a total answer, which goes to the bottom of things and completely.

I said at the beginning that Christ is the Word, the Word of an incessant dialogue. He is the *dialogue,* the dialogue with every man, although some people do not take part in it—not everyone knows how to—and there are also people who reject this dialogue explicitly. They move away.... And yet...perhaps this dialogue is in progress with them, too. I am convinced that this is so. More than once this dialogue "is revealed" in an unexpected and surprising way.

5. I note also your question why, in the various countries to which I go, and also in Rome, I speak to the various heads of state (question no. 2).

Simply because Christ speaks to all men, to every man. Moreover I think, rest assured, that there is no less to be said to men who have such great social responsibilities than to the young man of the Gospel, and to each of you.

To your question, what I speak about when I talk to heads of state, I will reply that I speak to them, very often, precisely of the young. In fact, "the day of tomorrow" depends on youth. These words are taken from a song that young Poles of your age often sing: "It is on us that the day of tomorrow depends." I, too, have sung it more than once with them. *Furthermore, I generally enjoyed very much singing songs with the young, for the music and for the words.* I recall this memory because you also asked me questions about my country (it is your 7th question), but to answer this question I should have to speak for a very long time!

And you also ask what France could learn from Poland, and what Poland could learn from France.

It is generally considered that Poland has learned more from France than the latter from Poland. Historically, Poland is several centuries younger. I think, however, that France could also learn various things. Poland has not had an easy history, especially in the course of the last few centuries. The Poles have "paid," and not just a little, in order to be Poles, and also to be Christians.... This answer is an "autobiographical" one. You will excuse me for this, but it was you who caused it. Allow me, however, to widen this autobiographical answer with the help of some other questions that you asked. For example, when you ask if the Church, which is "Western," can really be the "African" or "Asian" Church (20th question).

6. Of course, this question is much broader and goes further than the one about which I have just spoken with regard to the Church in France or in Poland. Both of them, in fact, are "Western," belonging to the field of the same European and Latin culture, but my answer will be the same. By her nature, the Church is one and universal. *She becomes the Church of every nation, or of continents or races, in proportion as these societies accept the Gospel and make it, so to speak, their property.* A short time ago, I went to

Africa. Everything indicates that the young Churches of this continent are well aware of being African. And they are consciously aspiring to act as the link between Christianity and the traditions of their cultures. In Asia, and above all in the Far East, it is often thought that Christianity is the "Western" religion, and yet, I do not doubt that the Churches that have taken root there are "Asian" Churches.

7. Let us now return to *our main subject, Christ's dialogue with the young man.*

Actually, I would be inclined to say that we have remained all the time in its context.

The young man asks, then: "Teacher, what good deed must I do, to have eternal life?" (Mt. 19:16)

Now you raise the question: *Is it possible to be happy* in the modern world? (It is your 12th question....)

As a matter of fact, you ask the same question as this young man!

Christ answers—to him and also to you, to each of you—*it is possible.* That is, in fact, what He answers, even if His words are the following: "If you would enter life, keep the commandments" (Mt. 19:17). And later He will reply further: "If you would be perfect, go, sell what you possess and give to the poor...and follow me" (cf. Mt. 19:21).

These words mean that man cannot be happy except to the extent to which he is capable of accepting the requirements that his own humanity, his dignity as a man, set him. The requirements that God sets him.

8. In this way, therefore, Christ does not only answer the question whether it is possible to be happy—but He says more: how we can be happy, on what condition. This answer is absolutely original, and it cannot be outdated, it can never be superseded. You must think about it carefully and adapt it to yourselves. Christ's answer consists of two parts. In the first one, it is a question of observing the commandments. Here, I will make a digression on account of one of your questions on the principles that the Church teaches in *the field of sexual morality* (the 17th question). *You express your concern, seeing that they are difficult, and that young people might, precisely for this reason, turn away from the Church. I will answer you as follows. If you think deeply about this question, and if you go to the heart of the problem, I assure you that you will realize one thing: in this field, the Church sets only the requirements that are closely linked with true—that is, responsible—married and conjugal love.* She demands what the *dignity of the person* and fundamental social order require. I do not deny that they are her demands. But the essential point of the problem lies precisely there: namely, that *man fulfills himself only to the extent to which he is able to impose demands on himself.* Otherwise, he goes away "sorrowful," as we have just read in the Gospel. Moral permissiveness does not make men happy. The consumer society does not make men happy. They have never done so.

9. In Christ's dialogue with the young man, there are, as I said, two stages. In the first one, it

is a question of the ten commandments, that is, the fundamental requirements of all human morality. In the second stage, Christ says: "If you would be perfect...come, follow me" (Mt. 19:21).

This "come, follow me" is a central and culminating point of this whole episode. These words indicate that *it is not possible to learn Christianity like a lesson composed of numerous different chapters,* but that *it must always be linked with a Person,* a living Person: Jesus Christ. Jesus Christ is the guide: He is the model. We can imitate Him in different ways and to different extents. We can make Him, in different ways and to different extents, the "Rule" of our own lives.

Each of us is a kind of particular "material" from which—following Christ—we can draw this concrete, unique and absolutely individual form of life that can be called the Christian vocation. On this point, a great many things were said at the last Council, as regards the vocation of the laity.

10. That does not change anything about the fact that this "follow me" of Christ, in the precise case, is and remains the *priestly* vocation or the vocation *to consecrated life according to the evangelical counsels.* I say so because you asked the question (the 10th one) about my own priestly vocation. I will try to reply to you briefly, following the pattern of your question. So I will say first of all: I have been Pope for two years; I have been a bishop for over twenty years, and yet the most important thing for me still remains *the fact of being a priest.* The fact of being able to

celebrate the Eucharist every day. Of being able to renew Christ's own sacrifice, by giving back, in Him, all things to the Father: the world, humanity, and myself. The correct dimension of the Eucharist consists, in fact, in this. That is why I have always living in my memory this interior development as a result of which "I heard" Christ's call to the priesthood. This special "come and follow me."

Confiding this to you I invite you to listen carefully, each one of you, *to these evangelical words.* It is in this way that your humanity will be formed completely, and that the Christian vocation of each of you will be defined. And perhaps you will also hear, in your turn, the call to the priesthood or to religious life. Until quite recently, France was rich in these vocations. She has given, among others, so many missionaries and so many missionary sisters to the Church! Certainly, Christ continues to speak on the banks of the Seine, and He always makes the same call. Listen attentively. It will always be necessary so that there may be in the Church those "chosen from among men," those whom Christ appoints, in a special way, on "behalf of men" (Heb. 5:1) and whom He sends to men.

11. You also asked the question about prayer (the 4th one). There are several definitions of prayer. But it is most often called a talk, a conversation, a colloquy with God. Conversing with someone, not only do we speak, but we also listen. *Prayer, therefore, is also listening.* It consists of listening to hear the interior voice of grace. Listening to hear the call. *And then, as you*

ask me how the Pope prays, I answer you: like every Christian—he speaks and he listens. Sometimes, he prays without words, and then he listens all the more. The most important thing is precisely what he "hears." And he also tries to unite prayer with his obligations, his activities, his work, and *to unite his work with prayer.* In this way, day after day, he tries to carry out his "service," his "ministry," which comes to him from the will of Christ and from the living tradition of the Church.

12. You ask me also how I see this service now that I have already been, for two years, Peter's successor (6th question). I see it above all as a maturation in the priesthood and as *permanence in prayer,* with Mary, the Mother of Christ, in the same way as the Apostles were assiduous in prayer, in the Upper Room in Jerusalem, when they received the Holy Spirit. In addition to that, you will find my answer to this question on the basis of the replies to the subsequent questions. And first and foremost the one concerning *the implementation of the Second Vatican Council* (14th question). You ask if it is possible? And I reply to you: Not only is the implementation of the Council possible, but it is necessary. This answer is above all the answer of faith. It was the first answer I gave, on the day after my election, in the presence of the Cardinals gathered in the Sistine Chapel. It is the answer I gave myself and others, first as bishop and as Cardinal, and it is the answer I give continually. It is *the main problem.* I think that through the Council there were verified for the

Church in our time the words of Christ in which He promised His Church the Spirit of truth, who will lead the minds and hearts of the Apostles and their successors, permitting them to remain in the truth and guide the Church in the truth, rereading "the signs of the times" in the light of this truth. That is precisely what the Council did, in accordance with the needs of our time, of our age. I believe that, thanks to the Council, the Holy Spirit "is speaking" to the Church. I say that taking up again St. John's expression. Our duty is to understand firmly and honestly what "the Spirit says," and to carry it out, avoiding deviations from the road that the Council marked out from so many points of view.

13. The service of the bishop, and in particular that of the Pope, is bound up with a special responsibility as regards what the Spirit says: as regards the whole Faith of the Church and Christian morality. In fact, it is this Faith and this morality that they, the bishops with the Pope, must teach in the Church, watching by the light of tradition, always alive, over their conformity with the revealed Word of God. That is why they sometimes have to note also that certain opinions or certain publications show that they lack this conformity. They do not constitute an *authentic* doctrine of Christian faith and morality. I speak about this because you asked about it (5th question). If we had more time, a more developed exposition could be devoted to this problem—all the more so in that there is no lack of false information and erroneous explanations

in this field—but today we must be content with these few words.

14. The work for the unity of Christians is, in my opinion, one of the greatest and finest tasks of the Church for our age.

You would like to know if I am expecting unity and how I view it? I will answer you the same thing as in connection with the implementation of the Council. There, too, I see a special call of the Holy Spirit. As regards its implementation, the different stages of this implementation, we find all the fundamental elements in the teaching of the Council. They must be put into practice, and their concrete applications must be sought; and above all it is necessary to pray always, with fervor, constancy and humility. The union of Christians cannot be realized otherwise than through deep maturation in the truth, and a constant conversion of hearts. We must do all that in accordance with our human capacities, taking up again all the "historical processes" that have lasted for centuries. But finally this union, for which we must spare no efforts or work, will be Christ's gift to His Church. Just as it is already one of His gifts that we have entered upon the way to unity.

15. Continuing with the list of your questions, I reply to you: I have very often spoken of the duties of the Church in the field of justice and peace (15th question), thus continuing the activity of my great Predecessors John XXIII and Paul VI. Tomorrow in particular, I intend to speak at the headquarters of UNESCO, in Paris. I am referring to all that because you ask: What

can we, the young, do for this cause? Can we do something to prevent a new war, a catastrophe that would be incomparable, more terrible than the preceding one? I think that, in the very formulation of your questions, you will find the awaited answer. Read these questions. Meditate on them. Make them a community program, a program of life. You young people have already the possibility of promoting peace and justice, where you are, in your world. That already comprises precise attitudes of kindness in judgment, truth about yourselves and others, their differences, their important rights. In this way an atmosphere of brotherhood is prepared for the future when you will have greater responsibilities in society. If we wish to make a new and brotherly world, we must prepare new men.

16. And now the question on the Third World (the 8th one). It is a great question concerning history, culture and civilization. But it is above all a moral problem. You rightly ask what must be the relations between our country and. the countries of the Third World: of Africa and Asia. There are, in fact, great obligations of a *moral nature* there. Our "Western" world is at the same time "northern" (European or Atlantic). Its riches and its progress owe a great deal to the resources and men of these continents. In the new situation in which we find ourselves after the Council, it cannot seek there only sources of further riches and of its own progress. It must *consciously,* and by *organizing itself* to do so, serve their development. This is perhaps the most important problem as regards justice and

peace in the world of today and tomorrow. The solution to this problem depends on the present generation, and it will depend on your generation and on those that will follow. Here, too, it is a question of continuing the witness borne to Christ and the Church by several previous generations of religious and lay missionaries.

17. The question: how to be a witness to Christ today? (18th one) This is the fundamental question, the continuation of the meditation we have placed at the center of our dialogue, the conversation with a young man. Christ says: "Follow me." This is what He said to Simon, the son of Jonas, to whom He gave the name of Peter; to his brother Andrew; to the sons of Zebedee; to Nathanael. He said, "Follow me," repeating then, after the resurrection, "You shall be my witnesses" (Acts 1:8). To be a witness to Christ, to bear witness to Him, it is necessary, first, to follow Him. It is necessary to learn to know Him, to place oneself, so to speak, in His school, to penetrate all His mystery. It is a fundamental and central task. If we do not do so, if we are not ready to do so constantly and honestly, our witness runs the risk of becoming superficial and exterior. It runs the risk of no longer being witness. If, on the contrary, we remain attentive to that, Christ Himself will teach us, through His Spirit, what we have to do, how to behave, in what and how to commit ourselves, how to carry on the dialogue with the modern world, this dialogue that Paul VI called the dialogue of salvation.

18. If you ask me consequently: "What must we do in the Church, we above all, the young?", I will reply: Learn to know Christ. Constantly. To learn Christ. The unfathomable treasures of wisdom and science are really found in Him. In Him, man—on whom there weigh his limits, his vices, his weakness and his sin—really becomes "the new man": he becomes the man "for others," he also becomes the glory of God, because the glory of God, as St. Irenaeus of Lyons, bishop and martyr, said in the second century, is "living man." The experience of two millennia teaches us that in this fundamental work, the mission of the whole People of God, there is no essential difference between man and woman. Each in his way, according to the specific characteristics of femininity and masculinity, becomes this "new man," that is, this man "for others," and as a living man he becomes the glory of God. If that is true, just as it is true that the Church, in the hierarchical sense, is directed by the successors of the Apostles and, therefore, by men, it is certainly all the more true that, in the charismatic sense, *women* "lead" her as much, and perhaps even more: I invite you to think often of Mary, the Mother of Christ.

19. Before concluding this testimony based on your questions, I would like to thank again very specially the many representatives of French youth who, before my arrival in Paris, sent me thousands of letters. I thank you for having manifested this bond, this communion, this co-responsibility. I hope that this bond, this

communion and this co-responsibility will be continued, and will deepen and develop after our meeting this evening.

I ask you also to strengthen your union with the young people of the whole Church and of the world, in the spirit of this certainty that Christ is our Way, the Truth and the Life (cf. Jn. 14:6).

Let us now unite in this prayer which He Himself taught us, singing "Our Father," and receive, all of you, for yourselves, for boys and girls of your age, for your families and for those who are suffering most, the blessing of the Bishop of Rome, the Successor of St. Peter.

Our Father, who art in heaven, hallowed be thy name. Thy kingdom come, thy will be done, on earth as it is in heaven. Give us this day our daily bread, and forgive us our trespasses, as we forgive those who trespass against us; and lead us not into temptation, but deliver us from evil. Amen.

CHRIST ACCOMPANIES MAN IN MATURING TO HUMANITY

The first event on the Pope's last day of his pilgrimage in Germany, Wednesday, November 19, 1980, was a Mass for youth celebrated in Munich's "Theresienwiese." The Holy Father delivered the following homily.

Dear brothers and sisters,
Dear young people,

1. When Christ speaks about the kingdom of God, He often uses images and parables. His image of the "harvest," of the "great harvest," necessarily reminded His listeners of that annually recurring and so very much longed-for time when people could finally begin to harvest the fruit that had grown at the cost of considerable human effort.

The parable of the "harvest" today sends our thoughts in the same direction, although, as people from highly industrialized countries, we can hardly imagine anymore what the ripening and harvesting of the fruits of the earth once meant for the farmer and people in general.

With the image of grain ripening for harvest, Christ wants to indicate *the inner growth and maturation of man.*

Man is bound by and dependent upon his own nature. At the same time he towers above it with the inner nature of his personal being. Thus, *human maturation is something different* from the ripening of the fruits of nature. This does not involve only physical and intellectual effort. An important part of the maturation process in man involves the spiritual, the religious dimension of his being. When Christ speaks of the "harvest," He means that man must mature towards God and then *in God* Himself; in His kingdom, he will receive the fruit of his effort and maturation.

I would like to point out this truth of the Gospel to you young people of today, both with great seriousness and at the same time with cheerful hope. You have arrived at a particularly important and critical time in your lives, in which much, or perhaps even everything, that will determine your further development and your future will be decided.

The knowledge of the truth is of basic importance for the formation of one's personality and for the building of the inner human being. Man can *only* be truly mature *with the truth and in the truth.* In this lies the profound meaning and importance of education which the entire educational system from the schools to the universities must serve. They must help young people to know and understand the world and themselves; they must help them to see what gives the existence and the works of man in the world their full meaning. *For that reason education must also help them to know God. Man cannot live without knowing the significance of this existence.*

STRENGTH TO BUILD
A MORE HUMAN WORLD

2. This search, finding of directions, and maturing with the basic and full truth of reality is, however, not easy. It has always been necessary to overcome numerous difficulties. It is apparently this problem that St. Paul refers to when he writes in his Second Epistle to the Thessalonians: "We beg you...not to be quickly shaken in mind or excited.... Let no one deceive you in any way...!" (2 Thes. 2:1-3) These words, addressed to a new group of the earliest Christians, must be reread today against the different background of our modern civilization and culture. Thus, I would like to call out to you young people of today: *Do not be discouraged! Do not be deceived!*

Be thankful if you have good parents who encourage and direct you into the right path. Perhaps there are more of them than you can recognize at first sight. However, many young people suffer from their parents, feel that their parents do not understand them, or even abandon them. Others have to find the path to faith without, or even against, the will of their parents. Many suffer as a result of the "achievement pressures" in the schools, and encounter insecurity with respect to the prospects for a professional future. Should one not be afraid that technical and economic development will destroy man's natural living conditions? And anyway, what will be the future of our world which is divided into military power blocs, poor and rich nations, free and totalitarian states? Again and again wars flare up in this or that part of the world, causing death and misery to men. And then in many parts of the world, near and far, acts of the rawest kind of violence and bloody terror are carried out. Even here, where we commemorate before God the victims who were recently injured or suddenly killed on the edge of this large square by an explosive charge. *It is hard to understand what man is capable of doing in the confusion of his mind and his heart.*

It is against this background that we hear the call of the Gospel: "We beg you...not to be quickly shaken in mind or excited...!" All of these troubles and difficulties are part of the resistance with which we must nurture and test our growth in the fundamental truth. From this we derive the strength to help build a more just and more human world; from it we derive the readiness and courage to assume a growing measure of responsibility in the life of our society, state and Church. There is truly great consolation in the fact that, despite many shadows and much darkness, there is a lot of good. The fact that too little is said of it does not mean that it is not there. *Often one has to want to discover and recognize the good that is hidden.* But it is at work and will perhaps at some later time become radiantly visible. Think, for example, what Mother Teresa of Calcutta had to do anonymously before a surprised world became aware of her work. Thus, I beg you not to be quickly shaken in mind or excited!

TEMPTATIONS TO FALL AWAY FROM THE FAITH

3. However, is it not the case that in your society as you experience it in your surroundings, not a few who believe in Christ have become uncertain, or have lost their sense of orientation? And does that not have a particularly negative effect on young people? Does this not reveal something of the numerous *temptations to fall away from the Faith,* of which the Apostle speaks in this Epistle?

The Word of God in today's liturgy gives us an idea of the *broad scope* of the loss of religious belief, such as seems to be emerging in our century, and makes its *dimensions* clear.

St. Paul writes: "For the mystery of lawlessness is already at work..." (2 Thes. 2:7). Would we not have to say that for our time as well? *The mystery of lawlessness, falling away from God, has an inner structure and a definite dynamic gradation in the words of the Epistle of St. Paul:* "...the man of lawlessness is revealed..., who opposes and exalts himself against every so-called god or object of worship so that he takes his seat in the temple of God proclaiming himself to be God" (2 Thes. 2:3-4). *Thus, we have here an inner structure of negation, an uprooting of God in the heart of man and an uprooting of God in human society, with the aim, it is maintained, of obtaining a fuller "humanization" of man, i.e., making man human in a fuller sense of the word and in a certain way putting him in God's place, "deifying" him, as it were. This structure is very old and known to us from the first chapters of Genesis, i.e., the temptation of replacing the "divinity" (of the image and likeness of God), given to man by the Creator, with the "deification" of man against God, and without God, as is becoming visible under the atheistic conditions of many systems today.*

Anyone who denies the fundamental truth of reality, who makes himself the measure of all things and, in doing so, puts himself in God's place; anyone who more or less consciously feels he can get along without God, the Creator of the world, without Christ, the Redeemer of man; anyone who, instead of seeking God, pursues idols, has always been fleeing from the sole, fundamental and saving truth.

There is also the attempt to escape by withdrawing into oneself. This can lead to giving up. "Nothing matters anyway." If the disciples of Jesus had acted in this way, the world would never have heard anything of the redeeming Gospel of Christ. Withdrawing into oneself can assume the form of attempting to bring about an expansion of consciousness. Not a few young people here in your country are in the process of destroying their inner beings by withdrawing into themselves with the aid of alcohol and drugs. Very often anxiety and despair are the reasons behind this, but often, too, it is based on a thirst for pleasure, a lack of asceticism, or the irresponsible curiosity of wanting to "try out" everything once. Withdrawing into oneself can also lead to pseudo-religious sects, which abuse your idealism and your enthusiasm and deprive you of the freedom of thought and conscience. *This also includes the attempt to escape through doctrines of salvation that pretend to be able to attain true happiness on the basis of certain external practices, but which, in the final analysis, throw the affected person back on himself and the unsolved problem of loneliness.*

Then there is the attempt to flee from the fundamental truth by moving outwards, away from oneself, i.e., into political and social utopias, idealized dreams of society. *As necessary as ideals and aims are, utopian "magic formulae" will not get us anywhere, since they are usually accompanied by totalitarian power or the destructive use of violence.*

THE GOOD SHEPHERD LEADS IN TRUTH

4. You can see all this happening, the numerous escape routes people take to flee from the truth, the mysterious power of evil and iniquity that is at work. Are you never *confronted with the temptations of isolation and despondency?* There is an answer to this question in today's reading from the prophet Ezekiel. He speaks of a shepherd who follows his lost sheep into the wilderness in order to "rescue them from all places where they have been scattered on a day of clouds and thick darkness" (Ez. 34:12).

The Shepherd who gathers up man on the dark path of his loneliness and disorientation and leads him back into the light is Christ. He is the Good Shepherd. He is ever present in the hidden place of the "mystery of iniquity" and Himself takes charge of the important matter of human existence on this earth. He does it in truth by freeing *the heart of man from the fundamental contradiction* contained in wanting to deify man without or against God, which creates a climate of isolation and disorientation. On the path leading out of the darkness of loneliness to true humanity, Christ, the Good Shepherd, in profound, pursuing and accompanying love, takes charge of every individual person, in particular every young person.

The *prophet Ezekiel goes on to say* of the shepherd: "And I will bring them out from the peoples and gather them from the countries and will bring them into their own land: And I will feed them on the mountains of Israel, by the fountains and in all the inhabited places of the country" (Ez. 34:13). "I will seek the lost, and I will bring back the crippled, and I will strengthen the weak, and the fat and the strong I will watch over; I will feed them in justice" (Ez. 34:16).

In this way Christ wants to accompany the *maturing of man* in his humanity. He accompanies, nurtures and strengthens us in the life of His Church with His Word and in His sacraments, with the body and blood of His Passover Feast. He nurtures us as the immortal *Son of God,* lets man partake of His divine sonship, "deifies" him within, so that he will become "human" in the full sense of the word, so that man, created in the image and likeness of God, will attain his maturity in God.

YOU ARE CALLED BY GOD

5. For this reason Christ says the harvest is "great." It is great because of the immeasurable destiny of man. It is great because of the dignity of man. *It is great in accordance with his calling.* This wonderful harvest of the kingdom of God in humanity, the harvest of salvation in the history of man, peoples and nations is great. It is truly great, "but the laborers are few" (Mt. 9:37).

What does this mean? What is meant, dear young people, is that you have been called, called by God. My life, my human life, is only meaningful if I have been called by God, in an important decisive, final call. Only God can call man this way, no one but He. And this call of God constantly goes out, in and through Christ, to each and every one of you: to be workers in the harvest of your own humanity, workers in the vineyards of the Lord, in the Messianic harvest of humanity.

Jesus is in need of young people from your ranks who will follow His call and live as He did, poor and celibate, in order to be a living sign of the reality of God among your brothers and sisters.

God needs priests who will let themselves be led by the Good Shepherd into the service of His Word and His sacraments for men.

He needs people for the Catholic orders, men and women who will abandon everything in order to follow Him and in this way serve man.

He needs Christian married couples, who will render to each other and to their children service leading to full maturation of humanity in God.

God needs people who are ready to help and to serve the poor, the sick, the abandoned, the afflicted and spiritually wounded.

FOUR GREAT FIGURES

The glorious, more-than-1,000-year history of the Christian faith among your people is rich in individuals whose examples can provide an incentive in the fulfillment of your great calling. I would like to mention only four figures that come to me as a result of the present day and the city of Munich. There is St. Korbinian in the initial stages of the history of your faith in Christ, whose episcopal work laid the foundation for the Archdiocese of Munich-Freising. We are commemorating him in today's liturgy. There is the sainted Bishop Benno von Meissen, whose remains were laid to rest in Munich's *Frauenkirche*. He was a man of peace and reconciliation, who preached non-violence in his time, a friend of the poor and the distressed. In connection with the present day, St. Elizabeth comes to mind, whose motto was: "Love, according to the Gospel." As the Princess of Wartburg she renounced all the privileges of her estate and devoted her life completely to the poor and the outcast. Finally, I would like to point out a man whom many of you or your parents knew personally, the Jesuit Father Rupert Mayer, at whose grave in the center of Munich, in the crypt of the *Bürgersaal,* many hundreds of people pause for a brief prayer every day. Despite the after-effects of severe wounds he suffered on a patrol mission in the First World War, he openly and undauntedly stood up for the rights of the Church and for freedom at a difficult time in history, and as a result had to suffer the hardships of a concentration camp and exile.

Dear young people! Open your hearts to Christ's call! Your human life is a "unique adventure and enterprise," that can turn into both "a blessing and a curse." In view of you young people, who are the great hope of our future, let us ask the *"Lord of the harvest"* to send every one of you, and every one of your young fellowmen on this earth, as laborers to His "great harvest," in keeping with the great wealth of callings and gifts in His kingdom on this earth.

I would like to close with a special blessing for our Evangelical Lutheran brothers and sisters, who today in this country are celebrating their *Day of Repentance and Prayer*. This day is dominated for them by a knowledge of the necessity for constant renewal and by the calling of the Church to commemorate our communion as a people and as a state before God in prayer. The Roman Catholic Church is united with you in this matter. Please include your Catholic fellow-citizens, as well as your brother John Paul and his ministry in your prayers this day. Amen.

BIBLIOGRAPHY

The addresses, documents, and letters of the Holy Father are published as they appear in the Vatican newspaper, *L'Osservatore Romano.* There is a weekly edition of this paper in English which prints the major addresses and materials. This is perhaps the best common source for on-going materials. There is also a quarterly periodical called *The Pope Speaks,* which prints the major addresses.

In addition, the Daughters of St. Paul have published a series of books (available either in cloth or paperback) on the various journeys John Paul II has taken to Mexico, Ireland, the United States, France, Africa, Brazil, Germany and the Far East. They have also two fine collections entitled *You Are the Future, You Are My Hope* and *I Believe in Youth, Christ Believes in Youth* which include many more of the talks he has given also to children and younger students.

Many of the writings of John Paul II before he was Pope, when he was Karol Wojtyla, in philosophy and theology, are also easily available.

The Pontifical Commission on Justice and Peace (Rome, Piazza San Calisto) has published a series of eight booklets on the texts and social teaching of John Paul II, which are available for $1.00 each, and represent the best current guide to the Pope's thought in this area.

INDEX

Daughters of St. Paul

IN MASSACHUSETTS
    50 St. Paul's Ave. Jamaica Plain, Boston, MA 02130;
      617-522-8911; 617-522-0875;
    172 Tremont Street, Boston, MA 02111; 617-426-5464;
      617-426-4230
IN NEW YORK
    78 Fort Place, Staten Island, NY 10301; 212-447-5071
    59 East 43rd Street, New York, NY 10017; 212-986-7580
    7 State Street, New York, NY 10004; 212-447-5071
    625 East 187th Street, Bronx, NY 10458; 212-584-0440
    525 Main Street, Buffalo, NY 14203; 716-847-6044
IN NEW JERSEY
    Hudson Mall — Route 440 and Communipaw Ave.,
      Jersey City, NJ 07304; 201-433-7740
IN CONNECTICUT
    202 Fairfield Ave., Bridgeport, CT 06604; 203-335-9913
IN OHIO
    2105 Ontario St. (at Prospect Ave.), Cleveland, OH 44115; 216-621-9427
    25 E. Eighth Street, Cincinnati, OH 45202; 513-721-4838
IN PENNSYLVANIA
    1719 Chestnut Street, Philadelphia, PA 19103; 215-568-2638
IN FLORIDA
    2700 Biscayne Blvd., Miami, FL 33137; 305-573-1618
IN LOUISIANA
    4403 Veterans Memorial Blvd., Metairie, LA 70002; 504-887-7631;
      504-887-0113
    1800 South Acadian Thruway, P.O. Box 2028, Baton Rouge, LA 70821
      504-343-4057; 504-343-3814
IN MISSOURI
    1001 Pine Street (at North 10th), St. Louis, MO 63101; 314-621-0346
IN ILLINOIS
    172 North Michigan Ave., Chicago, IL 60601; 312-346-4228;
      312-346-3240
IN TEXAS
    114 Main Plaza, San Antonio, TX 78205; 512-224-8101
IN CALIFORNIA
    1570 Fifth Avenue, San Diego, CA 92101; 714-232-1442
    46 Geary Street, San Francisco, CA 94108; 415-781-5180
IN HAWAII
    1143 Bishop Street, Honolulu, HI 96813; 808-521-2731
IN ALASKA
    750 West 5th Avenue, Anchorage AK 99501; 907-272-8183
IN CANADA
    3022 Dufferin Street, Toronto 395, Ontario, Canada
IN ENGLAND
    57, Kensington Church Street, London W. 8, England
IN AUSTRALIA
    58 Abbotsford Rd., Homebush, N.S.W., Sydney 2140, Australia